STEVE
"UNCLE CREEPY"
BARTON

Encyclopocalypse Publications
www.encyclopocalypse.com

Copyright © 2024 by Steve Barton

All rights reserved.

Hardcover Edition

ISBN: 978-1-960721-74-7

Cover art design and layout by Joshua Petrino

Interior design and formatting by Scott A. Johnson

Additional formatting by Sean Duregger

Edited by Sean Duregger and Joshua Millican

No part of this book may be reproduced in any form or by any electronic or mechanical means, including information storage and retrieval systems, without permission in writing from the publisher, except by a reviewer who may quote brief passages in a review.

14.	CHAPTER 14 *Night of the Living Dork*	159
15.	CHAPTER 15 *It Just Tastes so Damned Good!*	178
16.	CHAPTER 16 *Irregular Guests, Fuckin' that Puppet, and Ass Aid*	195
17.	CHAPTER 17 *What a Tangled World-Wide-Web We Weave*	206
18.	CHAPTER 18 *The War on Common Sense and Curses from Beyond*	218
19.	CHAPTER 19 *Chapter COVID 19*	230
20.	CHAPTER 20 *Part V - A New Beginning*	233
21.	CHAPTER 21 *I Did it All For the Spooky! The Spooky!*	244
22.	CHAPTER 22 *Terrifier Too*	255
23.	CHAPTER 23 *Turbulence 3: Heavy Mental*	264
24.	CHAPTER 24 *That's Another One for the Fire*	275
	About the Author	279

Contents

Acknowledgments — v
Foreword — vii
Obligatory (not-so) Blank Filler Page. — xi

Prologue — 1
1. CHAPTER 1 — 3
   Daddy's Home and He's Fucking Soused
2. CHAPTER 2 — 13
   A Rather Strange Brew
3. CHAPTER 3 — 22
   The Mourning After
4. CHAPTER 4 — 35
   The Vertigo Shot
5. CHAPTER 5 — 46
   The NUMBers Game
6. CHAPTER 6 — 61
   Little Orphan Anarchy
7. CHAPTER 7 — 75
   I Gather Speed From You Fucking With Me
8. CHAPTER 8 — 83
   Latino Heat
9. CHAPTER 9 — 93
   Cut a Hole in My Heart
10. CHAPTER 10 — 100
    Shine On, You Crazy Diamond
11. CHAPTER 11 — 119
    Sure! Blame Me For Everything!
12. CHAPTER 12 — 123
    Becoming Creepy
13. CHAPTER 13 — 144
    My Head with Fame!

A Tale of Suffering, Part 1 — 147
A Tale of Suffering, Part 2 — 149
A Tale of Suffering, PART 3: THE END! — 151
A Tale of Suffering PART 3: THE END! Part 2 — 154

Acknowledgments

For everyone who's never let me down, those who have instilled the kind of faith in me that I never had in myself...

Rob Barton, Kris Schlamp, Sid Haig, and George A. Romero. I cannot thank you enough for being in my life and making it a better place. Without you and your guidance I never would have been able to make some truly hard decisions. You gave me the courage to believe in myself. To say, fuck it, and face everything head on.

To Ann Barton, David Tirado, Lou Gentile, Thomas Barton, Tabatha Johnson, Kaela Beth DeJesus, and Jennifer Julian. Each of you were taken from us entirely too soon. Thank you for being the angels on my shoulders, even if at times you were wonderfully devilish. This is very much for you.

Also, I'd like to say a big thanks to the following folks who have made an impact in my life: Suzanne Grodetzky, my oldest friend, I love you, sis. Dennis and Betty Martin, James Martin, Andy Martin, Lucy Bianchi, Bridget Bonner, Alexa and Dylan Hummell, Estevan and Haley DeJesus, my grandkids (!WTAF?), Brian Markowitz, Sarah Clark, Brian Hoffman, August Lambros, Richard Lubinskas, Doug Blancero, Andrew Kasch, Buz Wallick, Scott A. Johnson, Katie Coy Johnson, Zak Bagans, Darren Bousman, Lin Shaye, Ashley Laurence, Ben and Alicia Rock, Michael Felsher, Daniel Farrands, Maria Mangone-Forte, Ricky Tirado, Scott Foy, Amy Allan, Matt Serafini, Nick Castin, Meredith Victor-Castin, Jeffrey Reddick, Cory Skier, Debi Moore, George Jensen, Bill Jensen, Adam Green, Joe Lynch, Malek Akkad, Ryan Freimann, Joshua Siebalt, Wendy Taylor, Matt Bolea, Shana Handleman, Jackie and Steven Smerling (hi, Mom and

Dad! A book? Who knew, right?), Sandy King Carpenter, John Carpenter, Joe Knetter, Sarah French, Marie Ciminello, Chris Cross, Pete Ross, Steve Martinez, Jaime Lathrop, Paulie Wohlmaker, Diedre Rosiello, Adrienne Lampasona, Dave Parker, Jeremy Posner, Travis Chambers, Ashley Goodbrand-Chambers, Tony Timpone, Sean Decker, Sarah Nicklin-Decker, Roro Battista, Matt Blazi, Melanie Cross, Danielle Ferraiola Shin, Justin Julian, David and Tiffany Hahn, Tim Leininger, Chris Roe, Chris Roe Jr., Chris Sembrot, Mandy Sembrot, The entire Gentile/Solano family, Jed Shepherd, Jonathan Barkan, Brad Miska, Josh Doke, Stephen Romano, Shawn Lewis, Jon Lewis, Mike Broom, Eva Schlamp, Kris Schlamp Jr., Joe, Gabby, and Matt Schlamp, Josh Petrino, Jess DuBois, Josh Stolberg, Local H, Pearl Jam, David McInerney, Ernie O'Donnell, Ben Reiser, Ben Carrasquillo, Josh Millican, Kevin Smith, John Camera, Mark Tortorella, Bob and Sandee O'Rourke, Dean and Morgan Sasser, Mark Redfield, Vincent Guastini, Tyler Mane, Renea Geerlings, Stacy Lynn S, Scott Straka, the Cabram boys: William, Peter, and Ely, Jon Scondotto, Oren Peli, Phil Nobile, Eileen Dietz, Marissa Feldmeth, Chuck Kratchwell, Ryan Russell, Alex and Jennie Cowperthwaite, Alex Noyer, Sue Procko, Jen Place, Aaron Thomas, Seb Bazile, Jesse Baget, Jennifer Martin, Doug Bradley, Spider-One, Adrienne Barbeau, Rob Lucas, Adrienne King, Ken Foree, Ed Sanchez, Dave Hagan, Barbara Crampton, Peter Anthony, Renee Maler, Suzanne Romero, Tina Burke, Claire Longo Closky, Franny Fonseca, Fallon Vendetta, Chris MacGibbon, Robert Dodson, Joe Sena, and Brandon Brooks. Your patience and belief in me helped to inspire me to believe in myself. Sorry about all the complaints you had to endure... well not really... But thank you just the same.

Finally, and most importantly for Danielle Barton.

You are the reason I keep breathing, the heartbeat that keeps me going. Words alone will never be able to fully illustrate the exact type of grateful I am to and for you. Thank you... thank you... THANK YOU!

Foreword

Happenstance tends to put all kinds of interesting opportunities and obstacles in our paths. If not for a curious, seemingly random moment, who knows where our lives would be?

Case in point: Many years ago, when my first novel was published, I was doing everything I could to try to market it. Part of that process was to scour this thing called the "Internet" and find other horror geeks like myself. The plan was simple: Infiltrate their ranks, befriend them, then casually drop the news that I had a book coming out. Little did I know that one particular message board would alter my life and introduce me to someone who can only be described accurately as a force of nature.

So, I joined the site, came up with my goofy username, and started the process of finding my people. People who understood me. People who liked the same things I did.

The administrator of this site was a guy named "Uncle Creepy." Yes, the same Uncle Creepy whose autobiography you're holding in your hot little hands. A few months of posting, replying, and expressing my own weird little interest in the paranormal, and I got a strange message.

Foreword

Gimme your phone number. Got time for a chat? -UC

To someone whose brain had been addled by horror movies, like mine, one of two things were going to happen. One, I was going to wind up in a building with plastic on the floors, or, two, I was about to become a made man.

I'm not sure what I expected when I picked up the phone that day. I mean, I pictured the voice I thought would come out of the comic book character of the same name. Imagine my surprise when the voice on the other end of the line had a New York accent, dropped f-bombs at any opportunity, and turned out to be one of the best friends a person could ever have in his life. That was my introduction to Steve Barton.

Over the years, Steve's been on one helluva journey. And through it all, there are a few constants that I'd like to relate to you, the reader. First, Steve's never lied to me. Never. He tells me something is true, I generally take it as gospel. Why? He's never given me a reason to doubt him. So, the stories in this book? Outlandish as they may be, I can pretty much guarantee, they're all true. How do I know? Because I was there for a few of them.

Second, I can count on one hand the number of people I consider to be my "found family," and I don't even need all five fingers. Steve's on that list. From our first contact to our first in-person meeting, Steve's lived up to every promise he's ever made to me, and then some. He's stood by me during some tough times, and I like to think I've done the same for him.

Third, and perhaps most importantly, Steve's hilarious. You have no idea what you're getting into when you're at a convention with him. The man has effortlessly transcended being simply a fan to become a true celebrity in his own right. He has the kind of swagger that only comes with a life well-lived and experiences that have kicked him enough times that a lesser person would've cashed in their chips by now. And through it all, he's still here.

Mostly, though, the thing that I feel best describes Steve is a word that is in short supply these days: Kindness. Say what you will…

Foreword

He's loud, he's brash, he talks a mile a minute and can swear with the greatest sailors on the planet. But for all of that, there's no one I would rather have on my side, whether going to war or playing darts (although, dollars to doughnuts, I'd bet he'd whip my ass at darts).

The fact of the matter is, there's a good chance I wouldn't have a writing career if I hadn't met him. At least, it wouldn't be as far along as I am now.

So, dear reader, do yourself a favor and buckle up. Grab a drink. Keep your hands and feet inside the vehicle at all times, and remember, there's no bailing out now. Steve's the genuine article. He's not just a horror fan, he's the king of the horror fans. He's the horror fan who befriended George A. Romero, Sid Haig, Ari Lehman, and every other horror celebrity that you can think of. The man has an encyclopedic knowledge of all things spooky and macabre and will gladly share his knowledge with anyone who asks.

To me, he'll always be Steve, my brother in arms and my dear friend. To everyone else, he is now, and will forever be, Uncle Creepy.

Scott A. Johnson
Author of *Through the Witches Stone*, *Ungeheuer*, and *The Stanley Cooper Chronicles*

Obligatory (not-so) Blank Filler Page.

Oh, so clever, eh? Feel free to scribble some shit of your own below. In fact, I encourage you to do so. If I ever meet you and you have a hard copy of this sliver of outrageous ridiculousness, not only am I genuinely curious to read your own scribblings, but I'll be sure to scribble under your scribbles thereby ensuring and preserving the integrity of the space-time continuum.

Prologue

If you're looking this over, I can only assume that something about it compelled you enough to want to read it.

My name is Steve Barton. I don't have much. I'm poor. I've been battered, broken, bruised, crushed, shattered, shit on, written off, and OF COURSE have been told incessantly that I "will never be anything" because I'm "just not good enough."

If any of that sounds familiar, I am so very sorry. Everyone has heartache and pain. But you know what? Despite everything I am STILL here. Still alive. So are you. If you can relate or are just morbidly curious go ahead and put this in your cart and head on over to "check out."

You see, I'm writing this record of sorts for only one reason - you. If my words or experiences can help just one person to feel that they are not alone, then every ounce of agony has been more than worth it.

First things first... There's gonna be nothing at all "pro" about this "logue." If you are easily offended by coarse language. I'd recommend that you stop now and return to your day, night, or whatever it is that you have going on. I don't know what the true purpose is of me writing this story... my story.

Hell, I don't know the purpose of much, but maybe, after getting all of this out of my system, I can gain some much-needed introspection. Am I exorcising my demons? Am I just ranting? I do not know, really. Nor do I care, either. I just feel the need to start typing away like I do everything else... like a driven madman.

Several paragraphs in, and I still don't even know what this book will be about. It's not a diet book, although I will talk a bit about being fat, as well as my own personal #WarOnGirth. It's certainly not a self-help book, as I don't recommend anyone ever doing what I did under any circumstances. I'm far from an example to be followed; more of a case study of how one idiot has learned to cope with adversity. I guess at its core it will just be about life in general, and how it can go both wrong and right.

Everyone has a story to tell. I'm not unique. There are gonna be highs, lows, even more lows, laughs, scares, and tears. What you're embarking on, kids, is a thought roller coaster which traverses my soul with at times reckless abandon. The events you're about to read about are, to the best of my recollection, completely true. However, I have changed names where I saw fit because who the hell needs hurt feelings and possible libel law- suits? I have enough problems. That being said, I will not be pulling any punches. This is my story... warts and all. Strap in... take a breath... and welcome to my life.

There's no turning back.

- SB

Chapter 1
Daddy's Home and He's Fucking Soused

It was a warm spring day in Brooklyn, New York. My older brother Rob was out with his friends, my dad was at work, and I was like anywhere between 3 and 5 years old. Today would be the day I suffered my first tragedy. It's actually one of my very first memories. The day that changed who I would be. My first scar and the loss of my innocence.

It was sometime during the week, and I was planted in front of what would become my best friend: a 22" Sylvania black and white console television. You see, in the 1970s TVs were sometimes encased in heavy wood and made to look more like furniture than an actual television set. When it would break, you could actually just put another TV on top of it. It was a different time, man. It took like three people to move this thing into our living room, and they were paid in beer. It was a cumbersome rectangular monstrosity that weighed probably as much as I did at my fattest, but more on the chub factor later.

Morning was in full swing, and I was watching my favorite show on WPIX, *11 ALIVE!*, as a slight breeze blew across the back of my neck from the open windows and doors of our home. It was one of those glorious days that you just don't forget. We're talking pure bliss. *The Magic Garden* starring Paula, Carol, and Sherlock the Squirrel was on the boob tube; and I was transfixed "from crafty fox to Goldie Locks (in storybox, in storybox)." That's kinda how one of the show's recurring songs went for you too young to remember this golden kid-friendly oldie.

I had two loves back then... television and toys. Oh, how I loved toys. Age be damned, I still do. The warbling duo threw to a commercial, and there it was... a dream toy! My favorite doll at the time was Colonel Steve Austin, The Six Million Dollar Man, which bore an incredible resemblance to Lee Majors, the actor who played him. Standing at 13" tall and rocking a telescopic eye, roll-up skin, and bionic implants, he was the coolest fucker in the world. Every boy I knew wanted to be The Bionic Man. This doll and I had become inseparable. It was my friend. Like the TV would eventually become, Austin was always there for me. The figure also came with a plastic engine of some sort. Why this was I'll never know. Maybe to illustrate that he was so strong he could pick it up easily? Who knows?! Later, said engine would ultimately end up becoming a primary tool in the clobbering of Bionic Sasquatch, and in the end that's all that mattered. Let's see... where was I? Oh, yeah! My dream toy!

Of course, this plastic marvel that had me salivating like Stephen King's Cujo would be a Bionic Man accessory, and though there were tons of cool ones available including different outfits for him... this one? This one was THE SHIT! I refer of course to the Bionic Transport and Repair Station. This thing was badass.

When closed shut, it looked like a rocketship. You could place Austin in it, and he'd be staring out of a clear plastic window. When opened up, it formed a repair center that was chock-full of fuckin'-A coolness! There were tubes that could be placed into Austin's bionic modules, several glow-in-the-dark dials that simulated X-rays of him, and more!

This transport was the ideal thing to have to go along with the official Col. Steve Austin astronaut suit. I HAD to have it. Oh yes, this would be mine!

Back then you couldn't just rewind TV or a tape of whatever you recorded on it for later playback. If you missed something on TV, you were screwed until it aired again. The struggle was real. My mom was in the kitchen talking on the phone. I needed to get her into the living room so that she could see what I was talking about... this HAD-TO-HAVE treasure. Even worse? The usual commercial lasted about thirty seconds. My success window was small. I grabbed my Bionic Man action figure and marched into the kitchen prepared to go to war for her attention. "Mom! Mom! You have to come with me," I said while tugging on her flowered house dress. I was relentless... I was annoying... I didn't care. "Mom! YOU HAVE TO COME NOW!" I was now holding up Austin as a means to plead my case. This was important, man! Maybe if she saw both of our faces she'd understand just how serious this was... I mean, everybody respected Steve fuckin' Austin!

My mother looked down at me... I'll never forget the rage in her eyes. She grabbed my Six Million Dollar Man from my hands furiously and threw it on to the floor... smashing it. He flew into a million pieces... plastic bits of him went flying as if he was exploded from the inside by a rogue bionic placed within his body by his evil nemesis, Maskatron. There was dead silence. My eyes began welling up as I dropped to my knees in front of the remains of my favorite possession. My friend. My closest ally. I remember my mom saying to whomever she was speaking to that she'd call them back. I never screamed... I was too shocked. This was akin to witnessing a murder to my young mind. I just sat there on my knees, tears profusely streaming down my face, barely even being able to breathe. My mom knelt beside me, still furious but obviously feeling very bad. She had never lost her temper with me before. As trivial as this may seem, this was the first time that I knew loss. That nothing was ever going to be the same. Shattered dreams, man. The doll was as irreparable as my heart. This day, unbeknownst to me, was about to get worse. A lot worse. My dad. My fucking dad. He was a real piece of work. I learned one thing and one thing only from my father... in the words of Maynard from A Perfect Circle's song "Judith" — *You're such an inspiration for the ways that I will never, ever choose to be.* Yep, that about sums up our father/son relationship.

Hours had passed. I was still completely traumatized, but my mom was doing her best to comfort me. She was doing laundry, and I was sitting cross-legged in the laundry basket. I love the smell and feel of freshly done laundry. It's comforting in some strange way... as if all of the dirt that was garnered all week was finally washed away... a clean slate if you will. It was now about 4:15 in the afternoon. I remember this because when my mom was home from work, once 4:00 p.m. would roll around, she'd immediately light a cigarette (she smoked Salems) and sit on the stoop of our house staring up the block and waiting for my father to come home. This time she was doing so while folding the laundry.

We lived across the street from what would become my grammar school. Good old PS 209! We had a corner house, and my dad would be coming from the opposite direction. Mom had an eagle eye. She could spot my father through the chain-link fence of the schoolyard way before he'd even turned the opposite corner of the block. One of two things would happen, and this scenario would continue to play out for the rest of my time with her. She would either see him walking swiftly up the block pretty carefree or she would see him staggering up the street like the pathetic drunk he normally was. Nine times out of ten it was the latter. My dad was a raging alcoholic. Not a friendly drunk. He was a volatile powder keg of hatred and impaired ignorance. Once my mother saw him doing the patented Mickey Barton Wobble of Drunken Stupidity, she would get up and start slamming things until he was up the stairs and in the house. From there a knock-down, drag-out argument would begin. This time, though, drunken dad didn't even make it into the house before my mom began lashing out. The battle began out on the front porch. "You selfish fuck! You're drunk again. AGAIN! This is the third time this week!," I remember her screaming...venomously waving her pointer finger as if it were a locked, cocked and ready to strike southwestern rattler.

"I ham noth, you fucken bitchth!" he slurred, barely able to stand and shifting his weight from one foot to the next to maintain his balance.

At just 5' 8" my father was the intoxicated Irish equivalent of Archie Bunker on four 8-balls of cocaine who hadn't slept in six months. He was a burly fellow and pretty intimidating given his hair-trigger temper. Not to my mom, though... there wasn't shit that intimidated Ann Barton. The arguing continued.

"All day long I clean..."

"Shuth the fukkupth, will ya fah christhakes."

"I cook..."

"I don't wanth to hereitth"

"I do the laundry..."

"FUKTH THE LAWNDREE AND FUKTH WHAT YOU DO!"

At that moment my dad knelt down to the laundry basket I was sitting in, my tears running like a river, and grabbed it with both hands. He lifted it up with me in it and dumped everything including my tiny body out onto the floor. I barely moved out of the way as he then began jumping up and down and stamping his feet on the once clean and fresh smelling clothes and towels. My mom, horrified, grabbed me by the arm, yanked me up and then stormed off into the bedroom where she locked her door, effectively putting up a barrier between us and the slurring lunatic running rampant throughout the house. My dad would begin beating on the door and yelling shit like, "Andth stay in thereth, you cunth!"

I'll never forget this day. Every moment of it—from *The Magic Garden* to being locked in the bedroom with Mom is clear as day. Every word. Every bit of spittle flying out of their mouths while they prowled around each other like hostile animals facing off in a fight to the death. I was so fucking scared. Even worse... my Steve Austin doll... my comforter... my best friend... was gone. I had nothing. This was the first time in my life that I felt true loneliness.

I can sit here and give you many other examples of the "woe is me" variety. Yes, my dad was a prick. Yes, he was drunk all the time, but at the end of the day all that pain I experienced at a young age helped make me who I am, and I like me now. There was one incident in particular in which I heard him telling my mom that I was a mistake, and they should never have had me. These words still ring in my ears. Something I needed to reason out inside of my head if only for the sake of my own sanity. It's tough to hear shit like that, ya know? I'm not justifying those words or their misguided sentiment, but I kind of understood them. See, I'm the youngest of four kids. Simply put, they couldn't afford me as they were struggling to make ends meet as it was. The way I understand it, when I was born, my mom had to get a job so that they could survive. This had to have crushed my father's ego as he was no longer able to support his family on his own. That's why he would hit the bottle more and more. Shame. Of course, though, it was my fault. Everything was. Everything I did was wrong. Every decision I made was stupid. I was never good enough.

You know what? Hey, Dad, in retrospect, suck my dick, man. I may be a lot of things, but I'm nobody's excuse and never will be. Asshole.

It wasn't all bad though... around the same age I had one of the single most important experiences of my life. One that defined me and put me on the path that I am on today. It was a few weeks after the Austin incident. My mom had replaced my Bionic Man doll with a new one that came with a faux-iron girder instead of the engine. I still had the engine, so fuck it! Bonus, right? But wait! Now that I think about it, useless things like an engine or a plastic orange girder came standard with the doll, but I have to buy the astronaut suit separately? Hey, fuck you, Kenner! You can suck my dick, right after my dad is done with his spooge-shooting face bath! "Hey, kids, here's a plastic engine... it does nothing! Enjoy!" You damned greedy fucks!

Sorry, I get derailed sometimes. My mind has a tendency to wander.

Anyway...

Rob and I shared a room. He was very much a rock for me. A safety blanket of sorts. We had separate beds, but even just being in

A Comedy of Tragedies

the same room as him would make me feel more at ease. My big brother remains a rock star to me, and nothing will ever change that. No matter what. I have two other siblings, Tommy "I Now Live Off-the-Grid as a Means to Hide From the Army of Bastard Children That I Sired" Barton and Camille "I Blew a Yuppie! He Liked It and Married Me and Now I'm a Rich Manipulative Cunt Who Reserves the Right to Judge Others" Barton.

I have lots of feelings about Tommy and Camille and believe me... you're gonna get an eyeful of them later, but for now—screw those cats. It was Rob whom I grew up with. He's my blood. A living Colonel Steve Austin, minus the bionics but every bit as heroic and cool in my eyes. I love him as much as I did back when I was a kid, but when he was gone and I was left at home to my own devices? Man, would I fuck with all of his shit and then absolutely deny it when I was questioned. That's what little brothers are for... to fuck things up and lie about them later. Ah, the good old days.

One particular weekend Rob was spending the night at a friend's house. I'm pretty sure it was a Saturday as I distinctly remember my dad not being drunk that day. Any day he wasn't drinking was a good day. He'd treat me like a human instead of the scourge of his loins.

I am a night owl. Always have been, always will be. Even at a young age I knew that the night was a special time. All bets were off, man. Reality took a backseat to the darkness. Anything could be there... creeping through the world at all ungodly hours. I dug the possibilities. I was never scared of the dark and I was always curious as to what it may be hiding. As children we used to have a simple MO: When Rob and I would hear our parents snoring, it was our queue to run to the living room and pop on the TV. The coolest shit ever would play in the middle of the night. I loved old '50s and '60s horror and sci-fi, and monsters were magical to me. Like unicorns. I always related to Frankenstein's Monster. He never asked to be here, yet here he was... forsaken by his father. How could I NOT understand him? Late night TV was like forbidden fruit to me and Rob, and

9

we'd watch it as much and as quietly as possible. This night though... I was alone.

My parents were snoring up a storm. I got out of bed and tiptoed to the living room, ninja-style... this was my mom's inner sanctum. She was a neat freak who could literally find footprints on the carpet, so I had to comb the rug when I was done or I'd be busted. No evidence of my late-night habits could be left behind. I popped on the old Sylvania and that familiar warm glow would fill the room. What wasn't familiar, though, was what would appear on-screen. This was no monster or kitschy tale of private eyes. This wasn't a war movie or a Three Stooges short. Tarzan would not be swinging from his vine, and Charlie Chan and Number One Son were obviously off on some adventure that I wasn't privy to. This was a newscast... and the most terrifying one I had ever seen.

> "It has been established that persons who have recently died have been returning to life and committing acts of murder," said a news reporter. "A widespread investigation of funeral homes, morgues, and hospitals has concluded that the unburied dead have been returning to life and seeking human victims. It's hard for us here to be reporting this to you, but it does seem to be a fact."

My jaw hit the fucking floor like an anvil being dropped from the Roadrunner onto the head of the Wile E. Coyote. The reporter went on about having to "get to rescue stations immediately." HOLY. SHIT. It was the middle of the night. Everyone was sleeping, and only the people like me who were awake enough to see the news knew what was going on. WHAT LUCK! I had to save my family! We had to find Rob. A million different things started going through my head. I had to move and do so with the utmost urgency.

I sprang up from the floor and dashed into my parents' bedroom as if the heated licks of a five-alarm fire were hot on my tail. I switched on the light...

"WAKE UP! WAKE UP! THE DEAD ARE COMING! WE GOTTA GO!" I screamed frantically while tugging on my mom's arm. She woke up dazed and my dad had also begun to stir. I was being a hero. A budding Bruce Campbell if you will. "GET UP! BOTH OF YOU! WE NEED TO GET TO THE RESCUE STATIONS!"

"Stevie, you're having a nightmare," said my mom. "NO I AM NOT! IT'S ON THE TV!"

"What the fucking fuck?" asked my visibly annoyed dad. "Go back to fucking bed, will ya?"

"NO! WE GOTTA GO! COME, I'LL SHOW YOU! WE HAVE TO GET ROB!"

Finally, my mom sat up and I dragged her by the arm to the living room with my dad aggravated and in tow. At this point I think he was just more curious than anything else. We made it to the living room, footprints on the rug be damned, and I pointed to the TV and exclaimed, "LOOK!"

Of course, what was on was George A. Romero's 1968 classic *Night of the Living Dead.*

"You woke us up because of a movie? A FUCKING MOVIE?"

I was dumbfounded and even worse I was in trouble. BIG TROUBLE. Not only was I up late, not only did I leave footprints on the sacred rug, not only was I watching TV, but I woke up both the Green and the Brown Gargantua and the words were about to get stuck in my throat and promptly stuffed up my ass.

Punishment was imminent.

My mom immediately got out the vacuum because fuck waiting for the morning like a normal person. Those footprints had to be smoothed out IMMEDIATELY, if not sooner. While she was doing that, my dad took me into my bedroom and grabbed his heavy leather belt and whipped me on the ass until I could no longer even feel the pain. That was the first time I felt agony. The first time I was actually hit. Violence was also about to become a close friend of mine, and this was my first meeting with him. He sucked.

After getting his licks in, my dad shut my room light off. I heard the vac cease and then heard them muttering to themselves until their bedroom door shut. As I lay there with my newly tanned ass throbbing, I became aware of something... I was terrified, but I was also 100 percent safe. How fucking cool is that? The pain subsided after a few moments, and it wasn't long before the monsters had gone back to slumber on Kong Island. Sounds of their sleeping filled my ears and I did what any other kid in my position should NOT have done… I made my way back into the living room to finish the movie.

It was at that moment, "Uncle Creepy" had been born.

Chapter 2
A Rather Strange Brew

I mentioned earlier that television was going to become my true best friend. It had brought me *The Six Million Dollar Man*, after all. Suffice it to say I developed a deep love for horror movies after my *Night of the Living Dead* experience. I consumed horror wherever I could find it. *The Twilight Zone, The Outer Limits, Night Gallery*, magazines like *Famous Monsters of Filmland, Starlog,* and *Fangoria*...comic books *Creepy, Eerie, Tales from the Crypt*. If it was even slightly horror related, I knew about it and was procuring it. One way or the other.

Sometimes I paid for my magazines and comics, sometimes I didn't when no one was looking. Not proud of stealing anything, but I was an addict and also a street kid from Brooklyn with no cash, so I was pretty much a true product of my environment. I did what I had to do. I told you at the onset that I was gonna be pulling no punches, so, hey, get used to the occasional confession.

Fast-forward to about thirteen years old, more or less.

No one ever really was there to teach me wrong or right. My mom worked five days a week from 2:30 p.m. to 10:00 p.m. as a phone operator at Brooklyn Hospital, so other than getting up for school and weekends I didn't see her much. Rob had been way into his teens by now and always out and my other siblings Tommy and Camille were already married and gone. As per usual my dad was too inebriated to bother checking in on me and once he came home with a load on, it wouldn't be long before he'd pass out. He was entertaining when he slept, though. He would randomly shout out things like "OH YEAH" like he was channeling Randy "Macho Man" Savage and then slap himself on the hip repeatedly and with astonishing force. This would happen throughout the evenings, and it made me giggle each time. With no one else around, I turned to my good old friend, the television set. Thanks to the wonders of the VCR, I discovered video stores and could frequently be found perusing their hallowed aisles. All it took back then was the right box art and I'd rent it. I had like a $10 a week allowance so I would pick and choose the goodies that would keep me company.

As you may have guessed, I raided the horror movie section countless times over and over again. It was from movies that I learned my values, the wrongs and rights, from people like Vincent Price, Boris Karloff, and in particular George A. Romero. George's movies struck more than just a chord in me. His films were so different, and in many ways, he actually raised me. I learned so much from *The Crazies, Martin, Dawn of the Dead,* etc. He became closer to me during my impressionable years than he ever could have imagined. Even when I didn't want to think, movies like *Creepshow* and *Two Evil Eyes* were there for me, helping me to celebrate what I loved. It was in my DNA, man. It still is.

My first job was working in Sal's Pizzeria on Coney Island Avenue. It was the summertime, school was out, and I had one mission in mind... I needed to buy *Night of the Living Dead*, the Media Home Entertainment edition, on VHS. I flipped pies and swept floors for two months straight to save enough money for it. What you may not realize (depending on your age) is the fact that VHS tapes were insanely expensive during that time when the market was in its infancy. *Night* clocked in at a hefty $89.99 plus tax. Working was the only way that I'd ever have enough scratch to buy it and this flick, for obvious reasons, was incredibly important to me. Still, I did it and I was happy to.

In early September I walked down to Parkway Video, also on Coney Island Avenue, and ordered my treasure. A week or so later I received a phone call that it had arrived. I cannot ever recall running so fast to get something. This was it, baby! It was finally mine to watch whenever I wanted to. I remember being ever-so careful opening up the tape. I didn't want to crease the packaging or damage it in any way. Words cannot fully describe how proud I was to own that and how elated I was that no one helped me to get it. This was my first accomplishment. The first thing I had ever purchased completely on my own with money that I earned. I wish I still had that tape. Over the years I would go on to buy about three-thousand different versions of *Night of the Living Dead* on various forms of home video platforms, especially when it and other flicks I loved became more affordable. A familiar chill was in the air, and I knew that Halloween, a.k.a. my Christmas, would soon be here to enjoy. I had my copy of my favorite movie. I was well-armed for the experience.

We lived in a corner house on Manor Court. It was a two-family house and me, Rob, my mom, Dad, and some old lady who spent her entire day sitting in a chair and watching the front door (I would come to find out that she was my great-aunt) all lived on the top floor. My grandmother and grandfather lived below us.

Before I go any further, I want to address my great-aunt. Her actual name was Eugenia, but for some reason everyone called her Sewagin. Maybe it was just their pronunciation or maybe it was a nickname. Truth be told, I don't know. The only thing I knew was that she would sit by my front door and sometimes would give me money for ice cream. For the first eleven years of my life, I had no idea who she was other than Sewagin, the old lady who sat on the chair.

If you couldn't have guessed by now I come from a dysfunctional family circus. Not knowing who this lady actually was wasn't at all strange for me. In fact, strange was very much commonplace.

Speaking of dysfunctional let me introduce you to my grandparents on my mom's side: Camillo (Camille) and Genoefa (Jenny)

Gentile. The two weirdest fucking people on the face of this or any other planet. I called my grandmother Nanny, so that will be how I refer to her from here on out. They were an odd pair. For starters, Nanny, never bathed and never came out of her house or opened any of their windows. It didn't matter how sweltering it was outside. Anytime they needed anything from the store it was always either me, Rob or my grandpa who would go. She rarely ever appeared to anyone as more than a disembodied head who peaked out of her front door. Whenever she needed anything that my grandpa wouldn't or couldn't do, she'd call. But not on the phone. No, phones had some form of germs, I guess. She would crack her door and yell.

"Robbbbbbiiiiitttttttttttttttttt!" "Steeeeeeeeevvvveeeeeennn!"

Even at just thirteen years old I knew this was annoying as fuck, and she would continue to howl our names until someone, hell, anyone, responded. She was so fucking strange, man. She wouldn't touch anything without a damp napkin in her hand, yet she wouldn't dream of bathing or cleaning her house. When she cracked open the door even a little bit, a foul stale stench would creep forward as a means to assault your nostrils. We're talking RANK. Super rank. No amount of sprayed air freshener would help. This was a tactic she frequently employed as opposed to bathing or cleaning. Trouble was that their musk was so fucking strong that once sprayed, her house would end up smelling as if someone had taken a shit in a bag of Froot Loops.

My mom regaled me with weird stories about her. Nanny apparently had an irrational fear of pregnant women. Apparently, one time when she first told them she was pregnant with my eldest brother, Tommy, my grandmother burned all of her clothing. What the fuck, right? She was also completely paranoid. I'm hard pressed to remember a time when she didn't start shit with the neighbors, complaining that they were doing all sorts of things to her and my grandfather. Everything from threatening them to giving them the evil eye or the *"malocchio"* as it was known in Italian. It's funny that word, now that I look at it all typed out. *Malocchio*. It's like Pinocchio's evil brother or something.

I can almost picture the scene. My balding grandfather peeking out of the door in front of my grandmother, extending his right hand with a candle illuminating the area around him, The flame flickering off his thick glasses as wax dripped to the ground. From behind him every now and then my grandmother would peek out her head and be pulling down her lower left eyelid while giving the horns with the fingers on her other hand, disdainfully spitting on the ground every few seconds.

Wax and spit. Spit and wax...

He'd bellow, "Maloooooooooochio," into the night air.

Furious spitting continues. "Maloooooooooooooochiooooooooooo....."

Here was a woman who LIVED to cause heartache and chaos. Seriously, there was not a normal or good bone in her body. If she ever had a shrink (not that she would ever leave the house to see one), I can picture him describing her Sam Loomis from John Carpenter's *Halloween* style:

> "I met her several years ago. I was told there was nothing left; no reason, no conscience, no understanding in even the most rudimentary sense of life or death, of good or evil, right or wrong. I met this... sixty-year-old woman with this blank, pale, emotionless face, and... the blackest eyes - the Devil's eyes. I spent eight years trying to reach her, and then another seven trying to keep her locked up, because I realized that what was living behind that woman's eyes was purely and simply... evil."

Yep. Sounds about right.

It was a December evening in 1985. I was 13 years old. The holiday season was approaching rapidly, and I decided that I needed a little levity in my life. I trekked to Parkway Video and rented the 1983 comedy, *Strange Brew*. Rob was out (as per usual), my mom was at work, and my dad was of course laying in a state of drunken slumber on his bed, slapping his hip every now and again as if he were forcing the world's fastest horse to go just a little bit faster. When he was in this state it would be near impossible to wake him up. Every night, I had to do just that so he could pick my mom up from the Sheepshead Bay train station by 11:00 p.m. I would start trying to rouse this beast about 10:45 p.m. We lived close to the station, but every second was crucial.

I would have to start yelling, "DAD! COME ON! IT'S TIME TO GET UP!" at least fifteen minutes before he needed to go in order to accomplish my arduous mission. I would sometimes have to shake him... move him... it was like trying to resurrect fucking Lazarus at times. I'd often be met with a quick slap on the mouth and a string of obscenities. This dude did not want to be disturbed. Sometimes he'd throw shit at me like ashtrays or anything that was handy. It was not fun. It was never fun. Though I did develop some catlike reflexes from all the dodging I had to do. This was my normal. It's important that I stress just how hard my father was to wake up because it's the only way you can truly understand what I went through that evening on December 23rd.

The time was 7:50 p.m. My dad had just fallen asleep and trying to wake him during this time would prove impossible. I remember the time exactly because I had just started my movie at 7:30 p.m. I was laying on the floor in front of the TV watching Canadian hosers Bob and Doug McKenzie prattle on about the rotten brew at the Elsinore Brewery. The clock struck ten until eight. I looked at my VCR's digital display as it was at that exact time that I heard it...

"Steeeeeeevvvvvvvvveeeeeen!"

It was my nan. She was sticking her head out the door and yelling my name as per usual. I figured that she'd wanted me to throw out her trash or something. I ignored her.

"Steeeeeeevvvvvvvvveeeeeeeen!"

It was fucking cold outside, man, and the movie was just getting good.

"Steeeeeeevvvvvvvvveeeeeeeen!"

Sometimes if I ignored her long enough, she'd just stop and leave the trash outside of her door for later collection. This time though? This time she was dead set on getting me downstairs. Getting me to her front door.

"Steeeeeeevvvvvvvvveeeeeeeeen!"

She sounded panicked. Shrill.

"Steeeeeeevvvvvvvvveeeeeeeeen!"

"ALRIGHT," I yelled. I paused the flick got my jacket and ran down the stairs to her door.

I saw her standing there...the door was fully open. She was wild-eyed. Hysterical, crying...nervous. I looked behind her and my grandfather was sprawled out on the kitchen floor. He was not moving.

"CAMILLE! CAMILLE! CAMILLE!" Nanny kept on shouting his name. There was no response. As I rushed in the house, its naturally foul odor hit me in the face like a ton of bricks. I asked what had happened.

"He just fell over," she said. I didn't know what to do.

"CAMILLE! CAMILLE! CAMILLE! HELP ME, CAMILLE!" I didn't think to grab her phone to call 911. I wasn't even remotely thinking clearly. I was thirteen for chrissakes. I needed to turn to an adult. I needed my father.

I ran back around to the front of our house as quickly as I could. Once up the stairs I sprinted by the old lady on the chair straight into my parent's bedroom. Dad was in full hip-hitting gallop mode. I was screaming at him, "WAKE UP! WAKE UP! THERE'S SOMETHING WRONG WITH GRANDPA!" Nothing.

Not even so much as a flickering of an eyelid. I was frantic. Beside myself. I grabbed the phone and finally dialed 911. "THERE'S SOMETHING WRONG WITH MY GRANDPA," I told the person who answered the line. They were remarkably cool-headed. I expected everyone to be as crazed as I was. The few moments of clarity they had given me while asking questions was so very much needed.

They asked for my address. I gave it to them. They asked if I knew if he was breathing. No.

Did I know what had happened? My grandmother told me he just fell off the chair.

Where was my grandmother now? She was with him. Was there another adult there? My dad.

Did I tell him? He won't wake up.

Is he breathing? The question made me stop dead. He was snoring, so, yeah, he was breathing.

Can I wake him? I would try again.

I left the phone hanging off the wall with the operator still on the line, the receiver was swinging back and forth in the air from its curled cord like a pendulum. No matter what I did, no matter how hard I yelled, I couldn't wake him up. My grandmother was now full-blown screaming. I looked at my dad and grabbed his ankles and began to pull. My general thought was that if I got him out of bed, he would be easier to wake up. I yanked for everything I was worth. This was like a 250-pound full-grown man. Finally, some movement. He sat up and swiftly slammed me across the jaw with the back of his left hand. I tasted blood in my mouth. I didn't feel it though. I wasn't in any state to feel anything.

"YOU FUCKIN' BASTID," he yelled as I dropped backward on my ass. He'd hit me full force. I went flying like a goddamned ragdoll.

"THERE'S SOMETHING WRONG WITH GRANDPA," I yelled through my tears. My face was beginning to throb. Pain was registering and settling in. Finally, my father grasped what was going on. There was an emergency. He ran right by me on his way downstairs to my grandparents. I got up and tried to haul ass behind him, but I was dizzy though from the shot in the mouth. I tripped and fell again. Finally, I got to my feet and began running. Dad had gotten there before me and when I looked into the room, he sat kneeling and cradling my grandfather's head in his lap. He was tapping him lightly on the cheek. Trying to rouse him, bring him out of it. My grandmother stood there still shrieking and crying, her back pressed up against the 'fridge as if she were hoping that if she got close enough to it, it could shield her from the events unfolding.

My dad began crying. Grandpa was motionless. Mouth agape, eyes wide open. I stared intently at his pale face, drained of all color, his glasses broken and laying on the ground next to him. I'd never seen an expression like that before. Sure, I've watched countless people play dead, but this was FAR different. All the muscles were loosened giving his face a skeletal quality even though he wasn't a very thin man. His eyes, man... wide... frightened... frozen in a gaze that would never change.

I knew then... he was dead.

After a few minutes the EMTs had arrived. They pronounced Camillo Gentile dead at the scene. They covered him with a sheet and began working on my grandmother who was now hyperventilating. My father stumbled out of the house and leaned against the brick fence that surrounded the property. He was weeping quietly. I approached him and put my hand on his knee. He looked up at me with an amazing amount of hatred in his eyes, as if his tears were snake venom.

He pushed me back with his left hand.

"If you would have just called 911 as soon as this happened, your grandfather would still be here," he said, verbally gutting me in the process. "This is your fault. I have to go and call your mother." He then pushed me aside and began walking slowly up the block.

Now, listen, I know what happened wasn't my fault now, but at thirteen the guilt that had dropped onto my shoulders felt as if I were strapped in place with boulders to make sure that I was weighted down for good. How could I face my mom? My brother? Everyone? Anyone? These thoughts raced through my mind as I watched them loading my grandfather's lifeless body onto a stretcher. The EMTs passed me as they were going to and from the ambulance. Were they looking at me with sympathy or disgust? I didn't know. I sat on the curb crying. Processing. Waiting for what certainly be some type of punishment.

Chapter 3
The Mourning After

Physical punishment never came. The next few days after my grandfather's death everyone was at their wits end. It was Christmastime. We didn't know what to do with the gifts. Should we open them? Was that appropriate? Nobody was celebrating, nor was anyone in the mood to. It was one of the single most confusing periods in my entire family's life. Everything was odd. Everything felt wrong. I couldn't even sleep. Every time I closed my eyes, I could see grandpa laying there. His eyes. Staring. It chilled me. For a while I'd sleep on the floor in my parents' bedroom, so I didn't feel so alone. Yes, I was far too old to have to sleep near them, but I was as scarred as I was scared. By this time Rob had moved downstairs so I was on my own. You see, my grandparents didn't need that much room as they managed to studiously contain their filth to a single bedroom-like apartment. As a result, the second bedroom was walled up and, since it had a separate entrance, it became Rob's lair. At his age, he didn't want me around. You know, typical big brother "I need my privacy" horseshit.

I had an aunt Josie (my mom's sister) and an uncle Sammy. They were over a lot after grandpa's passing. They were equally as eccentric and insane as anyone else in our bloodline. Josie embodied all of the worst traits of my grandmother. They were exactly alike, the only difference being that Josie liked to bathe, didn't smell of piss and shit, and would actually leave the house. She was an evil, evil woman, who, like her mom, thrived on chaos and negativity. Her husband Sammy was quite the character. A true Brooklyn Goombah if ever there was one. He was like a middle-aged greaser who loved Elvis and looked as if he'd hung up his leather motorcycle jacket (circa *The Lords of Flatbush*) to drink beer instead. He had it all... the Arthur Fonzarelli pompadour haircut, the hideous pinky ring, and a golden Christ head pendant hanging off a thick herring-bone chain that was so big you could literally see Jesus's entire profile when Sammy stood just right. His only other distinguishing characteristic? A ginormous bulbous gut that was so fucking hard I swear it could have repelled bullets. Like he had a medicine ball tucked under his shirt at all times, smuggling it constantly. I would muse during my teens that there's no way he and my aunt could ever really fuck right with Mount Saint Brewery protruding from his abdomen. She was a heavy woman too, so that shit would be like *Mission: Impossible*. I grew to really love them both, especially Sammy who didn't mind sneaking me a swig of Budweiser or some kind of booze every once in a while. He was a cool cat.

With my grandfather now gone, Nanny didn't need the whole downstairs apartment so she would move upstairs with us. BUT THERE WERE STRICT CONDITIONS:

1. She had to bathe. Frequently.
2. She had to cut her bullshit with the neighbors.
3. She had to resume normal bathroom habits.

She agreed to this, and our living space was as follows: My parents had their bedroom. My grandmother moved into the room with the old lady on the chair that once belonged to me and Rob, and I finally had my own room (formerly Rob's when he became too old to bunk with his little bro) that was above my grandparents' kitchen. Rob was downstairs in his lair and the space next door was to be refurbished, disinfected, and rented out.

Things were status quo for several years. Four to be exact. In that time my grandmother was forced by my mom to bathe, and she completely stopped her "the neighbors are evil" song and dance.

But condition three? Not so much. Make no mistake, Jenny Gentile was a deeply disturbed woman. She didn't want to use the same bathroom as everyone else. So instead, she'd pee off the back porch into the backyard (she vehemently denied doing so but, man, the smell was there) and she would shit in a napkin... in her hand... and then save it somewhere until it was safe to dispose of it. I kid you not. We would frequently see her washing it down the sink (fucking gross) or walking sideways down the hall with her back turned toward everyone like a crap toting crab miser keeping her "brown precious" safe. Of course, we'd bust her nine times out of ten and then all manner of arguments would ensue.

There was nary a quiet or even semi-normal moment in the Barton house. So, without our neighbors being the bane of the household existence, she instead targeted the old lady on the chair. You know, her roomie, Sewagin.

Her name was actually Eugenia Granieri, but no one ever called her that. We called her Sewagin, and my sister for whatever reason referred to her as Zizen. Truth be told I don't think anyone knew exactly who she was or what she was called beyond being my great-aunt.

Anyway...

These two were constantly fighting and a constant stressor. They would frequently even come to blows which I must admit was kind of entertaining in a strange way. Ever see two 80-year-olds brawling? I can assure you, there is nothing like it. It was like ECW (Elderly Championship Wrestling). It was both violent and completely fucking weird. It got to the point one time in which they were forbidden from speaking to each other. Didn't stop them though. I

A Comedy of Tragedies

remember one particular incident in which my grams pushed the lady on the chair right through the front screen door. It was constant elder-fuel chaos.

Having had enough of this constant fucking lunacy, we employed a house-wide gag order. They were no longer allowed to speak to one another under any circumstances. That didn't stop them from shooting lasers via their eyes at each other, but, hey, at least it was quiet.

Sewagin had two activities, despite her age she loved taking her little old lady shopping wagon and going to the store. Other than that, her pastime was sitting ever vigilantly on her chair making sure everyone "close-a the gate" by the stairs so that our dog "he no can-a get-a the loose.".

My parents had gone somewhere so it fell upon my grandmother to cook for me. During one of her shopping excursions, she went to around the corner to the Associated Supermarket, which she referred to as "Mets." I don't know why she called it that. Maybe it was called Mets before it became associated, or maybe she couldn't pronounce associated? Who knows? While she was there, she bought chicken cutlets for dinner. Not gonna lie, fried chicken cutlets with their yummy crispy bread-crumb-coating was my favorite meal back then and any time that they were on the menu I was ecstatic. Once the prized soon-to-be-dinner dish was wheeled home via Sewagin's old lady wagon, my grandmother would prepare them and cook them.

Man, if I close my eyes, I can STILL smell them cooking, and hear them frying, every pop of the oil an absolute delight.

Once dinner time rolled around, I was first there with my dish. Immediately I'd run into the living room, to pop on the original Star Trek which WPIX, *11 Alive*, would be running at 6:00 p.m. I cut a piece of my cutlet and immediately popped it in my mouth.

What.

The.

Fuck.

They tasted like death. I mean, sure, it was the breast of a dead

25

animal I was eating, but I cannot begin to describe how rancid this shit tasted. I went to my grandmother, who was just eating a sandwich, and asked, "Is there something wrong with the chicken cutlets? Do they taste funny to you?"

"Yes," she answered. "I knew they were bad while I was cooking them. They smelled really funny. That's why I'm eating a sandwich."

Furious, I asked, "If you knew they were bad, why did you cook them?"

My grandmother looked at me and with all the spite in the world and said, "If I would have said something, I would have argued with Sewagin, but you told me to not speak to her, so…"

I saw red. I swear to god I just blanked out. The next thing I remember was seeing my parents walking up the stairs, Sewagin yelling "close-a the gate," and the startling realization that I had my grandmother pinned down to the table while I was screaming and yelling in her face. Things were that bad. The tension and chaos in our home was always off-the-charts. If my parents didn't get home exactly when they did, who knows what would have happened? I shudder to think.

Between the ECW shenanigans, my dad's constant drinking and subsequent fighting with my mom, the corner house on Manor Court was a veritable vortex of hostility. To some degree or another this took its toll on everyone. Everybody was on edge… constantly. We were all at odds with each other, one way or another.

I was 17-years old now and I thought I was untouchable. The truth was I was a horrible person. An absolute asshole. I was a troublemaker who would look to beat people up for fun. I lived to inflict pain on others. Not mental pain, but physical pain. I once beat up a kid with a 2-liter bottle of Coke. That shit was fizzing everywhere as I was striking this dickhead, who did deserve to get his ass kicked, but didn't exactly deserve the carbonated thrashing I was administering.

I didn't give a fuck about anything. One time I was in a car with my best friend, Dave; we were coming back from a softball game and stopped at a red light. Members of the "gang" of miscreants known as The Avenue U Boys were hanging out. Standing on their corner.

They were eyeballing us. Of course, I wouldn't dare stand for this, so in typical Brooklyn attitude I yelled, "The fuck you looking at?" They were unamused and started spouting some kind of inane teenaged tough guy horseshit.

I grabbed Dave's steering wheel and forced him to pull over. There were about four of them. I reached into Dave's backseat and grabbed a baseball bat and got out of his car.

"Lookit this asshole! He's gonna need that bat," one of them snarled at me.

I took that bat and threw it on the ground in front of them. "No," I said. "That's for you, fucks." They looked at me, looked at each other and scattered.

I ain't telling you that story to make you think I was this extreme tough guy. I don't give a rat's ass about my image. Really, I was just an asshole. A completely different person than who I am now. The rage I had inside of me was always bubbling over. Always bleeding through. I hated me. Detested me. My family life had taken a toll on me by now, but that's no excuse for how I behaved. I chose to act like a fucking idiot. No one made me do it. It was my crutch. Typical teen angst. Everyone else was responsible but me... me... poor fucking me.

Kris Schlamp was always there for me. He is the most stand-up guy in the world. I have known him since I was about 13-years old. A mutual friend, George Jensen, introduced us. Standing in at 6'4" Kris is a giant in comparison to my vertically challenged 5'7." Blond hair, blue eyes, he has a heart of gold and is also completely and thoroughly insane. He's a couple of years older than I am but we bonded instantly, mainly because he was just as much of a fucking weirdo as I was. Here's a perfect example:

It was winter, Kris had come over wearing this big thick overcoat. We were sitting in my room watching TV. I think it was actually Peter Jackson's *Meet the Feebles*. Anyway, the AIDS bunny had just popped out of its cake and vomited.

Kris looked at me and said... "Hey, get a knife."

I was like, "Why?" He reached into the folds of his jacket and removed an entire Krakus Polish ham still in its formfitting can. Mind you, we'd been hanging out for over an hour by this point, and it dawned on me that he had this fucking ham in jacket pocket for probably a lot longer than that. Why? Just why? I'll never know and, truthfully, I'll never care. This was one of those instances that made Kris, Kris. I love him. He is my family. If I came home one night and found him naked and in bed with my wife, Dani, before I thought of killing him, I would rationalize that there had to be a good explanation for this. I have that level of trust in him, and I'd rather die than see anyone or anything hurt him. We had several really odd misadventures together which even managed to enter the realm of what could be considered paranormal. With two weirdos vibing off each other, what else could you possibly expect other than some type of strange fuckery?

Kris and I were always together. Inseparable. Kris had this friend named Richie. Simply put, Richie is a Class A filth-freak with one of the most annoying voices to ever vibrate a vocal cord.

"Hulloh. I'm Richie. Can I smell yah glohves?"

Sure, he never ever actually asked to smell anyone's gloves, but for some reason that sentence just embodies that voice to the tenth power in my head. I'm pretty sure Kris would just want to hang with Rich because he knew I couldn't stand the dude. He was just a gross and skeevy human being. Not trying to be a dick about him. Everyone is different and everyone has their own thing going on that should be celebrated. It's just that there are certain people you come across in your life that for whatever reason end up making your skin crawl. Richie, was that for me.

"Hulloh. I'm Richie. Can I shampoo yah toe haih? Hulloh? Ummm... hulloh?"

Richie lived in Gerritsen Beach, Brooklyn. Gerritsen is a really fucked neighborhood and so OF COURSE he lived there. Gerritsen was also a hot spot for Satanists who were rumored to have performed rituals and sacrifices there. Police were always finding remnants of candles and even the carcasses of slaughtered animals. Or at least that's how the stories went at the time. In New York, especially Brooklyn, every neighborhood had its own mythos, its own set of rules. You could be on a nice street one second, turn the corner and be in literal hell.

Kris and me? We were nuts. I remember one time I was with Kris in an old restaurant on Emmons Avenue called Mr. Philly's. They were famous for a sandwich called the Roman Burger which was a hoagie type roll with two beef burgers on them along with Genoa salami and Provolone. They also made kick-ass waffle fries.

Man, what I would do now for a Roman Burger.

Anyway, me and Kris made it up to the counter and the girl, probably around our age, looked at him and said, "Hey! I remember you! We played together when we were young! You made me pray to rocks!" They shared a laugh, while I was standing there slack-jawed and in disbelief. He made this chick "pray to fucking rocks"? Yep, that was Kris. Utterly and wonderfully deranged. I could tell you so much more, but some shit just has to stay between he and I.

Now, where was I? Oh yeah, Gerritsen Beach.

It was Spring of '89, and we had just dropped Richie back off at his house, and it was so nice out we figured we'd stop off at Gerritsen Beach to see if we could dig up any trouble. So brave, we were. Everyone knows that if you go looking for Satanists doing occult rituals, the proper time to go and investigate would be three o'clock in the afternoon. Yep, we were real warriors! Kris made it to the shore and decided it'd be best to taunt me with a horseshoe crab. If you've never seen one of these foul wretched denizens of the deep, Google it. Scream in terror. Then come back here to finish this yarn.

I'll wait. Thanks.

Back yet? Still screaming? Yep, I get it. Here now? Okay, good.

So, Kris picked up this black facehugger by its tail and began brandishing it toward me.

Let me be clear... I have three irrational fears: Bugs, heights, and nuns. Essentially if a nun ever sat next to me on a plane carrying a jar of fireflies, I'd be DOA. No, I didn't go to catholic school and have a bad experience with a sister. They just fucking scare me, okay? They float, man. They don't fucking walk... they float like Angela from *Night of the Demons*. No matter what you say to dissuade me from this line of thinking, I can assure you, you're shit out of luck. They fucking float and that's just that. Period.

So yeah, Kris was waving around this foul sea-bug at me and I was freaking out.

Another way of thinking no one will ever sway me from is the fact that any type of crab, lobster, or shrimp is, without question, a sea insect. I'm sorry to every one of you who eats them. Sorry to break it to you, but they are bugs. They walk funny (sometimes sideways), have claws, antennae, multiple legs, claws, and eyes. That equals fucking bugs to me, and it should to you too. Case in point: If you saw a lobster crawling on your kitchen floor would you say to yourself, "Hey, let me get a pot of frothy hot water going," or would you grab a fucking baseball bat and bash that thing to bits? If you pick the water option, take a moment to look at yourself in the mirror and admit that you are a liar.

That being said, Kris finally finished fucking with his tiny sea monster, and we decided to go and climb around on the rocks. I dunno why we were climbing the rocks, but one thing was for certain, we weren't gonna pray to them.

After a few moments Kris called me over. "Steve, Look at this? What in the fuck?"

In his hands Kris was holding one of the strangest and most out of place things I've ever seen, especially on a friggin' beach, wedged into some rocks... a heavy pewter pendant with one of the angriest faces I've ever seen. Think sort of the way the head of the Pazuzu statue looked in *The Exorcist*. It was about three inches long, two inches wide, and about an inch in height from the flat base. Like my Uncle's Christ Head pendant but way bigger and heavier. At the top it had a small hole so you could hang it on a string or thin chain. Total, I'd say it weighed in at about a pound, maybe a pound and a half. It looked old. Grayish in color, it had caked-on dirt and sand embedded in the creases of the eyes, nose, and mouth area. The back of what I shall now refer to as "The Idol" was flat and had some weird scratching on the back. Could have been markings or some sort of letters, or it simply just could have been scratches from being on the beach so long that appeared to be shapes or letters due to the power of pareidolia. Either way, this thing was weird. Kris handed it over to me. It was sinister looking. I loved it. Even at a young age I was always fascinated by the occult and all things spooky. This was so in my wheelhouse.

"We should leave that thing right here or where we found it," Kris said, extreme matter-of-fact caution resonating in his voice.

"No fucking way," I answered. "You found it, you don't want it?"

"No. It's not good, man. That thing could be evil," he said.

I could tell he was hoping I'd comply, but instead I scoffed. I knew deep down inside if he didn't want it, then this fucker was MINE. I took it home and threw it in my dresser drawer where it stayed for a week. Thursday rolled around and Kris and I were doing what we always did. We sat on my front porch playing Atari 2600 on this small portable TV I had for just such occasions. Tired of the usual suspects like *Jungle Hunt*, *Pitfall!*, and *Megamania*, we sat back and chilled as my dad, who was remarkably sober, went to the train station to pick up my mom. It was a delightfully warm and quiet night. The time was 10:45 p.m. and my dad had just pulled out of the driveway.

"So," Kris asked. "You still have The Idol?"

We called it "The Idol," mainly because we had NO idea exactly what to call it, and it's not like the word "pendant" rolls off the tongue.

"Damned straight I do," I said. "It's in my drawer inside." Funnily enough, even though I had this thing for several days I never once bothered to look at it or even touch it. As if it were in its new resting place and I thought better than to disturb it.

"Can I see it?"

I pushed my chair back from the table with the TV and the Atari on top and walked to my room and approached my dresser. Slowly I opened the drawer, half-expecting it not to be there for some reason. Yet, it was there. Seemingly waiting. I grabbed it and brought it back outside and handed it to Kris. By this time my mom was already climbing up the stairs after working her shift. It only took a couple of minutes for my dad to get her as the Sheepshead Bay train station was only a couple of blocks away from our house. We just didn't want her walking home alone late at night. I remember she had to go to the bathroom badly. Comically, each time she climbed a step she let out a little fart with every footfall. I remember pissing my pants laughing as she sped by. Now, in my Forties, I can fully appreciate the horror she was going through at that time on her way to the bathroom. Sometimes your bladder and your bowels just have their own agenda.

I sat back down next to Kris and handed him The Idol. We were both silent, fidgeting with this, to us, otherworldly object. For the life of me, I can't remember a single word we would have said to each other during this time, and I have a pretty damned good memory. I just remember the silence during the intent examination. The Idol still had the sand and dirt from the beach caked in its various crevices, as it never occurred to me to wash it off. I don't know how long had passed. Maybe ten minutes? My mom came out to the front porch with a now relieved look on her face and plopped herself down in a chair to have a cigarette. I can still smell her perfume when I think about it as she bathed in it before heading to work. Avon's Sweet Honesty. The familiar scent was now mixing with that of a freshly lit Salem cigarette. She leaned back and took a drag, observing Kris and I fiddling with something.

"Whatcha got there," she inquired genuinely curious. Kris and I told her the story of where we had gotten this thing from. She was, shall we say, less than pleased about us climbing on rocks in reputedly bad beach neighborhood. My mom was very protective of me. The thought of me in danger would drive her off the deep end. She was as over-protective as over-protective gets.

"Can I see this thing," she inquired. Of course she could. If I dared say no, I knew the wooden spoon, nay, the baseball bat, wouldn't be far behind and I had enough troubles.

I pushed myself off the chair and as I was getting up, I accidentally dropped The Idol.

Let me set the stage for you. In case you weren't paying attention (and who could blame you) we lived in a two-family brick house.

Under the front porch was our garage and adjacent to that, obviously, was the driveway. The porch floor was concrete surrounded by about four feet of brick work with only a few narrow openings. Conceivably you could be sitting on the floor of the porch, and no one would be able to see you from the street. I used this to my advantage many times when I was a kid.

I remember The Idol dropping from my fingertips. I fumbled at the air with both hands trying to catch it. It never made a sound when hitting the floor. I never heard it hit... I never even saw it bounce... and to this day I get chills thinking about its fall from my grasp. It was gone. I shit you not. As if it disappeared into thin air.

I looked at Kris, he looked at me and we both looked at my mom. As I said before this thing was damned heavy for its size. There's no way we wouldn't have heard it hit the concrete floor, but we didn't. My mom put on the porch light, we folded up the chairs, I grabbed a flashlight, and the three of us scoured the porch. Nothing. No sign of it. It's as if it just wasn't there.

My porch wasn't huge. Kris and my mother were always in my line of sight so I would have seen it if one of them had tried to pocket The Idol as a means of screwing with me or trying to scare me. We looked everywhere.

Finally, we even went down to my driveway and checked there too in case there was a remote possibility of this thing, this heavy ugly evil looking thing, bouncing off the ground and bouncing through one of the openings of the brick work surrounding my porch. I mean, we certainly would have heard that if that happened. But nothing was down there either. It was just... gone.

"You guys are funning me," my mother said in equal parts laughter and disbelief. "Very funny. Haha," she accused, equal parts slightly amused and annoyed as she took a drag from her cigarette.

She then gave us both a goodnight kiss, reminded us to clean up the porch, and put everything away before we went about our business. She turned, shaking her head, and made her way back inside to her bedroom for some well-deserved shut eye.

Kris and I just sat there looking at each other. Did that shit really just happen? It did, and to this very day I haven't seen hide nor hair of that thing.

I've always been curious what happened to The Idol. I probably always will be. It's as if this thing wanted to stay lost, and stay lost it has.

Chapter 4
The Vertigo Shot

Full disclosure: It's been nearly 48-hours since I've been staring at the three paragraphs below. Instead of continuing on, I stopped, fiddled with the title of this book, of which there have been several thus far, gone over previous paragraphs to make sure I wrote exactly what I wanted them to say. Anything I can think of to keep myself from detailing what's next. Hell, in all honesty just typing out this paragraph is kind of like my way of stalling. I know what's coming. I know how it is going to make me feel. The kind of wounds it is going to tear back open. I've never discussed in detail with anyone what transpired in July of 1989. Few people know a little. No one knows everything. I'm hoping that if I can just let this pour out of me once and for all that I can finally feel like it's out of my system. I don't think it ever will be, but these troubles have been swimming in my head for decades. It's time to face them. Maybe getting it out will help. Maybe it won't. Either way, I'm kind of scared. Writing this out is not an act of bravery to me. If anything, not opening up about this sooner is just an act of extreme cowardice, and a prolonged one at that. This door has been shut for so long. The thought of opening it and letting the light in may prove to be too much for me. I don't know. For the sake of trying to be a better person I am going to attempt to turn the knob.

Back in the day, my friends and I had formed a softball team. We were called the 209ers after the Public School whose yard we had always hung out and played in. What a fucking motley cast of characters we had there. There was me, Kris, my childhood friend Carmine, and his brothers, Franky and Antony. Who could forget Vinny, who had the distinguishing characteristic of having a bulbous swath of hair directly over his ass crack. He used to frequently moon people while shouting, "SPEAK INTO THE MIC!" Also accounted for were the Cabram brothers, William, Peter, and Ely, my currently friend/ex-friend Chilly who's going through one of his alcohol-fueled "I Hate Steve" moments as I write this, and finally a pair of best buddies who I would come to love dearly, Brian Hoffman, and David Tirado. I'll get to them soon, but for the purpose of moving things along in somewhat of a cohesive manner let's just stick to the rails for a few.

The 209ers had grown in notoriety. Some people even considered us a gang and the schoolyard of Public School 209 was our turf. So fucking silly. We were just a bunch of weird schmucks who enjoyed not only playing ball, but also each other's company. There were other frequent members of the team, but one of them is a person who would become rather integral to this tale. Franky's friend, Neal. This dude used to pitch for us, but he was always hanging around. Truth be told he was a chubby, Spanish, giant dude. I never really cared for Neal much, but Franky loved him, and he was an okay pitcher.

It was July 18th of '89 and I told my mom that I was going to be home that night very late. She was on her way to work and not happy with me at all. We were arguing A LOT lately. For all intents and purposes, I was a momma's boy. She was ALWAYS keeping tabs on what I was doing, and just like any Italian mother, she could sense me fucking up from miles away. No matter how bad I was screwing up and how unlikely it would be that she'd ever be able to find out about what I was doing, she was there, large wooden spoon in hand, ready to tan my damned hide. One time she hit me with the aforementioned spoon - which she wielded like Excalibur - across my ass and it broke. I made the mistake of laughing at her. Five seconds later she whaled on me with a baseball bat. She was not to be trifled with, but as I got older, I got bolder. That didn't stop me from fighting her and her wishes at every turn. This was a particularly bad argument, which ended with me saying the words, "Would you just drop fucking dead, already?" I stormed away.

Honestly, other than me staying out later than usual I do not remember just what in the world our argument was about. One thing was for sure though... we were both at our wit's end at the time. Without saying another word to her, I stormed off. There was important shit that needed tending to, like hanging out in the schoolyard and basically doing nothing. She had gone to work and after a while the 209ers had gathered for some impromptu softball practice. Neal had driven to practice and brought Franky along with him.

The clock ticked away and before we knew it, it was already late evening. I'd say about 10:15 p.m. At this point the only ones still hanging around were myself, Kris, Franky, his brother Carmine and Neal. Somehow or another we all decided that we should fuck around with a Ouija board. Neal had one with him. It was in the trunk of his car. And here I thought Kris was strange for smuggling meats or candy in his jacket. I mean, who the fuck drives around with a Ouija board in their car? Let me be clear, I am a skeptic and to this day I don't think that anything mass produced by Hasbro could be a key tool to contact the dead on the other side. Is there even another side to contact? Who the hell knows.

Of course we were all game. We were all freaks, and freaks who LOVED horror movies in particular. In my head I was wondering who'd be the first to start moving the planchette while claiming innocence. It was probably gonna be me. Again, I was a dick.

"Fuck it, let's do this," I said.

"If we're gonna do this we have to do it THE RIGHT way," said Neal, who was all of a sudden coming off as an authority on this hocus pocus. He went on to explain that he and his family were big time into Santeria.

No, not the Sublime song. Santeria is akin to Voodoo. There are drastic differences between them, but I'm not here to give you a history lesson, and there is such a thing as Google, so knock yerself out later.

Neal said that we needed a glass of water and a white candle to properly conduct our session with the Orishas (spirits) we were about to contact. Since I lived across the street and down the block I jetted home, grabbed the goods, and made it immediately back to the set of steps housed in the 209 school yard. I was excited. Spooky shit, even stuff I didn't believe in, was exhilarating. Upon my return we lit the candle and then placed it and the glass of water on either side of the board, respectively, and then began asking all manner of inane questions. Our otherworldly queries were so insignificant that I only remember one of them. I'll get to that in a bit.

After each question the board began moving. It never stopped on any numbers or letters. It had no pattern, rhyme, or reason. It was just moving and picking up speed as time went along. No matter what we asked it, we got ZERO intelligent responses. After a few minutes the planchette finally started sliding and stopping across various letters. I don't remember which or what was spelled out. Who was moving this thing? The only thing I knew for sure was that it wasn't me.

Gibberish. Pure Gibberish. That's all we were getting from this thing. It was like a colossal waste of time. There were no witty retorts. No sentiments that we could be used to rib each other later. Just random letters. Nothing resembling words. It wasn't funny. In fact, it was borderline annoying. What was the point of this? I sighed heavily and asked what the final question of the night would be.

"Are you just wasting our time to keep us here?"

The planchette moved immediately to "YES" and everything stopped. We all drew our hands back. "Okay, that was pretty cool," I said with an amused but uneasy laugh. "Who was doing it?" No one was taking any credit. There wasn't a single detectable smirk from anyone. No one fessed up. Weird. It was then that the board had been packed up, the water dumped out, and the candle extinguished. Many years later I learned that when using a Ouija board you were supposed to say "Goodbye" before exiting a session. We didn't do that.

My dad was actually sober this night because he didn't go to work. Once 10:45 p.m. had come, he'd gone to pick up my mom from the Sheepshead Bay train station and she'd be home sometime soon depending on which train she caught.

Having had enough schoolyard shenanigans for the day, I went home just in time to see my mom entering the front door. I went inside to put away the glass and the candle. She was standing in the doorway of her room. The time was 11:22 p.m.

"Are you still not talking to me," she asked? I didn't answer. "Come on, Steve, this is silly."

In my head I thought, "Oh fuck you!" but no words ever came out of my mouth. I turned away from her and went back out to the front porch where everyone was sitting on my stoop (that's Brooklynese for "stairs" as in the stairs leading up to the top floor of my house should any of you not be familiar with the term). Back inside I heard her bedroom door close. I trotted down the steps around everyone until I got to the bottom and leaned back on the metal railing. Everybody was pretty much silent. Neal was standing up. Looking into my front door. "What's up?" I asked. Neal looked at me for a second and then promptly returned his gaze to the doorway leading into the front door of my house.

"Steve. There's something in your house," he said with a hushed tone.

"What!?" I looked up and saw nothing.

"There's something in your house and it's not leaving until it gets something from you."

I scoffed. Did he think I was twelve and scared or something? Yeah, nice try, jackass.

"I'm serious, man," Neal said in sort of a desperate tone. "It's not leaving. It's staying and waiting. Waiting for you."

"Well, what is it?"

"I'm not sure," he said. "It's large and it's black. It takes up your entire hallway. I don't know what it is, but it's there."

The hair on my neck stood up a little.

"Okay, I'm going home," Neal announced and went immediately back to Franky's car without saying another word to anyone. We were all just sitting (or standing) there kind of dumbfounded. Franky and Carmine got up and said goodbye. They walked up to the car and Neal was looking forward. I could see him biting on this thumbnail. "Later," yelled Carmine and his brother flashed Kris and I a nod. They got in and sped away.

I turned to Kris, "What the fuck was all that about?" He shrugged, as perplexed as I was. He got to his feet and brushed off his legs.

"I should get going too," he said. We slapped hands and I walked him to his car.

"G'night, man," I said.

"See you tomorrow, asshole," he said with a smile as he started his car, a cherry red Thunderbird, and drove off.

I was standing there watching as his car turned the corner and kept going, taking some kind of weird comfort in his red taillights. I'm not too bold to admit I was spooked. I stood upon the bottom step, inhaled deeply and made my way to the front door. I locked it. The house was dark with the only illumination coming from some strategically placed night lights.

I made my way through the kitchen and stopped as I was about to turn down the hallway to my room. "Nothing there," I told myself and speed-walked directly to my bedroom. I entered, shut the door, stripped down to my skivvies and a T-shirt and jumped in my bed. "Fucking weird," I thought. I was asleep before I knew it, blankets pulled up to my chin, despite it being July.

The phone rang. My eyes fluttered a bit, my mom would surely answer it. That didn't happen. It kept ringing. By the third time I sat up and looked at the clock. 8:43 a.m. I picked up the receiver.

"Hello?"

"Hi, yes, this is [so and so] from Prudential. Would I be able to speak with Mrs. Ann Barton, please?"

"Yeah, just a second."

I threw my feet over the side of my bed and listened. I hadn't heard her snoring. I did hear the air conditioner in my parents' bedroom. Nanny and the old lady on the chair were in the kitchen preparing coffee. I could smell it. I stood up, stretched really fast, and approached her door.

"Mom," I said as I knocked. No answer.

I opened the door and peaked in. My mother was laying on her side with her back to me. I made my way around the front of the bed so that I could wake her. I stood there for a second and stared. Her face. Something was wrong. She was pale. I could see dental floss thin blue veins spider-webbing on her cheeks. Her eyes were shut, sunken, and dark. Her mouth... her mouth was open, but her lips were pulled back from her teeth and her gums, giving her mouth a horse-like appearance. Her tongue was purple and laying against the pillow. Completely dry. I never felt it, but I instinctively just knew that it was. Next to it I could see a bit of dried blood caked onto her pillow.

"Mom?" I asked.

I reached down and grabbed her hand. Her skin was like ice. I lifted up her right arm and it let out a sickening pop. I dropped it, startled.

What happened next was like something out of a movie. Alfred Hitchcock's *Vertigo*, to be specific. The background of the entire room sunk backward, while the bed and her body seemingly drew forward toward me. Then everything stopped.

My mother was dead. I'd come to find out she had a brain aneurysm in her sleep sometime after my dad had gone to work.

The house was remarkably silent. All I could hear were birds chirping. I walked slowly out of her bedroom and headed back to mine. I picked up the receiver of the phone and said calmly into it, "I'm sorry, but she cannot come to the phone right now," and hung it up.

I remember standing there still. I looked out of my window. It was gorgeous out. An incredible summer day was at hand. It was too nice out for something like this to be really happening wasn't it?

I turned back around to the hallway and looked back toward her bedroom. She was still lying there motionless. This was happening. I walked out into the kitchen.

"Good, morning," said Nanny.

"Hey," I answered. My dad had already left for work by this time, and I inquired if Rob had already left for whatever job he had at the time.

"He left about a half an hour ago," she answered. Our front door was open. The old lady in the chair was in her spot. We nodded at each other. I stepped out onto my porch.

Birds singing. Not a cloud in the sky. The neighborhood was still, almost frozen. "Such an incredible day," I thought to myself. I breathed in deeply before heading back inside. The air was fresh as newly folded laundry. The temperature utterly perfect.

Slowly I turned around, passed my grandmother who was now sitting at the table drinking her coffee, and made my way back to my bedroom shutting the door behind me. I picked up the phone and dialed 911.

"911, what's your emergency," asked a woman's voice on the phone. I didn't answer.

"Hello? This is 911, what's your emergency, please?"

"Yeah, Hi, my mom... she's dead."

The person went on to question me whether or not I was sure as well as ask all the standard questions. I was sure. I gave them our address, they told me paramedics were on their way, and I hung up the phone. From there I called my friend Vinny who I knew geographically was closest to me. I was calm as a cucumber as he answered his phone.

"Vin, hey man. Sorry for waking you. My mom's dead, do you think that you could come over?"

All I heard was Vinny hang up the phone. Assumingly, that meant yes. He would be coming over. I opened my bedroom door and never looked back toward my mom's bedroom. I knew what I would see.

What was the purpose? I knew what I had to do then. I went to tell my grandmother that her daughter had died.

"Nan. I'm sorry but your daughter is dead."

"WHAT," she gasped! "WHAT ARE YOU TALKING ABOUT?!? ANN? ANNA?" she shrieked, running back to the bedroom. "ANN WHAT'S WRONG! WAKE UP! ANNA? ANN?"

I stood there for a few moments. Nanny was screaming and crying at the top of her lungs, yet it kind of all faded in with the background noise. The stillness was back. The chirping of the birds.

I walked back outside and sat on my stoop, observing the beauty around me while in my head I knew that extreme tragic mayhem was unfolding just a few feet away. I looked up the block and saw Vinny running toward my house, full steam. He was just about thirty seconds away when the ambulance pulled up in front of our place. The paramedics got out and were prepping by the time Vinny got to my bottom step.

"Steve? You okay? What happened, man?"

I said nothing. Just sat there staring. Grandmother in the background screaming. The neighbors began to gather. Not approaching the house but standing around the street looking. Waiting. The paramedics were making their way up the stairs staring right at me.

"She's in the back bedroom," I said to them as Vinny put his hand on my shoulder. They went in.

Moments later my grandmother came out and asked me, "STEVEN, STEVEN! WHAT'S WRONG WITH YOUR MOTHER?"

I said nothing. Just sat there. Staring. Birds chirping. Neighbors gathering. Sun glowing. Beautiful. Quiet. Still. A few more moments later, one of the paramedics emerged from my house to the front porch. I stood up and walked up the stairs to meet them, Vinny close behind.

"I'm sorry. There's nothing we can do."

Grandmother screaming. Birds chirping. Sun glowing. Air still.

I began to shake, turned around, and ran down my stairs. I don't know why. Impulse maybe. All of a sudden, it all came crashing in. I began to scream. Vinny caught up with me and put me in what could only be described as a bear hug. I was hard to handle. Shifting violently, trying to escape, screaming so loud that I went silent. My mouth was open as if I were yelling but nothing was coming out. Vinny's grip tightened.

"It's okay, man. Everything will be okay. It's okay. It's okay."

I kept struggling, but I knew he wasn't letting go. Vinny was pretty friggin' strong. I became exhausted and eventually limp. He wrangled me back to my steps and sat me down. My neighbors tried approaching...

"Trust me, it's better for right now that you give him some space," Vinny told them while completely cutting them off. I remain so very grateful for that. I didn't know what was going on, but inside I did. I especially didn't know what I was capable of or what was going to happen from here.

My mother was dead at just fifty-three years old. The shaking continued as I sat there. Staring. The birds chirping. The sun glowing. The air still.

I have no idea how long I was sitting there for. Vinny went inside, got me some clothes, and began using the phone to call the rest of our friends. My dad's job, my two brothers, and my sister were called too. I have no idea who made those calls. I never bothered to ask.

Franky and Carmine were the next to arrive. They got out of their car and ran over to me. I stood up, walked over and got into the front passenger side seat. The vinyl was cool. It felt nice against the skin on the back of my legs as the day started heating up. It was definitely a lot more comfy than the stoop, and somehow more private. I remember feeling like a science experiment. Everybody was staring. "Should we poke him with a stick?" I imagined them thinking while reminiscing about my favorite scene from *The Blob* in which the old man poked a newly dropped blob filled meteor. My mind was all over the place. I do remember thinking that though, and fuck is that just typical me.

Tommy was the first member of my family to arrive. Kris, came next and he joined Vinny, Franky, and Carmine sitting on the brickwork which surrounded our house. Every once in a while, one of them would pop their heads in and ask if I needed anything. I didn't. I just wanted to sit. There was a crowd of people around my house now. A yellow taxi pulled up and my dad darted out screaming "NO, NO, NO!"

I asked Vinny to come over and call my friend Maria. Maria and I had grown very close, and I don't know why but I just wanted to be around someone pretty removed from the situation. She got there within an hour, and we went to the schoolyard for a little bit of quiet. I don't remember what we talked about, but I was glad she was there. After a little while, she left, and I went back to sit in Franky's car. One by one, everyone filed in. Rob, my sister, etc. None of them ever came to the car to check on me.

Somehow or another it was decided that my friends and I should go to Franky's house. I knew why, even though I never told them that I did. It was time to remove my mom's body and they didn't want me to see that.

I got into Franky's car and we drove away, the birds chirping. The sun glowing. The air still.

Chapter 5
The NUMBers Game

There was a lot going on after the passing of my mom. To this very day, I'm haunted by the twisted look upon her face when I found her that morning. I can still see it when I close my eyes. I never got to make up with her after our fight, and the fact that my last words to her were "Would you just drop fucking dead, already?" are amongst my biggest regrets. I said that and not even 24-hours later my "wish" had come to pass.

Words have weight.

My mind was on fire. I didn't sleep for days. Seeing her laying in that casket, her eyelids looked odd, as if they were made of papier-mâché instead of flesh. Her lips still looked alien, as if they were just draped around her teeth. Her mouth was closed, but the way the skin was hanging around it looked so strange, as if her jaws were jutting through. Upon closer inspection I remember seeing thin openings in her lips, no doubt the product of some ill threading or maybe not enough glue. I don't know the process. Maybe it was all in my head. The whole thing just fucks with me. We should never have open-casket wakes. People shouldn't be allowed to have their last memories of someone be tied to their death masks.

I only went to my grandfather's wake and was so horrified that I had to leave. It was too much for my tiny 13-year-old brain to handle. This was my mother. No matter how painful it was, I had to be there. The days of her viewing at Cusimano and Russo Funeral Home passed like months. Everyone was "sorry for our loss." It's impossible not to get sick of people whom you barely even know coming up to you and telling you how badly they feel for you.

"You're sorry for me? Who are you again? Oh, YES! RIGHT! You're my second cousin on my aunt's side from Saskatoon, west of Ottawa, who found out about her death through an old college friend that used to know my grandmother during her years in burlesque before she started her Rickshaw business in south Harlem next to the Little Sahara Gyro Shoppe on 110th Street with Johnny "Beebop Shop" Fitz, the world's most interesting Ferret smuggler. Gotcha! Thanks, man!"

For the record, my grandmother never did burlesque, though I accidentally caught her nude one day. It was like that scene from E.T. in which the alien is discovered for the first time, and both it and the person who found it began screaming. Lots of screaming. Many moons worth of screaming. I've never been able to look at a raccoon the same way. So much fur. So very angry.

Me? When I take my last ride, I don't want any part of wakes or funerals. The only way I won't be cremated is if someone I trust promises to encase my corpse in a formfitting glitter encrusted body bag and hang me from the ceiling like a piñata. Everyone in attendance could line up and whack at my lifeless body with Pixy Stix until glitter and sugar collide in a toxic cloud of fuckery that would have everyone equal parts cackling and coughing at the sheer absurdity of it all. I would also like a hype man at my funeral...

"ARE THERE ANY MOURNERS UP IN THIS MOTHERFUCK-ERRRRRRRRRRRRR?"

"IF YA BEREAVED, PUTCHA HANDS UP! IF YA GOT GRIEF, PUTCHA HANDS UP!"

About a week after her burial, I had the most vivid dream ever. In it, I was asleep on the floor of her room so I could enjoy the air conditioner. It was crazy hot out. I woke up to find her standing in front of her mirror, checking her hair and then spraying her perfume. She walked over to me and kissed me on the head telling me, "I love you. It's time for me to go." As she turned and walked away, I woke up for real, in my room. I swear to god, I could smell her scent, Sweet Honesty, in the air. That dream brought me a type of comfort I have never had in life.

Upon waking up, I realized that one particular vulture was circling: My bitch of a sister, Camille. This was her opportunity to raid our house of not only my mom's jewelry, but every other thing of value that was there. We wouldn't need the sterling silver spoons, forks, and knives or the fine china. She was literally going from room to room and taking whatever she wanted. My dad didn't care. She was, after all, Daddy's little girl who could do no wrong.

After my mom's death, her sister, my Aunt Josie, went batshit nuts. She was absolutely insane, and Sammy, her husband, was incredibly supportive of her lunacy. In her mind now that her sister had passed and we were living with mother, that somehow made her entitled to part of our home. Not sure just how this math adds up, but to her it did. Of course, my father told them to go and scratch their collective asses. They weren't getting jack shit. So, she resorted to doing the only thing she knew how to do... throw Italian curses! The fabled *Malocchio* was back and in full effect, baby! One time she literally stopped her car by our backyard, got out, and threw a dead chicken over our fence before pulling down her left eyelid and throwing the horns. Incidents like this became her pastime. Some people played ball; Aunt Josie threw curses. Needless to say, they alienated themselves from our lives.

Josie died sometime later. She had fallen while getting out of the tub in her bathroom and cracked her head open. Apparently, the sight of so much of her own blood was the gateway to a massive heart attack. Sammy found her dead on their bathroom floor. That's a sad and hard way to die, but I'm a firm believer in Karma and that you reap what you sow.

I'd be lying if I said that growing up without my mom didn't have its perks. My dad couldn't give the slightest shit about what I did or when I would come home. One night, Kris had brought Richie over and we were watching TV as per usual. We would frequently torture Rich without him knowing. This particular evening wasn't unusual. Kris and Rich had gone to Brennan and Carr over on Nostrand Avenue in Brooklyn for some chow. I declined the invite because I'm not a fan of the place, if only because it's always nighttime inside despite the time of day. There were no windows, and the lighting was so dim that you could barely see their menus. When it comes to food, I want to be able to easily identify what's in front of me and I want there to be lots of light so I can see where to stick my knife and fork. Make sure whatever is speared is of the cooked variety and not wiggling. Kris got his usual roast beef sandwich and Rich got a container of clam chowder to go.

Being that my mom was gone, and nobody really gave a fuck about anything anymore, Kris would just let himself in. I was in my room, lying on the bed with my dog, a Yorkshire Terrier named Corky. My mom named him. Corky the Yorkie. Yep, she never had such a great imagination. In any event Corky was stinking to high holy heaven. He needed a bath desperately, so I made a mental note and put "animal bathing" on my internal to-do list. I sat up when they came in. They both sat on the floor in front of me. *Ren and Stimpy* was on. I looked down at Rich's steaming soup. Kris was sitting on my left next to my bureau on top of which sat a small pair of scissors. I nudged his shoulder to get his attention and quietly mouthed the words, "Hand me the scissors." Kris had zero clue what I was gonna do but he was also delightfully intrigued. He handed me the shears.

"Hey, Rich," I said. "I have never tried Brennan and Carr's clam chowder. Can I try a little?"

"Sure," he said entirely too trusting. Mind you, he had heard me say that I HATED all seafood about one thousand times. You would think this request would have lit a few light bulbs in his thick skull, but nope. The inside of his dome remained, as always, dimly lit. He was captivated by the "Space Madness" episode of the toon that was on *Nick at Nite*. He reached back handing me the container of soup without ever taking his eyes off the TV. Kris looked back at me.

Corky was sound asleep. I took the container and positioned it right under my dog's ass and began snipping off a few errant dingle berries that were hanging there straight into Rich's meal. Kris's eyes widened in shock as a huge grin befell his face. He started laughing out loud, which prompted Richie to laugh too. He thought Kris was laughing at the TV. He had no idea. I mixed the dried dog fruit into the soup with the spoon and handed him back his newly minted Corky Chowder.

"Thanks, man!"

We watched as he ate every drop, maniacally laughing the entire time. This was a small victory. Cruel? Yes. Funny? Undeniably.

Hey, I said I was an asshole back then, right?

Later that evening it came time for Rich to go home. It was like 11:30 p.m. I decided to go with Kris to drop Richie off and then we were gonna stop at McDonalds and go back to my place to play some Nintendo.

Usually, it takes about twenty minutes to drive back and forth to Gerritsen Beach from Sheepshead Bay. I got in the front with Kris. Richie got in the back. He immediately began droning on and on about something and soon garnered Kris's ire. It never took too long for this kid to get on someone's nerves.

Now Kris? Kris is as evil as me and he decided to take Richie only a bit of the way home because "he was now tired." He pulled over by the side of a cemetery and told him to get out.

"Ok, Rich, now just walk through here and on the other side you'll find a train that can take you straight home," said Kris.

Rich got out and surveyed the situation. Before he could even say, "Wait, what? Hulloh?" Kris hit the gas and he was gone. We were cackling! Absolutely fucking crying. But here's where things got weird. We were nearly at my house when I looked down at the digital clock in his car. It read 2:45 a.m. Somehow, we had been gone for over three hours. Just to reiterate, we left my house at 11:30 p.m. It should have taken twenty mins max to go from my house to his and to make matters even more perplexing we didn't even drive Rich all the way home. It was far too late for McDonalds, and we were both really weirded out. To this day we have zero explanation for what we did for over three hours. It doesn't make any sort of sense, but that is what happened.

Kris said "g'night" and dropped me at home. It was about ten of three when I walked through my door. Had my mom been around, there would have been SWAT teams coming down the street for me, but those days were over. Forever done. It was the type of freedom every teenager longs for, but, man, did it come at a hideous price.

Things were a lot different now. Before her death I was an out-of-control lunatic who tortured her daily with the various outbursts I'd subject her to. In retrospect Ann Barton was a lot of things, but she only had one goal and that was for each of her children to be someone that she could be proud of. In the '90s that was about as far away from me as it gets. I promised her when she died, I would do my best to be that person. To use everything she had taught me and that I had taught myself to live a better life for everyone I cared about. I changed for her. No more drinking or dabbling any further with whatever drugs I was into. Ever again. This would all stop and stop immediately. I also gave up fighting and getting into trouble. Luckily by then I had developed such a reputation as a maniac, I really didn't have anything to prove physically to anyone. I was the beast you did not poke. Even when I did fly off the handle there would never again be any violence and I'd learn to channel my fury in different ways. This would be a complete 180 degree turn from who I was and be the genesis of who I am now.

Time passed and even though things were better, I still had never managed to find my direction. Horror movies remained my passion, but I also seriously embraced video games and music, specifically grunge. There's so much rage in that decade's music and it comforted me to know I wasn't the only one out there who was sick and tired of everything. Pearl Jam, Nirvana, Tool, Stone Temple Pilots, Alice in Chains... these bands were like my sounding board. They were saying, screaming, and singing the shit that was locked in my head. Especially Pearl Jam. I don't know what it is about that particular band, but they still manage to write songs about exactly how I am feeling without ever even knowing me. The wonders never cease.

The 209ers were still kicking ass, but then something strange happened. My dad decided to be a part of the festivities. He'd begun showing up for games and had befriended all of my friends. I resented this to no end. He still never even tried to reach me. Maybe he thought the damage was done and that I was too far gone. Was I? I don't really know. My entire life my father tortured me, and now he's super chummy with my friends, fostering the kind of relationships with them that he never even tried to have with me. They knew him as "Mickey, the super-fun old dude who won their hearts and wouldn't allow them entry into his house unless they had bought him Dunkin Donuts." I knew him as the drunken prick who seemingly LIVED to belittle me. That never stopped. It was one of life's little constants, despite his new friendly relations.

My father's drinking had for the most part ceased though he was still likely to tie one on at least once or twice per week. One evening my brother, Kris, and myself were in my room watching *Monty Python's Flying Circus*. My dad was boozed as per usual and was sleeping it off, slapping his hip every so often. We were watching the episode in which one of the sketches revolved around a bishop who was also a secret agent. *Monty Python* was so weird and gloriously funny. "THE BISHOP!" one of the character's would yell before slamming his staff down onto something. Each time it happened we'd laugh even harder. Then immediately after one of the final staff slams, we heard it. My dad let out a bone chilling scream and then there was a sickening thud, like a ton of bricks being dropped onto the floor. We ran into his room and turned on the light.

My father was on the floor with his head and his feet touching the ground and his midsection arched upward to the ceiling, he was making all sorts of noises and began foaming at the mouth while his eyes rolled back into his head. His fingers were rigid and moving scarily like claws, each one pointing in a different direction sporadically, almost rhythmically. He was like a piece of wood, stiff as a board yet writhing to some song only he could hear. I called 911 and told them what was going on.

"It sounds like he's having a seizure," said the operator on the phone. "You have to make sure that he doesn't swallow his tongue." I conveyed this to Kris who then ran to my dad's bedroom to tell Rob.

The paramedics were there in an instant, coming right through the front door. My dad was settling down. His eyes fluttered a bit as he sat up on the floor and looked around. "Sir, you've just had a seizure, and I need to ask you some questions," said the EMT.

"What happened?" asked my dad, bewildered but coherent. Now standing with the help of the medical technician and being angled toward his bed.

"Sir, can you tell me your name…"

"Robert Barton," he answered without hesitation.

"Do you know where you are?"

"Home."

"Do you know your address?" He gave it.

Once the questions were over and he answered each successfully, they put an oxygen mask over his face, asked him to sit upon the stretcher, and then wheeled him out. He insisted that he was okay and that nothing had happened. That's the fucking thing about seizures, once a person comes out of it, they have zero recollection of them. Unless you've been through this you can't imagine how frustrating this is for everyone else, especially if the person having one is a stubborn prick like my father was. Off to the hospital he went for tests. We followed along.

The results came back. He was diabetic with thick blood and that's what caused the seizure. He was put on Dilantin and some other med I cannot recall the name of and sent home. His routine was to be simple... take his medicine and he'd be fine. There was just one little catch: he wasn't allowed to drink or smoke anymore. They may as well of told him he was forbidden from breathing. Mickey Barton was not happy, and Rob and I both knew we had an uphill battle ahead of us. One that we were not prepared for.

As you may have guessed, old Mickey didn't wanna play nice.

Life became a series of late-night trips to the hospital. At least once per week. He couldn't (or wouldn't) understand that these episodes were happening. He didn't remember them, so why should he give up drinking to prevent something he insists is not happening.

"I'm just probably having a nightmare," he'd say.

Yeah, that's it! We wanted to spend night after night in the emergency room of the hell pit that is Coney Island Hospital just to annoy him into cutting out the booze. Makes total sense.

It got to the point where he couldn't work any longer and was forced to retire. He joined my grandmother and the old lady on the chair in their daily elderly torments. With more time on his hands than expected, Dad decided he'd do something he always wanted to... visit my sister in Long Island. He'd head out there for days at a time. Sometimes without even telling us he was leaving.

It was Christmas Day of 1993. Rob and I woke up and exchanged whatever gifts we had for each other. My dad was nowhere around. Didn't say he was leaving. Didn't even call us on Christmas to say, "Merry, merry." He hadn't gone shopping and there was no food in the house. Rob was in college, and I was between jobs. Collectively we didn't have a pot to piss in. Even if we did, no stores were open so couldn't even buy food if we wanted to. Plus, we had no car and no way to get around. It never occurred to us that old Mick wouldn't have bothered stocking up on chow for the holidays. We had one thing and one thing only in the cupboard... spaghetti. Yep, it was gonna be one of "those" holidays.

That evening we fired up the pot of water and diligently waited for our Yuletide "feast" to cook. When it was ready Rob dumped the pasta into the colander and let it drain. Thinking it was done draining I picked up the steaming hot dripping noodles to toss it in the bowl where a liberal amount of sauce and Parmesan cheese was to be applied. Unfortunately for me as soon as I lifted up the colander scalding hot water splashed on my hand and I dropped it.

Yep, the spaghetti hit the floor. I shit you not. There was our Christmas dinner laying in a pitiful pile on the kitchen linoleum. Rob was PISSED. That's all we had. He began picking up the spaghetti with his bare hands and tossing it into the sink. I was helping... handfuls of noodles dropping between my fingers. We began washing the pasta. Yep, you know things are fucking bad when you have to wash off your dinner before eating it. Most of the spaghetti ended up circling right down the drain. We barely had enough to split. Merry fucking Christmas.

About an hour later Kris called to wish us a happy. We told him what had happened, he immediately hopped in his car to drive us to go and get something to eat. What heathens we felt like, shopping for fast food on Christmas night. We settled on the now defunct Kenny Roger's Roasters because at least we could get some kind of turkey there. The night was saved.

I don't write this to elicit sympathy. Far from it, actually. Truth be told I found it funny then, and I find it funny now. Sometimes you have just got to laugh. It's the only way to keep your sanity.

For the better part of the year my dad spent his quality time with my sister and came home for what felt like some sort of weird obligation. Oh, how he loved daddy's little girl. Camille wasn't the one who took care of him. She didn't spend any time at all holding his tongue during seizures or going back and forth to the hospital. That was all me and my brother. Tommy would show up every now and again to make sure everything was cool. Things were not cool. In fact, they were declining rapidly.

Some tough choices needed to be made. With Nanny and the old lady on the chair fighting so often it began to take a toll on my dad's nerves. He'd get nervous, then dizzy from the anger caused by the nonstop octogenarian-laden bickering. That and for whatever reason the household bills were becoming too much to maintain the house. Rob and I were kicking in whatever cash we could, but it still wasn't enough to cover costs. Enter my eldest brother, Tommy. He had a plan to keep the house in the family. It was simple...

Nanny and the old lady on the chair were to be shipped off to separate nursing homes thereby removing that bit of stress from everyone's lives. Nan was in her late Eighties by this time and Sewagin was well into her Nineties. Despite their arguing, they had particular needs as old folks that we just couldn't shoulder at the time. Even though they were extreme pains in the asses I always felt bad about seeing them go. It sure would be a lot quieter around Manor Court and that would be a good thing.

Once the ECW participants had moved on to far more forgiving pastures, my dad and I were to move downstairs to my grandparent's old pad. Rob would stay put in his section of the house and Tommy, whichever wife he had at the time, and their children would move in upstairs. For a while things were cool but then again if growing up in the Barton house had taught me anything it's that the fuse to the next powder keg would soon be lit.

Tommy began arguing with his wife. Divorce was looming. Dad's seizures were as frequent as ever, and on top of everything else that was wrong with him, he had a heart attack. Dealing with him was maddening and he wouldn't do a damned thing that he was supposed to do, except of course when he'd go to Long Island to see my sis. Then he was a well-behaved angel. Rob was in his final years in college, and I was working my ass off somewhere as always. The relationship with my dad improved a little bit. He had even apologized for being such an asshole to me for the majority of my life. There was just too much for me to forgive. So much pain and agony being distilled on the regular.

"It's cool," I told him halfheartedly.

He still didn't give a fuck about me though. I remember soon after his apology my bed broke. I forget what had happened to it exactly, but it was fucked. Completely fucked. I told him and he said he'd buy me a new one as soon as he had the cash. In the interim I resorted to sleeping in Rob's old sleeping bag every night on the floor of my room. I was curious to see how long it would take my father to provide a bed for his son. Months had passed. He'd taken countless trips to my sister's lavish place. Finally, a year had passed by, and I was STILL sleeping in that infernal bag. I could have bought myself a bed after a while, but I just wanted to see if Mickey Barton would make good. He never did.

Finally, tired of sleeping on the floor, I bought myself a futon because I had gotten really used to a bed not taking up space in my room.

Thanks, Dad. You're a gem.

It was now 1994. My dad's heart troubles had subsided, but his seizures were at an all-time high frequency. Sometimes he'd have a full-blown episode, and sometimes we'd find him just sitting up in bed, his head twisting around wildly and talking to people who weren't there. That was pretty scary. What was he seeing? Who was he talking to exactly? Was it his imagination? Was it death? Only he knew, and when he came out of it he never remembered. Things had gotten pretty standard:

- Sometime between midnight and 3:00 a.m., dad has a seizure.
- We call 911.
- I pack him a bag so he had some of his stuff with him in the hospital.
- After a few days he'd be home.
- After a few more days during the night dad had a seizure.
- We call 911.
- Wash, rinse, repeat.

It was our new normal and it sucked every bit as much as you think you it did.

This went on for months. My dad was always a burly dude, around 230lbs would be my best guess. He'd begun to lose weight and the pounds were dropping off fast. This alarmed us all. The doctors couldn't find any reason for the weight loss. For the rest of the year and into 1995 we spent the majority of our time going from hospital to hospital and doctor to doctor. Everyone believed he had some form of cancer. Finally, he ended up in one of the biggest cancer hospitals in the country, Memorial Sloan Kettering Cancer Center in New York City. He would be there for several weeks. They found nothing and eventually had to send him home. He was now just over 110lbs. Frighteningly thin. It was July. The air was hot and sticky. Rob and I gave up watching *Monty Python* at night because every time we did our father would have a seizure. The show officially had "the cooties." To this very day I haven't seen another episode.

The majority of my fellow 209ers were on vacation in Florida and I was pretty much alone. Kris had moved away to Queens at this point in my life, and I didn't see him anywhere near as much as I used to. I missed him. I never told him how much, but I did. I still do. He is my brother. Every bit as much as Rob, and way more than Tommy could ever be. He found himself a wonderful woman in Laura and he would go on to marry her and have a bunch of awesome kids.

Midnight had passed, making this day the anniversary of my mother's death. July 19th. A day that still haunts me. It was about 2:00 a.m. and my dad began talking to the invisible people again. This was no longer alarming. We were sadly used to it. The paramedics carted him off to Coney Island Hospital. I then began my ritual of packing his overnight bag. I opened up his underwear drawer and there it was, the reason for my dad's sickness. In the back of his drawer, I found what had to be over a week's worth of food. Food he said he'd been eating. We never watched him eat. Hell, we never even thought to. We brought him his food and came back for the dishes. The rotting meals were wrapped in bags... bread... chicken... potatoes... steak... veggies... whatever was on the menu. I sat down on his bed looking at all of this. All this waste. I came to a realization...

My dad was committing suicide. He was trying to starve himself to death. There was no sickness. No cancer. This was a premeditated plot to die and one that showed both a tremendous amount of willpower and an immense amount of sadness. I called Rob and Tommy into the room. Showed them what I had found. We were all silent. Just looking at each other in bewilderment. Finally, things were crystal-clear. Our father wanted to die.

The next morning when he was coherent enough to speak, he confessed. There was no more hiding it. His face began streaming with tears - the product of his personal perdition.

"I don't want to live... I don't want to live anymore without your mother," he shook his head using any little bit of energy he had left to complete the gesture. He tried in vain to raise his hand and slam his fist down.

This scene remains one of the saddest things I've ever witnessed.

"It's my fault she had the aneurysm... all the fighting we did. All my drinking. All the stress. This was all my fault. I did this. I should have been a better husband. She is my life. I was trying to make sure that I died on the anniversary of her death. I wanted to share that last thing with her. It's all I have."

We all went home after a while, shell-shocked. We didn't say much to each other. My brothers and I were all processing in very different ways. This was so fucking much to take in at once. So much agony. My father's broken heart had finally given out and in the process he managed to break ours yet again.

It was now July 20th, and we went to visit him. There'd been no news overnight, and at this point, no news was good news. The doctor had stopped Rob and Tommy, but I continued on to his room. I looked around at the beds, but I couldn't find him. Had they moved him? I approached a nurse who was handling another patient in the same area.

"Nurse," I asked. "I'm looking for my father, Robert Barton. Did he get moved or something?"

"No." she answered. "He's right over there."

She pointed to the bed directly behind me. I turned to look and was just frozen. My father was lying in his bed, oxygen mask over his face and hooked up to every conceivable machine you could imagine. I didn't recognize him. I was standing right fucking next to him and yet could not see him. This wasn't the monster of a man I was used to, the mountain of drunken fury. This was a frail, skeletal old man laying on what would no doubt be his deathbed.

"Dad," I asked softly? "Dad?"

No response. I moved over to the side of his bed and saw that his eyelids were half open with only the whites showing. He didn't move. I could see the color draining from his face. I put my hand on his.

"Dad, it's Stevie. I'm not sure that you can hear me, but I wanted you to know something." I paused, carefully choosing my words. "I forgive you. It's okay. It's all okay."

Did I though? I'm still not sure. I just felt like it was something he needed to hear, and I was okay with that. We'd all led such a tormented life, and no matter what he had done to me—from flipping me on to the floor out of the laundry basket to never buying me a bed—I wanted to extend him some type of comfort, whether he deserved it or not.

Rob and Tommy entered the room, visibly shaken and upset. The doctor stopped them to find out if they would sign a DNR (Do Not Resuscitate). We spoke briefly about it and decided that's what was best. Mickey Barton was no longer in there. This was someone else. A hollow man. Before we left, I knelt over him and carefully removed his most prized possession: a tiny Saint Anthony medallion that was lying limp on a cheap gold chain.

"That's a good idea," Tommy said. "Someone in this shithole would probably take it from him while he was unconscious."

At 7:45 a.m. the next morning the call had come. Robert Michael Barton passed away on July 21st 1995. He was sixty-three. Mickey was never a lucky fellow. If someone had found a dollar, it usually meant that he had lost it. He couldn't hit the lottery if someone gave him the winning numbers, yet somehow, some way he found a means to nearly die on the exact day as my mother. Impressive, no?

In the words of Maxwell Smart, "Missed it by 'that' much."

Chapter 6
Little Orphan Anarchy

Holy shit. I was officially an orphan. For the first time in my life, I felt truly alone. But to be completely honest, I was also relieved. The hell of my father's "illness" had drawn to an end, but I was also free of his over two-decade long reign of mental and physical abuse. There would be no more hospital visits, seizures, tongue holding, or slights against my person. I never cried for my father. Not a single tear. The irony that I had to spend the last year of his life taking care of him even though he never gave a rat's ass about how I was will never be lost on me. I didn't do it because I loved him. I did it because it was my obligation as a son and nothing more. Just because he didn't do the right thing doesn't mean that I shouldn't. When I laid my head down on my pillow at night, I knew that I had done everything that day for him that I possibly could have. This gave me something priceless: peace of mind.

Unfortunately, for the next few years that peace is all I'd ever know. Sorting out my dad's estate brought some startling revelations to light. One was that my eldest brother, Tommy, had opened up a credit card under my dad's name to—as he put it—"help him pay some bills."

Bullshit. Complete and utter bullshit.

Even though everyone called my dad, Mickey, his name was Robert Barton. We found out about this card because Robert Barton is also my brother's name. He's a junior. Of course, he opened this bill thinking it was his and let's just say that the expenses on it were questionable for a man in his Sixties. Typical Tommy. Always scheming. Always trying to get ahead by taking as many shortcuts as possible. In his twisted mind since he was "helping my dad keep the house," well then he would be entitled to perks that didn't need to be made public to anyone.

Even worse were the actions of my sister. Daddy's little girl was a diabolical bitch. It's been a while since I mentioned Camille so allow me to bring you up to speed. She married into a wealthy family and moved to Long Island, the suburb area of New York. She had no further need to sully herself with her by blood-related family. She was no doubt embarrassed by her middle-class upbringing and the loonies which populated our family. Not sure I can blame her for that, but it's still a shitty thing to do. It came to light after my father's death that she had pretty much drained his bank account as a means to add another wing onto her home. Ponder that. Another fucking wing. I guess her embarrassing alcoholic dad's money was just good enough to take. Or maybe my dad was just showing off in front of her in-laws. I wouldn't doubt that either. Could lavishing his daughter's family with a new wing of their home be enough to make him feel like their monetary equal? Maybe regain some of that machismo he had felt he had lost when my mother had been forced to go to work? No one will ever know as Mickey Barton took his warped way of thinking with him to his grave. But one thing is clear: Camille knew everyone's financial situation and the last thing that she needed was money. She was well aware of the fact that when dad passed, we (Rob and I) would have nothing. This was a thoughtless and selfish case of vanity which ultimately led to her brothers, with the exception of Tommy, never speaking another word to her again. Good fucking riddance. If you're reading this, KARMA IS A BITCH. Please fall off the Earth. No need to wait. Thanks.

With my dad leaving behind what we were told amounted to nothing more than pennies after the financial reaping of our eldest siblings, the family home would have to be sold and it was. Rob and I got ten thousand dollars each which honestly we didn't even want. To us it was blood money. Tommy and Camille would also get 10k each. To Tommy it was reparations of some sort. To Camille it was pocket change which she no doubt spent on something unneeded and extravagant. With the exception of Rob and I, we had all gone our separate ways. This was for the best, as just about every person in our family had let us down. We quickly learned that family will be the first to fuck you, given the chance. Just because the people around you when you are born are technically considered relatives doesn't mean they're family. You choose your own family. It's better that way. Just because your bloodline is shared with others shouldn't have to mean that you need to stick around for their circus of selfishness.

Rob and I got our very first apartment—The Koutsoflakis. That was our landlord's last name. We had rented an apartment on Avenue U and east 18th street from an elderly Greek couple who would become a never-ending source of both stress and comedy. These folks were fucking nuts. They lived below us and would make our lives hell by literally yelling at us for making even the slightest of sounds. Old or not these fuckers had the most extraordinary sense of hearing we had ever encountered. Living in The Koutsoflakis was akin to life in that flick, *A Quiet Place*.

Listening to a Pearl Jam "Unplugged" performance at 2:00 p.m. in the afternoon at a ridiculously low listening level? They complained and then called the cops for noise.

Listening to our answering machine message at 8:00 a.m.? They complained and then called the cops for noise.

Closed our cabinets too often? They complained and then called the cops for noise.

You had to be a rice-paper-walking ninja to live there. Even worse, there was a massive noisy staircase in their house leading up to our apartment, and each time we either went up or down it they would peek their heads out of the door to give us some kind of static and whatever Greek form of *malocchio* they saw fit. We dealt with this for a year. Having company was nearly impossible. We'd all have to be quiet as mice.

One night in particular, the unthinkable happened.

There are few things in this world that I consider life's little constants. Cat shit will smell awful, Midian is where the monsters live, and if Kris comes over to your house, he will have some type of food with him. This night he had come over with what could only be described as a literal smorgasbord of Italian food. There were rice balls, there was garlic bread, there were husks of pepperoni and or salami and of course spaghetti. No one ever ate spaghetti. It was always just there. In fact, as an Italian, I can tell you that I personally HATE pasta. Growing up in a poor Italian household there was pasta to spare. We ate that shit at least three times a week. No matter the shape and/or size it may come in, to me it all tastes exactly the same. I remain sick of it.

After gorging ourselves on one of Kris's impromptu food banquets, it came time for him to go. We had to walk him out so we could lock the door behind him. That damned staircase. That noisy damned staircase. It was about 2:00 a.m. and Kris had gathered up the leftovers (spaghetti) and we were all creeping down the staircase to let him out and lock up. Normally it would have just been Kris and either me or Rob, but for whatever reason it was all three of us this time. Each step of ours was precisely measured. Every footfall spaced out to be as quiet as possible. But then it happened...

Kris somehow lost his footing and, in turn, the whole plate of spaghetti went sailing through the air. We watched it in a state of horror, frozen in place, the pasta strands sprouting tendril-like arms, whirling recklessly as it flew through the air like an angry jellyfish in slow motion.

Somewhere in the distance of our minds, Jim Morrison crooned "The End."

The plate landed on its side and bounced once, heaving all the remaining non-airborne pasta on the front door of The Koutsoflakis.

A Comedy of Tragedies

This was our worst nightmare. We were slack-jawed and staring at each other. Our heads darted in every conceivable direction like raptors trying to detect any noise, any stirring, of the old man and his wife. This would be it… we were certainly about to have the police called on us for unlawful usage of sauce-covered macaroni.

Seconds passed like hours. We couldn't move. All three of our backs were against the wall of the inner staircase as if cowering in its sturdy silent safety. There wasn't a sound. We watched as the spaghetti—now a pasta-based antagonist—dripped from the walls, to the door, to the floor. Rob clasped his hands around his head as if he were holding in an inaudible scream. Kris stared at me wide-eyed as if pissed-off, hungry Greek raptors were shadowing his every move. We fucked up and we knew it. Consequences were inevitable. Yet there was nothing. No one had heard or seen what had happened but us. We had gotten lucky, but now we had a new problem… how do we clean up this mess without rousing the elderly ogres from their slumber?

I darted as stealthily as possible back up the stairs and grabbed paper towels and Windex. Why Windex? Why fucking not? It was the first thing I saw, and we needed to work quickly. Kris made his way back down the stairs and began extracting strands of the tomato-soaked abomination from the walls, door, and floor. I tossed the paper towels and cleaning fluid down to Rob who caught them both with the ease of a wide receiver on his best day. Rob looked at the Windex puzzled and looked back up at me. I shrugged.

The game was afoot.

I held out a plastic bag for trash, Kris was picking up stray bits of spaghetti and putting them back into the warm tin plate, and Rob was wiping down every surface he could see where sauce may or may not have landed.

"Windex. Fuckin' Windex," he muttered under his breath incredulously while shaking his head.

Within minutes the area was clear, but now we had to spray and clean the door of the great and terrible Koutsoflakis. We stepped back. The only sound hanging in the air was that of our collective breathing as Rob took aim at their doorknob. With a gentle squeeze of his finger the blue liquid hit its target with a soothing splash, immediately breaking up the sauce. "PPssstthhhh."

We wiped with precision, every move deliberate, daring not to even look at each other for fear of the temptation to make some audible form of communication during this chaos. The deed was done. Kris had left with his filthy pasta in tow, Rob had locked the door, and then we both crept back up the stairs completely drained mentally. If there is a god, they were with us that evening. The Koutsoflakis never learned of the Pastacalypse. Dear lord, FINALLY, a crisis had been averted, but one thing was abundantly clear: We had to move. It couldn't get any worse, right? Wrong.

Rob's longtime friend Gene was a weird one. Somewhere in his Thirties, he often wore a pink tank top, daisy duke cut length blue jean shorts, Timberland boots, and a work belt. Attractive! He was the quintessential *cugine* construction worker who always had some sort of scheme cooking, and no matter what, was always on the clock. Soft spoken, Gene was always listening and his two go-to responses for anything that would come up would be either "Not a problem," or "I hear ya." He let Rob know about a house that was for rent back in Sheepshead Bay over on 35th Street. It was owned by the Zarzana family, and for all intents and purposes this place, like The Koutsoflakis before it, will only be referred to from now on as The Zarzana. We were desperate to break our rental imposed vow of Greek silence, so we jumped at the opportunity to be able to make some form of noise without penalty.

"Gene, Thanks for letting us know!"

"Not a problem."

"We gotta get outta here."

"I hear ya."

The Zarzana would be the complete opposite of The Koutsoflakis. With no landlord on site, we could do whatever we wanted. But we never expected, nor could we have predicted, the chaos to come. With freedom came a price.

We gave our notice to The Koutsoflakis and used the month leading up to our departure to pack, etcetera. The plan was for us to get to the main floor of The Zarzana. The basement was already rented to someone else. More on that in a bit.

This was the Zarzana family home and has been so for years. It was understandably sacred ground to them, but it was also a holy mess of angst, ill feelings, and confusion. There was static in the family and there were relatives who didn't want the home to be rented out. At the end of the day though, money talked. There was also an issue with the family's elderly matriarch who was living there. She was supposed to be moved out the day we were scheduled to move in. This didn't happen. Upon the first days of our occupancy, she was still there and, unbeknownst to us, we were to be at her service until she was moved out. We thought the reign of elderly tyrants had come to an end, but no. It was, instead, two solid days of torture. We couldn't begin unpacking because the Zarzana's weren't completely out yet. We could however start cleaning and, man, did this place need it.

Opening up the kitchen cabinets I began spraying down the inside of them with some form of liquid cleaning agent. What I didn't notice was that the contents of a box of instant mashed potatoes had been dumped in the cabinet and as soon as it was met with any form of liquid, mashed potatoes began growing on the fucking shelves like The Blob oozing to life. The more I cleaned the bigger it got. IT WAS NEVER-ENDING! An ever-growing NIGHTMARE! I was horrified. How was anyone supposed to deal with this? This couldn't be taught or learned. Everything tried proved to be futile. Once I scraped the now liquid mush out of the cabinet more kept on growing like one of those dried sponge toys you toss into water to watch grow larger and larger. I decided to let it fester. Let nature take its course. When the liquid absorption stopped creating mush from flakes, I'd spoon it all out and then clean again.

Perplexed and slightly grossed out, I stepped outside for some air, visions of that bulbous misshapen thing that was currently pouring and growing out of the cabinet dancing through my head.

Leaning against the house, I inhaled a deep breath. Silence. A moment of actual silence. You forget how precious these are until you really need one. It was a gorgeous spring day. I let the warm air fill my lungs with renewed focus, my eyes closed. I was suddenly jarred back to reality by the feeling of something weighty hitting my right shoulder. Looking down, the realization that the impact came from a dead pigeon who had just fallen out of a tree and struck my person left my mouth agape. Was this a sign? Was it my Aunt Josie spitting *malocchio* from beyond the grave? What fresh evil was this? There was no peace to be had inside, and no peace to be had outside either.

Shit.

One of the Zarzana brood came by to see if his grandmother was okay. We had bought her a ham sandwich from the store for lunch. He was grateful and before he left, he asked to use the bathroom. Of course! Rob and I were standing just outside of the commode and from within we could hear the distinct sound of cocaine being inhaled behind the door. Was this really happening? You betcha! After a few moments the Zarzana emerged from the bathroom sweating bullets with his eyes the size of headlights. He was wired to the tenth power and sniffing like a madman. Upon close inspection, there was a tiny bit of blood pooling around the inside of his left nostril. Now that we had a potential coke-fueled maniac to contend with, we were relieved that instead of hanging around he opted to hop into his car and split. Ah, sweet relief.

A few minutes passed and we suddenly heard it.

The old woman was calling out from her room that she needed to go to the bathroom. At first, we weren't sure why she was telling us, as we were only there for a few hours at this point, but it quickly became apparent that she was for the most part bedridden and had huge issues getting around. Rob, the saint that he is, went to her, helped her up, and brought her to the bathroom. I was standing outside the door as we exchanged "WTF" glances while he was escorting her. She stood against the sink, propping up her frame. Rob was about to turn and leave so she could have her privacy.

"Wait," she said pausing, her raspy voice launching spittle like tiny rockets of disgust. "I need help taking off my bloomers."

GOOD CHRIST! NO! These are words that you NEVER want to hear. What had we ever done to anyone that had led us to this point?

A mask of horror formed over Rob's face. I leaned back against the wall, squirming. Rob knelt down, turned his head, and helped the woman off with her undies. He was visibly repulsed. We were both in some form of octogenarian genital induced shock. What place is this? Was this to be the new norm? When was this woman leaving? My god, what's gonna happen when it's my turn to help? The elderly woman's anus erupted into an explosive symphony of fresh bile splattering thunder. It sounded like someone got a peach pit stuck in swamp slime inside of a blender. It would not cease. Finally, she quieted down and was able to wipe. She did so herself much to Rob's relief. He helped her back up, brought her back into her room and then quietly assumed the embryonic position on the front stoop while I brought him beer, after beer, after beer. Nothing could dull this pain.

Later that evening she called out again...

Rob fled. This time it was all up to me. I removed her bloomers and for a moment caught myself staring face to face with a dead grayish forest. It was so tangled. This was a place of violent despair. So wrong. So disturbing. I turned away, waiting outside the lavatory. I was praying quietly...

"Please, God. Please don't let her poop again. I'm not the man that Rob is. I couldn't shoulder such a responsibility. I'm ill prepared!"

But then the sweet tinkle of urine on water danced audibly through the air. It was music to my ears. A toe tapping bladder draining ditty. After about thirty-five minutes it stopped. She called out, "I'm ready!" I walked back into the bathroom, arms extended hands open wide, ready to whisk her back to her lair. I was met with resistance. My head turned to meet hers. Our eyes locked.

She smiled, "Wait... Let me drip."

I've known all manner of horrors in my life but this... those three words...

"Let... me... drip..."

What have I become? What has brought me to this moment? Was I Judas Iscariot in a past life?

The tinkling began, drop by vaginally expelled drop.

Each one hitting the water and—I'm sure—taking a minute off my mortality in the process.

She did the deed, and I brought her back into her bedroom, shut the door, and immediately showered. In the back of my mind, I pictured her walking into the bathroom like the old woman in *The Shining* from Room 237. Her arms would be outstretched, and she'd have a ghastly grin upon her face as she cackled. Pendulous breasts swinging comically from left to right with each step she advanced. Her nappy pubes writhing and twisting around each other like a network of greasy gray tendrils with a life all their own. Each hair fat like an earthworm. Thankfully this did not happen, but it wouldn't have been surprising if it did.

Within a day or so the woman was moved out and all traces of the Zarzana family had been removed. We settled in, getting the lay of the land. There was a heavy bag and a weight bench in the backyard garage, but there was a problem: Little Marky, the other tenant in the basement apartment, owned a 150 pound, always furious pit bull who was chained to the wall in the backyard behind the house. The dog's name eludes me, but it wasn't like anyone would be able to get close enough to befriend the pooch. This fucker was angry 24-hours a day. It never slept. It just quietly grimaced and growled. Yep, the heavy bag and weights would have to wait until a much safer time.

The first week we lived there we learned what Little Marky had done for a living. He was, we thought, a quiet and unassuming guy. Standing in about around 5-feet tall with a jail yard stocky build, dark skin, and distinctly Latin features, Little Marky would prove to bring a lot to the table in regard to the "Are you fucking kidding me," variety.

One night Rob and I were in our respective rooms playing Xbox when we heard the front door open and then the distinct tapping of high heels. Hooker boots with clear heels to be exact. "Marky," some mysterious tart called out. Rob and I went out into the living room and before us were two scantily clad chicks, one with a cut off blue breast length fur coat, cut off shorts, and the aforementioned clear platform heels. Behind her stood her friend, wearing thigh-high orange boots, sequined silver hot pants, and a leopard skin tank top. These two made Mercy from *The Warriors* look like Beyoncé.

"Why don't ya strap a mattress to yer back? I don't like the way you live." Oh, Swan, we know you are warchief. I mean, everybody knows that. But where were you when we needed you?

"Who you? Where's Marky," Miss Clear Heels asked, while her friend popped her gum frantically.

"Who me?" Rob said. "NO, WHO THE FUCK ARE YOU AND WHAT THE FUCK ARE YOU DOING IN OUR HOUSE?"

"I'm looking for Marky."

"Marky lives downstairs," I chimed in.

"Oh, my bad, boo! We'll hit him dere den," said Clear Heels, and the two began sauntering out.

gum popping

hair flip

Rob and I looked at each other. "What in the hell was that?"

"Dunno," Rob answered, "But we're never leaving the front door unlocked ever again." About five minutes later there was another knock on the door; it was Marky. "Hey, yo... I'm sorry yo," he said. "Dems mah girls and dey went inta the wrong door 'n shit, nahmean? Wonhappin again, yo."

Over the next week or so we'd hear Marky talking to his girls and it became clear from their conversations that he was their pimp.

"C'mon, yo, you know I ain't think you dirty. I wouldn't love up on you if I tought you was."

"Ay yo, when you done out dere, use summa mah money to bring me back some Nathan's, yo. Don't be comin' back hea' without dat shit either."

Some would think that living with a pimp below you would be an amenity of sorts. Believe me, though it was fucking gross. Things were about to get even more fucked up. Dangerous even.

One evening Rob went out to the store to grab some chips. He came back like 15 minutes later, looking furious.

"Stevie, grab some weapons man we got trouble. I gotta make some calls. I'll grab Gene you call Kris. There's problems."

Rob went on to explain that when he was coming back from the store he saw a car parked out in front of the house. The dude in it got Rob's attention and motioned to him to come on over to the car. He did, and the dude pulled a gun on him.

"You live here?"

"Yeah," Rob answered.

"You Little Marky?"

"No."

"He live here?"

"Yeah, downstairs."

"He home? You see him? Don't fucking lie to me."

"Dude, I just moved in. I've barely said two words to the fucking guy and, honestly, I don't give a fuck if you kill him. None of my business."

"Aight, you can go."

That's when Rob came inside and alerted me. He called Gene and put him on speaker and explained what transpired.

"Dude, shit may go down," Rob told him. "We need you."

"I hear ya," Gene answered.

"Come now," said Rob.

"Not a problem," said Gene.

I called Kris. We had a similar conversation minus the "I hear ya's" and "not a problems."

Rob was in full-blown emergency mode. Gene came over with 2x4s, heavy chains, and hammers. Kris brought, I shit you not, a fucking sword. Rob and I immediately started gathering whatever we had including three baseball bats, a heavy wooden cane, a machete, and several D cell batteries. We started loading the batteries into tube socks for swinging purposes. Those fuckers can hurt, and when you grow up in Brooklyn you learn to be inventive in terms of protecting yourself. Gene went to work hammering the door to the basement leading to Little Marky's dwelling shut with the chains and wood. It was like watching Ben from *Night of the Living Dead* shoring up the house while wearing ill-fitting daisy dukes.

The stage was set. Within 20 minutes we were armed to the teeth and ready for whatever. We heard Marky's door open. Rob crept up to the living room window and peaked out of the blinds. He held up his hand… Gene, Kris, and myself braced. Nothing happened though. Marky was in the car with the guy for what seemed like an hour. Finally, he got out. The car sped away, and he just walked back to the house and went in through his door. It was silent. Not a peep. We were all sitting there staring at each other. So quiet you could literally hear a pin drop.

After about fifteen minutes Kris spoke up.

"So, should we order a pizza or something?"

There was very little sleep to be had that evening. Gene stayed over because it was not a problem and he totally heard us, as did Kris. We played video games until dawn and gorged ourselves on pizza from Lenny and John's Pizzeria. The next day Rob was on the phone bright and early to our landlord. Little Marky the killer pimp had to go, or we were leaving. Marky and his dog were gone within two days. The hookers and the gunmen never returned. Even better? We could finally use the heavy bag and the weight bench. It was a small victory, and in a life filled with absolute anarchy and mayhem, you learned to cherish such things.

Things quieted down at The Zarzana. The only odd disturbances would come periodically when one of the brothers would swing by with some type of something or other to sell. The bell would ring at any time between noon and three in the morning; one of us would open the door.

"You wanna buy a vacuum? 20 dollahs. I fig'yid I'd axe ya. You know in my yute they called me, Beebop Shop," the crab-like humanoid with the horribly dyed slicked-back black hair would grouse, gray roots peeking out of his scalp like pre-cum from an erect penis. This dude was always soused and disheveled; he always wanted to talk. He was Beebop Shop, after all, and he had plenty of tales from his "yute".

Aside from the occasional ruckus things were pretty standard for a few years. We moved out of The Zarzana after a time and then got another place in Marine Park, Brooklyn in early 2000. Life was good for the most part, but the pain that was on the horizon was something no one could have expected.

Chapter 7
I Gather Speed From You Fucking With Me

Full disclosure. I originally wasn't going to include the following part of my life for a multitude of reasons. Said reasons range from me wanting to forget this time period to not wanting to say things about the people responsible for it as they would have no chance to speak up for themselves, thereby leaving me with a rather one-sided account of what happened. At the end of the day, my main reason is simply me being just plain ashamed of how far I had fallen.

After much mental wrestling—sans loincloth because that's how I roll—I decided that it's probably integral to my overall tale. I've changed some of the names because I don't want to cause anyone anymore pain.

Let me start from the beginning, a look at the unbridled hell that was my love life. I've had five great loves: Adrienne, Shana, Kimberly, Debi, and finally Dani.

I met Adrienne when I was just fifteen. She was a Puerto Rican and Italian spitfire who awakened teen lust in me times ten. Our relationship was instantly sexual and even at that age it was—not gonna lie—absolutely white-hot. I grew to love her as much as I could possibly love anyone at that young and impressionable point in life. After a couple of years, we split and she broke my poor naive heart, but I'm happy to say we remain friends and every now and then she pops up on Facebook or texts me to say hi. She's one of the funniest people I know and I'm genuinely happy to hear from her every so often.

When I was 17, I met a person who changed my life. Her name was Shana Handelman, and our relationship began with a lie. She's probably blushing as she reads this. You naughty lil' thing! She told me that she was 16, BUT she was younger! I didn't know about this until we got serious, and she finally figured, "Well, I guess I had better tell him."

This was our first hurdle, but we stayed together for many years and totally overcame it. Shana—to this very day—is one of the single smartest, beautiful and incredible people I have ever known. She is WAY smarter than I will EVER be. I'm talking way, way smarter. What the hell she was doing with this douchebag, I'll never know. But, hell, was I lucky.

Even more special to me was the fact that her parents, Jackie and Steven, liked me. They still call me "their son." Let me be clear. If I was in their shoes, I would have told Shana to run from me as quickly as she could. But they didn't, and she didn't. That's just mind-blowing to me. We were both so young and we grew up together, figuring out who we were along the way. This was the relationship in my life that remains invaluable to me.

My mom was gone, my dad too, my world askew. Yet, her parents took me in. Fostered me in a lot of ways.

I learned more from Jackie and Steven than I ever did from my own parents who pretty much left me in the lurch. Oh, poor fucking me, right? No. Not even close. The pain my parents caused me lead me into the arms of Shana's family and all of that has contributed to who I am. My pain is mine. My life is mine. My tears are mine. I'm grateful for it all, good and bad.

As you would have expected given our ages, Shana and I did not last. But our friendship is as strong now as it ever was, and I love her and her folks dearly. Always will. I'm proud to be their Stevie.

For many years post-Shana, I played the field. Even got back with

A Comedy of Tragedies

Adrienne for a short time. But, in the end, she broke my heart yet again. Le sigh.

Really, A? I was damned good to you! I even bought YOU a gift on MY fucking birthday!

From what I know of her now she has a daughter, and she's now a Christian. After dating me twice it's no wonder that she needed to go and find Christ.

When I was 26, my world was turned upside down again. I met Kim online. I don't think anyone has ever clicked with someone faster in the history of the world. She quickly became my everything. The only trouble? She lived in Chicago and I was in New York. It didn't matter though... we used to talk on the phone for hours at a time. Every time my phone rang or my email went off, my heart would stop. We consumed each other's every thought. She was like an extension of me. We loved each other to a staggering degree. Everything that happened was for us.

The first time we met in person I took a plane to Chi-town. This was the first time I'd ever been on an aircraft of ANY kind, and I'm ludicrously scared of heights. That didn't matter though. In just a couple of hours I'd be holding her in my arms and that's all that mattered to me. It was the reason I was put here for.

And hold her I did. It was amazing to me how well we "fit" in each other's arms. Like we were always supposed to be there. She had this way of looking at me, that remains indescribable. Like, for the first time ever, someone finally saw "me." Just me.

The reason for my first trip there was that her birthday was coming up and I didn't want her to be alone. She deserved better than that and I was going to make sure she got it no matter what.

The next morning, I purposely woke up extremely early and went out without her knowing. She NEEDED to remain asleep for my plan to work. I began walking around this city that I was completely unfamiliar with. My plan was simple: "Walk straight so that I wouldn't get lost and hopefully run into a florist." There had to be one on the main drag. I set out and within about twenty minutes I found one.

After I traced my steps back to her place I entered quietly. Peeked into her room and she was still very much asleep. I began decorating her house with birthday stuff and of course, flowers. She woke up... it was magic. Whatever she wanted, she got. I ended up putting myself in debt going back and forth to see her and getting her whatever in the world she wanted, whether she knew she wanted it or not. Looking back, this was a really bad idea. But fuck it... what the heart wants it gets without a second thought of the consequences.

After a few months she came to me with a confession.

"I have to tell you something," she said. "Something I didn't want you to know because I was afraid you would treat me differently."

She could have told me she was a shapeshifting troll and I would have been completely okay with that.

"My mom and dad... they're very wealthy."

Let me be crystal-clear about something. I never gave the slightest shit about money, and I never will. All it does is complicate everything. Happiness is all that matters. Of course, I didn't care in the slightest bit. It didn't make her any more or less attractive to me. Didn't change a single thing as far as I was concerned. She could have told me she was incontinent and I would have been there to change her diapers without a second thought.

Like *The Lego Movie* said, "EVERYTHING WAS AWESOME."

After a while, she made a big move to another state where her parents live. Her parents were a big part of her life and she wanted to be nearer to them. That actually made me happy because it made her happy. Now she was even farther away. That didn't matter though... have airplane WILL TRAVEL!

The time came to meet her parents. I was beyond worried. Amazingly enough, they liked me. Her dad had even told her that I was "pretty smart," as I was able to answer a sales question of his correctly that few people were able to. I couldn't have been more on top of the world.

We discussed me moving there. Yes, this had to happen. For the first time in my life, I was on a road that I could actually see clearly.

The time came for me to visit her again. We, as always, had a blast. The night before I was supposed to travel back to New York, we were to have dinner at her parent's house. I remember sitting in their porch/yard area. Her dad said that her mom wasn't feeling well and wouldn't be joining us. Kim went to go in and check on her.

She was back in about ten minutes. She was smiling but I could see something was bothering her. Something behind her eyes.

That night we went back to her house, and she hugged me ridiculously tight. This was normal on our last nights together, but there was just something there. I figured her mom was, god forbid, "really sick" and that was eating at her inside. That was okay though. I was going to be there to hold her up no matter how much weight was on her shoulders.

The next day I was back in Brooklyn and, as per usual, coming home S-U-C-K-E-D. All I could think was, "Why am I back here and when am I getting back to Kim?"

She called me on the phone and said, "I need to talk to you about something."

FINALLY I was gonna hear what was bothering her and I could start putting plans in place to repair whatever damages would come her way. No one person, no earthly force, nothing was going to stop me from making DAMNED SURE she was okay.

"When I went to talk to my mom," she said as she began to cry, "She told me that [they wanted me] out of her life." That I was not good enough for her. Her parents had given her an ultimatum—it was me or them. They would disown her if she stayed with me.

The shades go down...

Panic was setting in. I began bawling, feeling like I was fighting for my life. I assured her that we could work through this and pleaded with her to let me speak with her folks. She said she'd make it happen.

The next day her father got on the phone with me and read me the riot act as her mom would spout out venom intermittently like the hype man did in a rap act, while Kim cried feverishly in the background.

This was my worst nightmare.

"You're not good enough for my daughter. She has a college

degree. You have a GED. You have nothing to offer her. You will never be anything. Love is not enough. Love. Is. Not. Enough. If you do love our daughter as much as you say that you do, you will let her go."

The call, and what seemed like my life, was over in a manner of minutes. From then on Kim became very distant. I would call, begging, pleading with her to make this work. We can't let this end. She eventually stopped taking my calls. She eventually stopped listening to my messages. She eventually was just... gone.

You know, I had been through some shit. I found my mother dead and yet, this shocked me even more. To this very day I do not think anyone could have ever fathomed the depth of my love for her.

I was lost. I found myself wandering around, ending up in places with no knowledge of how I had gotten there, with the exception of a few lucid moments. One day as I was wandering, Shana's dad, Steven, found me walking blankly around Sheepshead Bay and he put me in his car and took me to his home. Shana wasn't there but Jackie was. I told them everything. I cried my eyes out. This was pain so savage, so undeniable, I could barely breathe. They tried to tell me how wrong Kim's parents were, but I couldn't hear them.

All I could do was hurt and continue to fall apart bit by bit. There was no taking me off "self-destruct."

Remember, before when I said I put myself into debt? It was bad. I'd spent the majority of my savings and then some. I even took money from my brother without his permission. I'm very ashamed about that too.

It was impossible to get lower, to feel more worthless. More days had passed, and my friend Dave began hounding me to snap out of it. I didn't want to leave my house. I didn't want to talk to anyone. I didn't want to be. I once upon a time told Kim that I would die for her. I meant that too. I just never thought it would be like this.

The time came. There was only one answer, and I knew what it was. I simply didn't belong here. I simply didn't deserve to be loved. I was never good enough, and Kim's parents knew it. They called me on it. They reinforced everything that anyone has ever said about me.

Alone in my room. Dave was calling nonstop. I didn't answer. Rob was oblivious upstairs. Me? I was fashioning a noose out of a belt. This was it. Over. I lived in a basement apartment. I had piping along my ceiling and walls. I tied the belt, went across the room, picked up my chair and brought it to where the makeshift noose hung. Before I could even put the chair down out of nowhere Dave appeared and kicked it out of my hands. He tackled me right down onto the floor. I didn't move. I didn't fight. I just lay there in his arms and began to shiver. He held me tight. He didn't let go. Hours passed. Neither of us said a word. There were no words. Just emptiness. Dave stayed the night.

The next morning, we woke up and we had a long talk. Dave shadowed me for a long time and at the end of the day pulled me back from the brink. There's no doubt in my mind I would have shut the lights off had he not of arrived when he did. I was ready.

I remain incredibly ashamed of myself for falling that far. For getting that lost. For dropping my arms and taking the beating instead of fighting back like I always had. If it wasn't for David Lawrence Tirado I would not be here.

He said he would never tell anyone what had happened. I believe he kept that promise as no one has ever brought this up to me.

To the people whom I care about—from my brother Rob to everyone else I love—I'm sorry I didn't tell you. I'm sorry I kept this in. I'm sorry I never reached out for help. I'm sorry, sorry, sorry.

Today, I hold no malice toward anyone but myself. I was being selfish. I was being a coward. Kim's parents believed that they were doing the right thing for their child. Who am I to begrudge them that? As for Kim, I hold no anger toward her. She was put into an impossible situation and honestly, I don't know what I would have done if in her place. For a long time, she'd message me every once in a blue moon out of what I can only guess was pure guilt.

There's one thing for sure though. I will NEVER, EVER, let another human being on this planet talk to me the way that her parents had. I haven't since and I won't ever again. No one will ever get the better of me like that. I am better than that.

I ended up working for about two years, without having an extra dime to my name to pay Rob back every cent I owed him. I did it too. I will always own and fix my mistakes.

On my right arm right now, I have one of my favorite lyrics from the song "Rearviewmirror" by Pearl Jam.

I Gather Speed From You Fucking With Me.

Kim's parents would HATE IT, but ironically, they are very much responsible for it. I will prove them, and everyone else who doubted me, wrong. I'm a fucking force of nature.

This quote embodies who I am and what I have been through. It reminds me just what it took to get through. It IS me. It has also become my first line of defense. If someone reads it and is offended, if someone judges me for daring to have something like that emblazoned on my body, well, they have one of two choices:

Accept me for me for who I am or turn around immediately and forget I exist. Either one is fine by me.

To be brutally honest though, looking back at it all, every single thing that I've ever cared about in my life has been ripped from me. As a result, there remains a part of me that is very much STILL broken. A part that is afraid to love and more importantly afraid to be loved. That's about as honest as I can be.

Chapter 8
Latino Heat

With Kris now married to Laura and living his own life, I had a huge hole in my heart. Don't get me wrong... I was and remain happy for him, but I'd be lying if I said I didn't miss him dearly. He's my Tonto, man. I had time on my hands now, and as a result I was lucky enough to grow close to one of my fellow 209ers... David Tirado.

Standing in at about 5'6" Dave had a slight, but muscled build, and a smile that could light up a room. His skin was smooth and tan, and his hair shaved all around his head with the exception of the top. This cut in the '90s was known as "The Caesar." He was the epitome of the fabled Latin Lover, and chicks would flock to him by the dozen. It wasn't just because he was good-looking, which he most definitely was. It was because he was also absolutely beautiful on the inside as well. Dave's only shortcoming was that he, well... he wasn't the sharpest tool in the old shed, and I mean that with every ounce of love in my body possible. That didn't matter though. Whatever it was that he lacked, and it wasn't much, he made up for it with warmth and heart. People genuinely liked being around him. He was so fucking funny.

Dave was the kind of guy who would do anything for anyone. I ended up loving this dude as much as I do Kris, and he loved me right back. We became inseparable.

Rather than drone on and on in some chronological order about some of my favorite Dave stories I'm just gonna spout out some random shit that we'd been through together. Through them, you'll get to know him. You may even find yourself loving him as I do. I share these because they're like snapshots of some of the best (yet absurd) times of my life. Times when I found myself laughing impossibly hard. I've always been the jokester, but Dave was one of the few who genuinely made me laugh. These instances need, no, *deserve* to be immortalized in print.

Dave was so delightfully weird. When we were all hanging out in the schoolyard, there was a steady stream of girls showing up to hang out with our motley crew. The main reason they were there though? Dave. Without question. As soon as a chick entered the school yard Dave would drop whatever he was doing, run up to them while they were in mid-stride, and sit on them. Yes, this would happen exactly as it sounds. They would playfully and flirtatiously "struggle" for a moment and then Dave would be there sitting on their backs, in their laps, whatever. He was gentle, good looking, and this act was so weird that they adored it. We all would have a great laugh at this behavior, and as nuts as this sounds, it became like a thing, an oddball sign of respect and affection. Dave weighed probably less than most girls his size... if he was a buck twenty-five soaking wet with rocks in his pockets it would be a lot.

I'd come to realize (and I say this with all of the humility in the world) that together we were the perfect one two punch. People would flock to us because I was the tough badass guy who was not to be fucked with—with a sense of humor that was so random and wacky I'd have people regularly screaming with laughter—and Dave he was the good looking, ridiculously funny and charismatic young stallion who could win your heart with the quickest of smiles. Even more than that though, we were brutally honest. We never judged anyone, and everyone was welcome. Color, race, sexual preference, none of that shit mattered in the 209 school yard. The only requirement to be in our little club was that you were not a fake asshole. Misfits? We had em! Lunatics? There by the dozen. But the one thing we all had in common was our hearts, which beat together with the type of solidarity that's rarely found. It was like a small pocket of sanity. A sanctuary if you will. No judgment. No pretenses. Just fun.

Dave and me? We were always there for each other. Through the good times, the bad, and everywhere in between. Dave was the type of person though that was never on time for anything. It took me like a month to realize that if we needed to be somewhere at 9:00 p.m., I'd have to tell him we'd have to be there at 8:00 p.m. so when he showed up inevitably at 8:15 p.m. it was never a big deal. One time he strolled into the yard about a half an hour late for something and we playfully questioned him, "Dude, take yer time much?"

"Sorry, I passed out."

Now, he didn't mean that he fell asleep or anything. He meant that he literally lost consciousness. You see Dave, when he saw the sight of his own blood, would faint. Apparently, he had cut himself shaving and BOOM down he went, only to wake up—according to him—like twenty-minutes later. This was never worrisome to us. This was just classic Dave. Of course he lost consciousness.

It was midsummer and Dave got what would become his favorite car: An AMC Eagle. You may be asking yourselves, "What the fuck is that?" Hell, none of us knew as we had never heard of such a car. But Dave? He loved it. He loved it because it was his. He bought it. Admittedly, it was a piece of shit car, but he didn't care. It was his girl. The car was constantly on the fritz and every week he could be found fixing it or bringing it into the shop. It didn't matter though. To Dave, this car was legit. It may not have run very well, but he'd installed a banging car stereo, and the air conditioner ran second to none. If there's one thing the Eagle did well, it was temperature control. In the winter the car was hot as a Puerto Rican summer. In the summer it was cold as an igloo.

One time, it was a sweltering day mid-summer and his AC was

fritzed. Dave was gonna pick me up to go with him to get a new one. Getting into the car, it was a gazillion degrees, and I could feel the backs of my legs immediately begin sticking to the car's swampy interior. Dave looked at me and said:

"Hey, bro. I got us a couple of ice-cold Arizona Peach Iced Teas."

He handed me one and I began shaking it before opening it. He reached and grabbed his, and also began shaking it up. But he had already opened his and was now shaking its sugary contents all over us and the interior of the car. He realized how stupid this was, and he began laughing... no, cackling!

"Dave! What the fuck, dude! Your shit is open! Stop shaking it!"

He continued, so bemused by this stupidity that it took him an extra few shakes and splashes before he stopped.

He pulled over. We were soaking wet. Iced tea was everywhere, all over us. I was furious. He was deliriously laughing to the point that I couldn't help but laugh too. We giggled like idiots for what felt like forever before proceeding. It was magic and our love for one another made it all okay. Uncomfortable for sure, but totally okay.

Another time we were driving somewhere and were stopped behind a car at a red light. The light changed twice before Dave, who was furious about the jackass in front of him making him sit through two revolutions of a traffic light cycle, was blowing his horn like a maniac. I just sat there staring at him. I started to laugh.

"I'm gonna fucking kill this idiot! Hey! Dickhead! Your mother's in my backseat!" he yelled out the window before looking at me. I was hysterically laughing at both the situation and the bizarre statement of "Your mother's in my backseat!"

"What's so funny?"

"Dave," I said. "The car in front of us is parked. You're not in a turning lane. You're in a parking spot. You're blowing your horn at nobody."

He paused. Leaned forward laying his head against the steering wheel and we just both damned-near pissed our pants.

We'd get lost in thought and circumstance dozens of times. During my dad's illness, we had to drive to Staten Island. We were both talking. I was mentally spent. Whatever was going on medically with my father was taking a toll on me and Dave was there, as always, to lift my spirits. We were so deep in conversation that neither of us realized that Dave had missed his turnoff, and we were now making our way onto the Verrazano Bridge, at the end of which we'd have to pay a (then) $7.00 toll just to turn back around and head back to the proper turn off.

"Shit!" Dave exclaimed. "I ain't paying no toll!"

So what does he do? He knocks over a divider and pulls a fucking U-turn on the damned bridge. In my head I could almost hear the traffic report overhead from a helicopter:

"Things are moving along swiftly on both lanes, and it looks as if... wait... what? I'm not sure I'm seeing this correctly but... yes... Yes, it does appear that someone has decided to make a U-turn on the Verrazano Bridge. He's screwing up traffic both ways! This is highly irregular, and highly illegal! I hope someone got his plate number. This person is a menace to everyone around him."

There were no repercussions though, no tickets or police car chases. Just another typical Dave moment. Absurd, hilarious, and largely unexpected.

The 209ers eventually boiled down to five main players. Myself, Dave, Brian Hoffman, Augie Lambros, and Chilly Cross. I love each of them equally and I still do. Even Chilly, who I have every intention of never speaking to again. Though I'd be lying if I said Dave wasn't the most special of them all to me. Dave grew up with Brian and that made Brian family by default. Augie and Chilly bonded with us three. Well, truth be told, Chilly and Brian never really got along great. They kinda just tolerated each other for the sake of keeping the peace. Next to Rob and Kris, these guys were my brothers. My family... my REAL family. Chilly's mom and dad took us all in as strays. To say I love them both dearly is an understatement. Augie and I were the oldest of the bunch, so we bonded on that level. Brian, like Dave, wasn't always the brightest bulb in the room but, Christ, he was lovable all the same.

One time Augie, Bri, Dave and myself were playing that board game, Outburst. In it, you had to get your teammate to say a specific word by telling them about it. Aug and Bri were on the same team. Aug drew a card and had to get Brian to say the word, "China."

Aug gave his clue... "Not Japan, buuuttttt..."

Brian blinked twice and asked in earnest... "Japots?"

I shit you not. We broke up laughing so hard that the game couldn't be continued.

Japots. Ja-fucking-pots! Holy shit. It still kills me.

When I first met Chilly, he was in tight with a local gang called TBR which was short for The Bay Road. There was a pool hall down in Sheepshead Bay where they used to congregate—when they weren't out on the corner drinking, getting high, and engaging in the usual street "gang" activities—like acting like idiots, fighting, and being a general menace to everyone around them. Several members of TBR lived on Chilly's home block. Around the first time I met him we all went back to my house for a moment. There were always people in and out of my house. One day it came to my attention that a gold chain that my brother Rob had given me had disappeared. No, let's be frank... it was stolen. Never found out who had taken it.

I surely didn't think it was Chilly. I mean I didn't know him that well, but that's not something I thought he would do. Many years later, Augie told me that one night while he was there Chilly had come in bragging about stealing the chain and sold it to one of the pricks there. Augie knew how close Chilly and I were. When I found out it was him, I was hurt. I had no doubt that Aug was telling me the truth. Chilly, God bless him, was a storyteller. He was constantly lying as a means to impress people. I was hurt. Incredibly hurt, but it was many years later and I forgave him. I was now close with his entire family, including his younger brother Chris (who's one of the smartest people I know) and his lovely, troubled sister, Melanie. She became like a little sister to me. I treated them with respect even when they were young, and they respected me back. I'm sure it will hurt them to find out what their brother had done. But, hey, water under the bridge, right? I never told Chill that I knew.

A Comedy of Tragedies

If you're reading this, YOU'RE BUSTED, MOTHERFUCKER! So long and thanks for the fish.

There's more to the story with Chilly but I'll get to that a bit later. For now, back to one of my favorite people... Dave Tirado.

It was Christmas eve and Dave, Brian and I were over Chilly's house, voraciously eating his mom's homemade Christmas cookies. These things, man, they were like crack. Between these and her rib recipe, Marie not only owned my heart but my appetite as well. After eating, we all went out to do whatever it was we would do. Usually, it'd be me and Dave playing video games and watching Brian and Chilly get extremely high. Bri was first to go home, and since he lived within walking distance from my house, he stumbled his way home, no doubt giggling the entire time. Chilly was not only high, but he was also piss drunk. Fucking inebriated. He sloppily loaded himself into the back of the Eagle. It was about midnight and Dave was gonna drive him home. I took the ride with them, in case Chilly needed help getting into his house. Because of his drunken tomfoolery, someone would have to bear his weight, and Chill outweighed Dave by about 50lbs. During the ride home Chilly kept spitting out of the window of Dave's love machine. The only hitch was the window was closed. Joy. Then, as we made the turn onto Chill's block, Banner Avenue, Chill began violently puking everywhere. All over the back seat of Dave's car, Dave's windows, and himself. He was like a bile spewing fountain, and at this point Dave and I were just happy to not have any of Chilly's puke on us. The smell was horrendously vile. We pulled up to Chilly's house and much to our surprise he was able to get up and inside on his own steam. Marie, his mom, would later tell us that he was so drunk he stripped naked and accidentally jumped into bed with her and his dad by accident thinking it was his.

I got back into the car with Dave. We opened all the windows.

"Dude, I'm gonna drop you off and then head to my house to clean up my car."

"No way," I said. "It's Christmas, man. I'm not leaving you to clean up vomit by yourself."

Dave looked at me and didn't say a word. He just nodded, and it was then that we both knew. No matter what happened, no matter how bad, he and I would tackle it together, and so we did for many years.

It took about an hour to fully clean up the car. It was a mess, but I had a copious amount of cleaning products at my disposal. We got through it. Tired, Dave hopped up on the hood of the Eagle and I joined him. We laid there staring up at the sky. It didn't even feel that cold even though it was the ass end of December. We both just started laughing. Time passed and it was time to say goodnight.

"Merry Christmas, man," Dave said. "I love you, dude."

"I love you too, you filthy spic."

"Eat six dicks, Dago."

"Munch on these nuts, son."

After that exchange, Dave turned and got in his car.

He made it three feet.

"Fuck! Motherfucker! What the shit? FUCKING BULLSHIT! FUCK YOU, WORLD!" he yelled furiously.

"What's the matter?" I asked.

He got out of his car and walked around the rear passenger side tire. It was flat.

"Welp, I guess we're not rid of each other yet," I said as I approached his car again. "Get the jack out of the trunk and let's throw yer donut on."

"I can't," Dave said sheepishly. "I don't have one."

"What?"

"I don't have one."

I sighed and took a seat against the Eagle. He sat down next to me.

"So, what do we do?"

"I've no idea, man."

"Do you even have a spare?"

"Yeah, I got one. Just no jack."

"Okay, let me try something," I said and stood up. I cupped my fingers under the back of the car and lifted. All in all, I was able to raise the back corner of the car a few inches.

"So, here's what we do. You unscrew all the shit around the tire, from there I'll lift it and hold it up until you can slap the donut in place. Then I'll lay it down gently and you tighten everything up."

Dave looked at me like I was some kind of fucking nut, but figured we'd give it a shot. I can still feel my arms burning from holding up the Eagle. Dave was so fucking amused by what was happening that he was trying (in vain) to hold in his laughter as I went through a litany of profanity as my arms shook and sweat poured down my face. Within a few minutes the deed was done. "Good, now get the fuck out of here before some other Yuletide disaster falls upon us. And buy a fucking jack, you dickhole, because I'm NEVER doing this again!"

Dave said nothing got in his car and turned the key. "Oh, and Dave," I yelled out. "Merry Christmas." He nodded, still holding in his laughter. Red faced.

As the car pulled away, I heard him bust a gut as he drove down the block, like Santa bidding the children a final goodbye before heading back to the old North Pole.

"Merry Christmas to all… and to all a good night filled with less drunkenly spewed vomit and air-filled buoyancy."

Dave and I bonded over a number of things. Video games, music, you name it.

Later that same year I met some folks who would change my life… Pete Ross, Steve Martinez, Jaime Lathrop, and Paulie Wohlmaker, collectively known then as the indie band Five Cent Hero. Aside from Pearl Jam and such, their music directly spoke to me, and I ended up managing them. No one was more surprised at this turn of events than I was. The band was genius and I fell crazy in love with them. So did Dave and he would be there to support us through thick and thin. He had a show flyer, an old show flyer, taped into the window of his Eagle. We'd spend many a night singing together driving around with the windows open like we were the real rock stars. FCH's music was personal to us. Not only was it good, it was ours. If you're curious you can check them out on Spotify, as I will always make sure that shit will live on forever.

Nothing could stop us. The future was a blank canvas and the world was ours. We were young, hungry, and rocking enough balls to take anything the world could possibly throw at us. With Dave by my side, and me by his, there was nothing we couldn't accomplish. We forged a bond that would carry us forever.

Bring it on world...we fucking got this.

Chapter 9
Cut a Hole in My Heart

The Booze Cruise. That's what we called the first ever concert Five Cent Hero was to play on a boat that would sail around New York's harbor. Dave, of course, was late and ended up missing the boat. He showed up right as it set sail and we saw each other. Him on the dock and me on the boat. We both shook our heads and laughed. He gave me a smile and a wave, and I returned it wishing he could have actually had the experience with us. The voyage went off without a hitch and there wasn't even much puking, given the amount of alcohol everyone ingested. Tomorrow, much to everyone's chagrin, would be a workday. A poorly timed workday, but a workday nonetheless.

At 8:00 a.m. I left my house in Marine Park to catch the bus to the Sheepshead Bay train station. The Q Train, to be specific. The air was crisp and warm. Incredible weather for early September. It was a perfect Tuesday morning and the last thing anyone would want to do was head into another average work week of bullshit before the coming weekend. Once at my train station, I got on at a stop that was usually empty so I always got a seat. Somehow, having a seat for the long ride into Manhattan always softened the blow of traveling. In tow I had my copy of Bruce Campbell's book *If Chins Could Kill:*

Steve Barton

Confessions of a B-Movie Actor under my arm so I was ready for come what may.

> **Author's Note:** At this point in the writing of this book it was July 18th, 2018—the day before my mom's death day. I knew this chapter was going to be a lot to process and as a result I stepped away from it until I felt I could come back and cope with these memories. The time is now September 11th, 2018. It's 12:15 a.m. I think I'm ready.

Every train ride would be the same for me. Once we got to DeKalb Avenue, I'd vacate my seat and stand by the doors as we crossed the Manhattan Bridge into the city. Now don't get me wrong, Campbell's book is entertaining as fuck, but it would be nothing short of a criminal shame to miss this view. The water, impossibly blue. The massive skyscrapers of the New York City skyline, even from a speeding train, were nothing short of breathtaking. I stood as always by the doors. Drinking it in.

Then something caught my eye. A plane flying impossibly low I thought it was making a descent into an emergency landing. But it never even came close to making ground. Instead, it crashed right into the North Tower of the World Trade Center. The time was 8:45 a.m. The crashing sound was audible even over the roar of the subway car. A collective gasp resonated through the speeding metal box as everyone gathered around the windows and doors, speculating about what had just happened, this terrible accident, the worst anyone had ever seen. By about 8:50, the Q had arrived at the Canal Street station in lower Manhattan and I, like many, started making my way topside to head on over to the Trade Center.

The one thing about New Yorkers, when shit hits the fan, we are there for each other. If help was needed on the scene, help was going to be in abundance, and it was. The crowds were massive and gathering.

As we all made our way to the Twin Towers another rumble vibrated what felt like the entire city. I remember looking up to see another plane come careening into the South Tower. The time was

A Comedy of Tragedies

9:03 a.m. This changed everything. This was obviously no accident. This was very deliberate. The sound the plane made when crashing through the building was like nothing I've ever heard, and hopefully nothing I will ever hear again. People were screaming, crying, running. There was no time to think, only act. By this time both Towers were engulfed in flames and smoke. Fire engines and police cars roared down the streets, not all of them making it to the scene, with some police and fireman just pulling over and running toward the blaze. Whatever it takes. That's a special kind of bravery.

I knew it was best to let the authorities handle the situation, so I headed to work at the School of Visual Arts on East 23rd Street. By the time I got there, everyone was huddled around TVs. It was then that I first learned of the Pentagon being struck by a plane as well. This was madness. Chaos. An unrealistic reality.

Collectively everyone decided it would be a good idea to get the hell out of the City. As I was leaving the word came... the unthinkable... The South Tower fell. This reverberated throughout the city. Manhattan was now engulfed in an endless cloud of rubble and debris.

It began, for lack of a better term, raining paper. I'll never forget that. The sheets of paper blowing in the wind, forced into flight by the dropping of a massive building. I decided to head back down to the Towers. There would be no doubt that help would be needed. I could see the North Tower burning in the distance. Things falling from it amid the paper rain... things that would turn out to be people. People falling to their death so as not to be burned alive. Poor souls with no choice. Husbands, wives, brothers, sisters. Bodies just dropping indiscriminately. Screams... Roaring flames... billowing smoke... ashes... thick ashes... rubble... dust and debris, the smell of burning flesh, all accompanied by the first scent of death... the raining paper. This was a new type of horror that could never be put away.

There was nothing else I wanted to do more than turn around yet with every step I moved toward the Towers the more I felt like I needed to stay. I needed to help. I had to do something. Then it happened... the North Tower fell. The time was 10:28 a.m. The smoke was so thick, the air incredibly dense. A cloud came rolling down street level with a ferocious velocity. I ducked into a bodega. Lights were blinking. The screaming and crying hit new heights of absolute terror. Strangers were holding on to each other as tightly as the closest of families. The ground was just shaking. It felt like the end of the world. In a lot of ways, it truly was. Some guy put his arms on my shoulders, and I hugged him right back, nodding to each other. Just holding on, just trying to hold on. Waves of debris and dust crashed against the windows and doors of the store we were in for what felt like hours. In truth maybe 5-minutes had passed but it felt so very much longer.

In less than two hours the entire world had changed.

The situation had become dire. There would be no helping. The only thing left to do was to try and make it home. There was just one problem... all exits to and from the city had been closed. Manhattan was on lockdown with only one way left to vacate. If you wanted out of the city, you'd have to hoof it over one of the many bridges. Through lots of routing, walking, and rerouting, I ended up at the Williamsburg Bridge amid an ocean of people, all of us shell-shocked and covered in dust. Crying. Holding on to each other. In that moment nothing else mattered, other than people helping people get to where they had to go. Color, race, creed, nothing mattered in that moment. People were just helping other people. In that moment of chaos, it was as if everyone came to the realization that we're all the same...just people.

We were about a quarter of the way into crossing the bridge when the word began traveling. First as a murmur and then into a full-blown panic.

"The bridge was wired to explode."

That was to be the next phase of the attack, and with that word, which traveled like lightning, everyone, myself included, started running for their lives. Just trying to make it to the other side. People were dropping, running, crying, screaming. As I ran, I started saying goodbye to the ones whom I loved in my head. I then cried out to my parents and God to please keep me safe. Please let me reach the other side. Please let me live longer than I had. Of course, the bridges were never wired to explode and everyone made it safely to the other side. People who owned stores, etc., were waiting at the other end of the bridge with bottles of water and assorted drinks for anyone who needed them. Gasping I gladly accepted some water, and I hugged the guy who gave it to me. We were alive and lucky and, despite the paper rain, we had made it. This was the best of humanity set against the backdrop of the worst-case scenario. It was impossible not to feel hopeful among these horrors... there was love in the air. Pure unconditional love. Love for each other and love for our neighbors. The worst was over and now it was time to make it back home.

I walked for hours until finally I found a bus line that was running so that I could get home. There was no charge to ride it. Everyone on the bus was commiserating. Some were worried, and some, like myself, were extremely grateful that they didn't know anyone who had worked there at the Trade Center. At about 3:00 p.m. the bus dropped me off by my house. I turned the corner and began shuffling toward my residence. My feet were killing me. I could feel a hot mixture of both sweat and sticky blood swimming around my shoes. Rob was there waiting. When he saw me, he ran toward me and I kind of collapsed in his arms. He hugged me extremely tight. He had no way of knowing where I was. You see, when the Towers fell, that knocked out a lot of the phones in and around the city. This was before the big cellular boom too, but even if they were commonplace—the cellular towers had gone down with the buildings. Landlines and phone booths were still the standard. He pretty much carried me to the stoop where I sat collapsing into a heap.

"Stevie," Rob said. "I don't know how to tell you this, but Dave is missing. They think he was in one of the buildings."

"What buildings," I asked, knowing full well what his answer would be.

"The Towers."

No. Impossible. It couldn't be. I just couldn't be. Dave didn't work there. He would have had no reason to be there.

Rob looked at me, staring through me. I began unlacing my boots, they were filthy and as predicted my socks were covered in soot and blood.

"Rob, can you get me a drink? I think I really need one." He went inside and emerged a few moments later handing me a beer.

"Drink this, man. Please."

I took the beer and gulped. I put my head in my hands and sat there. Him standing next to me. This nightmare was just beginning. Just. Fucking. Beginning. The worst had not passed. It was yet to come.

The rest of the night felt as if it happened in slow motion. I showered the thick layer of dust and ash off me and wrapped up my feet in bandages, band-aids, and gauze. From there, our good friend Karen drove me to Dave and his fiancé Danielle's house. Upon arriving everyone was sitting gathered around the TV. Every time the phone rang all eyes were on whoever answered. Unfortunately, all we got was more questions than answers. Every minute that passed felt like hours and every hour that passed felt more and more bleak.

Our general consensus was that maybe, just maybe, Dave was just either unconscious somewhere, or he hadn't been dug out of the rubble yet. There was no way he was dead. It couldn't possibly be. We were there for hours. Nothing. No news whatsoever beyond our own speculation. Finally, it came time to go home. There was just nothing that could be done. The next day was bound to have answers.

None ever came.

There are things about 9/11 that you don't know unless you were there. Things no one ever talked about. The sea of "Missing Persons" posters, puddles of water that when you stood in would leave a pinkish residue on your shoes. Blood? Who knows. Then there was the smell. A mixture of burning materials and human remains. It was abysmal. Something you could just never forget and something that no one should ever have to experience. This was the new normal.

After a few weeks hope was painfully abandoned. All of us spent a lot of time in various states of denial and disbelief. The American flag waved everywhere, but none of our loved ones who were lost ever waved back. There was never a trace of David Lawrence Tirado found. There was nothing to bury. It was as if every bit of him was just gone. That's been the hardest part. The best we could hope for is that he died instantly and painlessly.

I know that this may sound cliché to say, but he truly was the sweetest guy in the world, and he deserved better.

Once upon a time Dave saved my life. Dave is my hero, through and through. Knowing that I couldn't do the same for him or be his continues to dig at me. Gnaws on my soul. It probably always will.

Everyone who lost their lives or were affected in any way deserved better. There's not a day that goes by I do not miss him. Thankfully though, this wouldn't be my last interaction with Dave, as he's been integral to my life and has helped me to become who I am. More on that in a bit. Things were certainly about to get dark, and dawn was a painfully long way off.

Chapter 10
Shine On, You Crazy Diamond

You expect a lot of things in your life. You expect to love and to lose. There's going to be a time when the people who care about you and make your life special leave you. I expected to lose my parents. That's just a fact of life. People grow old and fade out. You're the one left carrying on, and carrying on is in most of our DNA. The one thing you don't expect is to lose your best friend. After all of the pain I had been through. Nothing had prepared me for this. I was broken. Beaten. Shattered. Destroyed. There are times I'd find myself just walking and ending up in places without ever remember going there. It's like I would snap in and out of lucidity. I couldn't get on the subway anymore. Luckily my employers, SVA, were very understanding and allowed me to remain on paid leave instead of firing me. They even sent me to a therapist. I don't really know how good therapy was for me or even if it helped me at all. Just telling a stranger about your life is bizarre. Especially because you know that they're just listening because that's what they're paid to do. Not to say all therapy is a waste as millions of people are helped by it every day. Said therapist diagnosed me as having Post-Traumatic Stress Disorder. Another feather in my cap? I was just too far gone. Farther than I have ever been. I couldn't "brain" anymore. Thinking or rationalizing the slightest thing was a chore. Full-blown panic attacks were hitting me over the head. My blood pressure was through the roof. I didn't want to leave my house.

Rob would come down to my basement room to check on me frequently. Many years later he said he did so because he was afraid I would have done something stupid. I'm not going to lie... I have been that desperate and low several times already. One time I came dangerously close to checking myself out, but that's another story and it's one I do not wish to share. There are lots of variables. Lots of people involved, that it would be unfair to tell you about it because they're not here to defend themselves, and everything would read seriously one-sided. Maybe I'm just not that good of a writer? Who knows.

Having been through the "Kim Incident," I wasn't thinking about checking out. Suicide is NOT me. I'm a fucking cockroach. I don't quit. I may get lost like everyone else, but I'll never quit. That's just not who I am or who I will ever be.

Still, I cannot ever remember a time in which I felt more alone. There was nothing to live for and living just felt like a chore, man. Just going through the motions of existing until the big checkout.

They say when one door closes another one opens. That is true, but to be perfectly honest I was really tired of going in and out. There was only one thing to get me through this and it was the last thing I ever expected.

Love.

Before 9/11 went down I met a woman named Debi on a news group. A Pearl Jam news group. To this day Eddie and the band possess the uncanny ability to write songs about whatever is going on in my life. The same was true for Deb. After a couple of back-and-forths about P.J. tattoos, we spoke on the phone. I quickly learned that I could talk to her about anything. She's thirteen years my senior but that didn't matter. She got me and never pushed me to be anything more than what I was. Of course in true Steve self-destruct manner I tried pushing her away, but she's about as tenacious as me. No matter how hard I pushed away she pushed closer. During the events of that September, I was broken and lost. Debi was always there. It didn't matter that she was in California and I was in New York. We'd spend time with each other on the phone and even watch movies together by simultaneously pressing the play button on whatever it is we wanted to watch. She became a constant in my life and was so for twenty years. Thankfully. Deb fed all of my hopes and dreams. She knew I was a big horror fan and she also knew that deep down inside I was just a big kid. My childhood was pretty much nonexistent, so I still found myself lost in varying degrees of wonder over even the littlest things. Especially horror toys. I'll get to that in a bit.

You see I'm not done with the Dave story. He was... well... he was haunting me.

I know, I'm crazy, right? I couldn't be more sane and reasonable. Over the months after 9/11 little things would happen around my place.

I was a cute little fucker, wasn't I?

A COMEDY OF TRAGEDIES

My parents, Ann Barton and Robert Barton Sr.

Sewagin, Mom, Dad, Grandpa, and Grandma.

Steve Barton

Here it is. The house of pain, also known as the house I grew up in. It even looks like a place where bad shit happened.

Chillin' in my room in the House of Pain: Brian Hoffman, Me, Augie Lambros, Dave Tirado

A COMEDY OF TRAGEDIES

My besties back in the day: (Left to Right) Brian Hoffman, Augie Lambros, Me, Dave Tirado, Chilly Cross

This pic encapsulates all that I will always love about Dave. He was both effortlessly and fearlessly goofy. I will ALWAYS love him and my career is dedicated to his memory. Thanks for looking out for me, man. 'Til we meet again!

Steve Barton

Probably my most cherished photo of Dave and me. This was like an hour before Chilly threw up in his backseat on Christmas Eve.

I swear this was a picture I took of my call waiting. In retrospect, I probably should have answered.

My best friend now and always, Kris Schlamp

Steve Barton

My brother Rob and me. I love this fucker so much. We drive each other nuts but that's what brothers do.

A Comedy of Tragedies

One of the best to ever investigate the paranormal, the incomparable Lou Gentile. I love you, brother.

I dedicated an episode of my Internet radio show, Brianwaves Horror and Paranormal to Lou. He's the only reason I ever even wanted to do it. I'm glad I did. I hope I made you proud.

STEVE BARTON

The illustrious Johnny Butane and me goofing around first at Rock and Shock. Decades later we recreated the moment!

have no idea why I love this picture of me so much. It just really captures me.

A Comedy of Tragedies

While waging my #WarOnGirth I realized while hiking that my shadow looked like a hard on.

STEVE BARTON

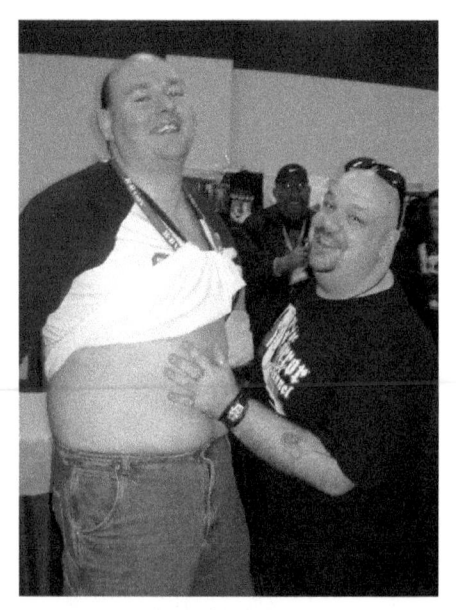

Joe Knetter and I at Rock and Shock.

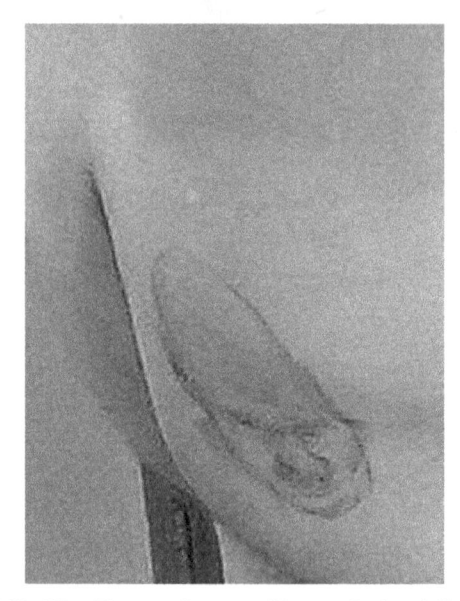

ASS-AID—The tattoo Joe got on his ass at Rock and Shock

A Comedy of Tragedies

The first time I ever met Sid Haig. A true motherfucking legend!

The "Other" Happy Couple at Sid and Suzie's wedding!

Steve Barton

And, oh, how we danced!

The Terrordome in full effect, yo!

A COMEDY OF TRAGEDIES

Our fictitious band's tour poster.

Our fictitious band's live album.

I knew when I saw you that night that it was gonna be one of the last times I'd ever be graced with your presence. I didn't want to let go. I still don't wanna. I never will.

Me on the set of the Amityville Murders pre-twisting my ankle, thereby falling victim to the Amityville Curse.

A Comedy of Tragedies

Copy of a poster that appeared in the supplemental features of one of the Friday the 13th Blu-ray releases

Steve Barton

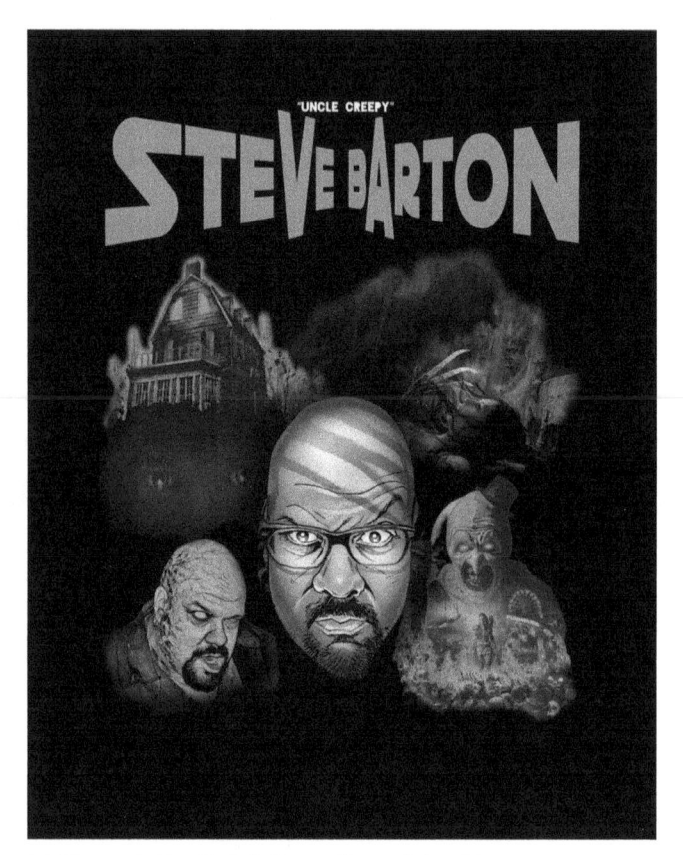

My Homage to Tom Savini's Scream Greats. I sign this at conventions.

Hugging Chris Sembrot's son, Ryan, at my ScarePros signing.

Chapter 11
Sure! Blame Me For Everything!

Now, I will be the first one to admit, after the events of September 11th I was not in my right mind. I wasn't crazy by any stretch of the imagination, but there was truly something busted in my head. I was just apathetic. Disconnected. Nothing mattered. Nothing at all.

Let's fast forward a few months. I finally worked up the courage to head back to work in Manhattan. That was a huge step. Slowly, very slowly, I began to normalize. I became more aware of what was going on around me. The second I left my house, I just wanted to turn around and go back home. I knew that wouldn't do, so I forged ahead.

It was a Friday night. I was lying on my bed. I had to sleep with the TV on because one of the most golden things about PTSD is that I became unsettled by silence and darkness.

Was this what death was like? That's kind of how I imagine it.

It was about 1:00 a.m. and I was spent from a long hard work week. I was drifting to sleep on my stomach when it started. This pressure... it came on like a wave, started from my thighs and creeping up my back. I had never felt such a tremendous weight. It literally was pushing me deeper into my bed. I couldn't scream, couldn't move. I was being held down. Whatever sleepy goodness that was on its way was now completely gone. I was WIDE awake. I pushed myself up and broke free. I sat up, looking around. I remember thinking to myself, "Well, that was different." A couple of minutes passed. I was genuinely unnerved, but convinced myself that this was just some weird byproduct of mental instability and exhaustion. I laid back down on my stomach. I couldn't have been more awake. Within seconds, the pressure was back. This time even stronger. I could not fucking even come close to moving. It felt like I was being suffocated. Like this was it. I was gonna die in my bed for some unknown reason. Then I gave one last push. It took EVERY SINGLE THING that I had and I even kinda let out a mini-scream... the kind you'd hear a weightlifter make after a very heavy deadlift.

I sprang to my feet and looked around. This time I made sure every light in my room was on. What the hell was that? I was scared out of my mind. The next day I tried looking up if this had ever happened to anyone else. The closest I came to answers was sleep paralysis. Never heard of that before. Was it some hag sitting on my back? Some entity holding me down. No clue. No fucking clue. The only rock-solid thing that I knew was that it had happened.

About two weeks later I came home from work to find all the batteries taken out of my remote controls. The remotes themselves were turned over to reveal their battery compartments. The lids were laid down next to them. On my table there were about eight Double A batteries lined up in a neat row. This freaked me out. I know I didn't do this. I asked Rob but as usual, he found some colorful way to call me an idiot. Par for the course. At least that weird pressure sensation hadn't come back. Thank God for small favors. Another few weeks passed. Nothing. No oddities. Status quo. Maybe I was just kind of nuts. Sleep deprived. Depressed.

It was a Thursday evening. Rob called out to me. "Stevie! What the fuck did you do? Get up here and clean this shit up"

Huh? What in the world was this lunatic talking about. I left my room to find him in the kitchen UBER-pissed-off!

"How in the fuck did you even do this?" he snarled.

"Do what?" I asked, genuinely perplexed.

He pointed to the inside of the fridge. I looked in and spied maple syrup dripping all over EVERYTHING. I mean EVERYTHING! It was as if this particular bottle of pancake topping had exploded everywhere. But how was that even possible? It was a plastic bottle, and the contents were hardly under pressure. There was no conventional reason that this could have happened, yet it did.

It took about an hour to clean everything up. Rob was convinced I did it because he "certainly fucking didn't." Let me be honest. I may have been guilty of doing things like leaving an empty box of cereal (or five) in the cupboard instead of throwing it away, but I'd never have done something like this, if only because I'd have to clean it up. I'm too lazy for this kind of shit.

There was only one logical conclusion that was completely illogical... the house was haunted. Maybe it was all the pain I was in that was making these things happen, the energy of my agony, like a poltergeist manifestation. I kept doing my research and happened upon something that struck me pretty good. In one of the many articles I poured over, someone had described a strange incident that seemed to be on par with my "bed incident." They wrote something to the effect of when a person dies suddenly or tragically, they will sometimes go to their loved ones and try and communicate. Sometimes they could make said loved ones "feel" what they had felt during the moment of their demise. Dave would have been crushed while being burned to death. Is that what happened? I couldn't say for sure because no one knows exactly what happened to Dave. Sitting back in my chair and glancing around my room I said aloud:

"Dave, man. Is that what happened to you? I'm so fucking sorry, dude. So. Fucking. Sorry. If that's what you wanted to do, let me know how you felt, I will hold that. I will remember it here for you whether you want me to or not. Thank you for sharing that. I wouldn't want you to hold onto that forever. I have big shoulders, bro. I can help you shoulder whatever you need me to."

Thinking more about things I asked:

"Hey, was that you with the batteries and the fucking syrup, you dirty motherfucker!?" I said with a laugh. "Were you trying to get my attention? You have got it. You will always have it. I'm so sorry you're not here to share your life with the world. How about I always share mine with you? I love you, man. I'm always here."

Touching my heart and then my head.

"You'll always be right here. Now and forever. Rest easy, brother. I will live one hell of a life for us both. I swear to you."

I've held tight to that promise. I will never break it. One thing is for sure, I knew that if I hoped to fulfill my word to Dave... fuck, I had my work cut out for me. Did I ever.

Chapter 12
Becoming Creepy

That was it. I was done. 9/11 affected me in ways I never would have imagined possible. In fact, it still does. It's gotten a little easier, but it still sucks. I hadn't been to work at the School of Visual Arts in weeks, but this place gave me whatever I needed, including sending me to a shrink. I remember thinking, "Man, oh man... Whomever this therapist is has no clue about the overflowing bucket of fuck that they're about to ingest." And that's exactly what it was. Funnily enough, I didn't even tell them everything, like I have here, but I could see that they were overwhelmed just sitting there. My official diagnosis was "depression, post-traumatic stress disorder, and anxiety." Within weeks I was put on Zoloft, and I'm still on it to this very day. Dr. Z evens me out. I'm extremely thankful for it, but there was a HUGE inhibitor for my progress, Zoloft or not. It was a giant-ass city with an open and bleeding wound called, Manhattan, New York. I just couldn't be there. I still freeze when I visit "The City"—as we New Yorker's call it. For me it's like walking through a ghost. It hurts me to the very core of my being. My heart starts racing. My hands get sweaty. I sometimes have to fight back tears. For me, Manhattan has become a sprawling cemetery. I don't ever think that will change.

One thing was certain, if I was going to survive, I had to leave behind everything and everyone I knew and loved. My first stop was moving in with my girl, Debi, in Venice, Florida. It's such a beautiful little city nestled on Florida's western coast. No matter where you were, you were only ten minutes from the beach. Florida was, like, the polar opposite of New York. The people themselves were different. I wasn't used to things like nodding at a fellow driver on the road just because they were your fellow traveler, or people taking their time with, well, everything. I was constantly moving at a million miles per hour. It didn't take me long to acclimate and eventually love the slower lifestyle. But it wasn't all good.

You see, there's a lot of things that weren't in the Florida brochure. Looking at literature of the place before moving, it was all people in bathing suits, playing volleyball on the beach while someone was squeezing oranges nearby. It looked like paradise. I mean, yeah, that kind of thing was there, but it was surrounded by chicks with sideburns who were wearing NASCAR jackets and giant fucking bugs.

Now, we had wildlife in New York too, but it was mainly winos and rats, with the occasional shitting pigeon and rabies spreading squirrels who steal pizza. You saw the video. Florida's was different. Completely different. I was a fish out of water with no clue of my surroundings. I loved the fact that everywhere I looked there were tiny lizards running about that would do push-ups to assert their dominance if confronted. That was probably my favorite part.

The only problem with Venice was that it was goddamned boring. There was literally nothing to do and everything closed down at 8:00 p.m. It was so dull that we had to be really creative to have a good time. One day I was laying on the floor of the bedroom while Debi was surfing the Interwebs.

"I'm bored," I said. She answered with a silent nod. I sat up and exclaimed, "Wanna do something stupid? I have an idea!" Always game, she nodded and I got up and told her to stay put while I went outside. I came back in with a small rock.

"What's that?" she asked.

"Entertainment!" I said cheerfully. "Let me get the computer chair."

A Comedy of Tragedies

She got up and I sat, immediately clicking over to eBay. This was still the time of the Internet's infancy, where you could do wacky things like buy a "haunted toaster," or a "cursed mirror." I looked at Debi straight in the face and told her, "Deb, you see this rock? It's haunted and we're gonna try and sell this fucking thing!" She looked at me completely confused.

"It is?"

"Yes," I answered with a smile. "It sure fucking is!" In reality I just went outside and found a cool rock in our yard and brought it in, but I'm also a bit of a lunatic and, even worse, like I said, I was bored. Being a paranormal buff, I had heard many a story in my life including one regarding the cursed ghost town called Bodie, California.

Situated in the eastern Sierra Nevada mountain range, Bodie was founded in 1859 after the discovery of gold in the area. Of course, once there's ghosts, there are eventually ghost stories to go along with them! However, this town's, shall we say, "curse" was a particularly interesting one.

By the early Twentieth Century, the mines were depleted, and the population sank like the nutsack of an octogenarian. By the 1940s, Bodie was all but abandoned, left to the mercy of life's biggest bitches: time and the elements.

Legend has it that the curse of Bodie originated from the—SURPRISE—mistreatment of a Native American chief by the town's early settlers. As the story goes, the chief's daughter fell in love with a miner from Bodie, but he wasn't having any of it. The white man had already taken enough, and the chief wasn't about to let this dude mine his daughter's.... well... you get it. When the chief refused to allow the marriage, the miner and his daughter fled into the woods. Understandably pissed off, the chief cursed the town, proclaiming that it and everyone there would suffer misfortune and ruin for generations to come.

Immediately the curse took hold. Visitors reported all sorts of strange shit, from unexplained noises to sightings of ghostly apparitions. However, the most famous part of Bodie's curse involves a tourist who allegedly stole a piece of jewelry from one of the abandoned houses. Shortly after leaving Bodie, the thief was haunted by a series of misfortunes, including—but not limited to—financial ruin and illness. Having learned not to have sticky fingers the hard way, and as a means to break the curse, the thief returned the stolen item to its rightful place in Bodie, to try and appease whatever restless spirits were haunting the land.

That story was all I needed. I looked at Deb and said, "Bodie is the source of our haunted rock," and began writing our description. To the best of my recollection, it went something like this:

HAUNTED ROCK FROM BODIE CALIFORNIA

My wife and I are paranormal investigators who are always on the hunt to personally test the boundaries of what we know as 'reality.' Our thirst for knowledge led us to a ghost town known as Bodie located in California. It is said that if you take ANYTHING from Bodie, you'll be cursed and followed by bad luck until it is returned. We visited, looked around and left with only the rock that you see pictured here.

It all started with our flight home being canceled. We joked about the supposed curse being the cause, but then little things started here and there. Flat tires, broken glasses, misplaced valuables, nothing huge, but it was about to get bad. Our home state of Florida was hit with not one but four deadly hurricanes in the span of a month which is easily verifiable with a quick glance at the weather news over the past several weeks. Is this rock and the curse of Bodie responsible? It's hard to say, as it could all be unfortunate coincidence, but this is enough for us to want to be rid of any shred of our trip to Bodie.

Unfortunately, we don't have the money or time to fly back and return this rock to where it belongs. Our hope is that either A: someone on the West Coast will buy it and return it, or B: someone will buy it who has the know-how to remove whatever evil intent is nestled within this stone. If you too are a risk taker or a skeptic, this is the auction for you.

A Comedy of Tragedies

Immediately our eBay inbox was flooded with questions and inquiries, the best one read: "If I buy this cursed rock, can you mail it to my ex instead of me?" We laughed for hours about that one. At the end of the day, the "cursed rock" sold for about $25 bucks with shipping. Not bad for a rock from our yard. The person who bought it informed us that they "knew how to remove the curse" and that "the rock will be stored with their personal collection of haunted objects."

Yes, this whole situation is indeed a "dick move" on my part, but I was bored, dammit!

That was probably the most exciting thing that happened in Venice, Florida during our stay, so we decided to move somewhere a little more "city-like." We planned on moving to Tampa. Little did we know that some really strange shit was on the horizon.

There were a lot of reasons to leave Venice. Especially to get away from our next door neighbor, whose home and person reeked of Chef Boyardee SpaghettiOs 24/7. Seriously, the smell of that shit would hit us like a thick ghost-filled fog bank every time this middle-aged dude opened his window or door. Between him and the constant hurricanes, I always had to fight back the urge to stand on the porch with an industrial fan raised over my head just to blow shit back at 'em for spite. Yep, we couldn't get outta there soon enough, but there was just one thing... apparently our condo didn't want us to go.

You know they say that when an area goes through a major change it can sometimes kick up a haunting if any spirits were present. Nothing weird ever happened in our place the entire time we lived there, but the week before we left things started happening. Strange noises and shit. Nothing to be alarmed about as they could have very well all have had a logical explanation, but our last night there was like living in fuckin' Amityville.

I'll never forget it. I was lying on the bed backward, resting on my stomach while watching TV. We had just finished the last of our packing, and being that our computer was going with us instead of movers, Deb was on it surfing around. The Phantom of the Chef Boyardee was particularly strong this evening, but thankfully it was mid-winter and we could sit comfortably with the air conditioner off and the windows closed. To our immediate right was the bathroom which was connected to the bedroom. By the door I saw a light. A flickering light, which looked like a piece of tissue paper drifting slowly to the floor.

"What the fuck was that?" I yelled.

"What?" Deb answered inquisitively.

I told her what I saw. I got off the bed and put the lights on. I couldn't find anything around the bathroom door. I looked everywhere. I am POSITIVE I saw it. The blinds were closed so it wasn't any lights from outside or anything even remotely like that.

"Steve, you're scaring me," Deb said.

I told her I wasn't exactly happy about it either. I laid back down on the bed and she went back to surfing, but my eyes never left that area where I saw "the lights." After a few minutes one of our cats came in to go to the bathroom. His litter box was in there. He stopped before entering the bathroom, waited like 5 seconds, then turned tail and ran out.

"Did you see that? Klassik wouldn't go in the bathroom."

We were both uneasy. Bedtime came, and I had a routine. Brush my teeth, get a glass of water, and bring it to my nightstand which was also the computer desk in case I got thirsty. I did that and got into bed. Then out of nowhere, the printer started going off. Over and over and over again. As if it were just turned on from being off. It kept repeatedly resetting.

"Maybe just unplug it," Deb said.

I turned around to do so and noticed my glass of water was no longer on the desk. It was placed, not a drop spilled, on the floor at the foot of our bed.

What the actual fuck, dude?

I got up and turned on the lights. Looked around everywhere. There was no way that glass could have moved on its own. ZERO. We were both freaking out a bit. To make matters worse, our cats, of which we had three, wouldn't come near the bedroom and they slept with us every night. After about ten minutes of panic and to be honest a bit of terror, I unplugged the printer, which was STILL going, making its shifting noises, turned the lights off, and got back into bed. We were laying there, almost afraid to keep talking when all of a sudden, the vertical blinds began swinging back and forth as if some mad breeze were blowing them, but again—the windows were shut tight and the air conditioning was off! Neither of us slept a wink that night, and the morning couldn't come soon enough. Once it did, we were in the fucking car and Tampa-bound, the spooky and the SpaghettiO's be damned!

We moved into a place called Wild Wood Acres and lived in a condo complex whose trash center was located at the opposite end to our place. When it was time to take out the trash we'd have to walk about a quarter of a mile down the road. I came to realize in no time that Floridian trash areas were much like New York public toilets in that whoever uses them instantly forgets everything that they've been taught about cleanliness and hygiene. It was a true shit show. The only difference really was a lack of graffiti and the occasional jump-scare provided by eager frogs who were just trying to score a meal.

Let me be clear... just like everyone else, I have a tendency to be lazy. In fact, my goal in life is to be bored. I mean that too.

Anyway, the trash had to be taken out, but it was like 10:00 p.m. Deb had already gone to bed, and I wanted to play video games. Instead of walking the trash down to the dumpster I just put it outside of my front door with the intention of taking it the next morning. I fired up the Xbox and began my long journey into digital nightmares. I'll never forget, I was playing one of the *Resident Evil* games, which are auditory wonders, with the audio masterfully delivering the ambience and scares when I heard it. some type of scratching. I thought it was the game at first and ignored it. It persisted and it wasn't long before I heard the unmistakable rustling of a plastic bag accompanying it. I thought to myself, "Oh, it's probably a cat," and I got up to go outside and scare it away. I grabbed the doorknob and before I knew it, I was face-to-snarling fang with a creature I had never seen before. This thing was the size of my adult cat and looked like the Lou Ferrigno of rats! It looked up at me from within the now clawed upon bag with its eyes catching in the light like a wolf, and it fuckin' snarled at me! It literally growled and snarled. its thin snout completely lined with sharpened teeth. The noise it made still sends shivers down my spine. Immediately I shut the door, my heart was pounding.

WHAT THE FUCK WAS THAT!?!

I did what any red-blooded male would do in this time of huge animal, *Food-of-the-Gods*-like crisis. I grabbed a newspaper and rolled it up into a weapon. I have no idea what in the world I was gonna do with it, or even how that was supposed to protect me from the fucking alien-like hound of the Baskerville. Maybe I was gonna smack it on its nose and give it a stern lecture? It didn't matter. I NEEDED to protect my home and loved ones. I put my hand on the doorknob, took a deep breath, and emerged from my home with violent intent and a weaponized newspaper held high.

It was gone.

What horror was visited upon me that night? Instantly, every sound I heard that night was magnified by ten. This hideous thing of unknown origin was the stuff of nightmares. Make no mistake, that night I slept with one eye open. The next morning, I told Deb about what happened. She asked me to describe what I'd seen in detail. After about five minutes she called out from the bedroom and asked me to come to where we had the computer setup. There it was on the screen.

"Yes! What the fuck IS that?! Some kind of a cryptid?"

The answer was "No, it's a possum."

Excuse me?! A *possum*? Now, before this incident all I knew of possums I learned from cartoons in which they played dead and hung cutely from their tails off branches and shit. I would NEVER have imagined this creature being a fierce motherfucking beast. But it wasn't over. As the weeks passed, I'd see the possum, and I know it was the same possum because it was scary everywhere. What did it want? Why was it eyeballing me?

My birthday rolled around and me and a few friends decided to go to our favorite Thai restaurant, Lai Thai. We'd been there countless times and I LOVED their food. I also very much loved the bottle of red wine I consumed before dinner, so to say I was tipsy was an understatement. We got there and the lady who worked there was holding the door open.

"How nice," I thought. "They're opening the door for us."

As we got to the door the lady held up her hand and said...

"You no can go in."

Huh?

"Why not?" I inquired thoroughly tipsy and a bit confused.

She looked at me with the most serious stare you could imagine and said words that sent shivers down my spine.

"There's a possum loose in there."

I looked over her shoulder and sure enough, there were four panicked Thai folks with brooms chasing this feral furry juggernaut of spiteful Steve-fueled hatred, running to the right, then to the left, then back to the right again. All that was missing was the *Benny Hill* chase theme. How in the fuck could this be? Not only was this motherfuckin' thing stalking me, it was now out to ruin my birthday dinner. I was just standing there slack jawed. Then it happened: the possum and I locked eyes, and it hooked a hard right with its pursuants doing their best to shoo their restaurant to safety. It was now running for the door, and straight for me. I jumped into the waiting arms of my friend Mike like Scooby Doo leaping to safety in Shaggy's arms, and the evil hightailed it out of there.

"I think we should go somewhere else," Deb said laughing, but I was persistent. I wanted my good chicken Tom Yum soup badly! Nothing was gonna deter me. We all went in. The staff was still flustered due to their recent invasion, but as soon as they caught their breath, dinner was served.

Then I saw something out of the corner of my eye. I could swear that the drop-ceiling over the table adjacent to us looked as if it was beginning to move, but that couldn't be.

"That wine was fucking delicious, yo. I'm still buzzing," I said with a laugh.

I dismissed is as the fruits of my fucked-uppery, but it kept happening. Then it started to buckle. From my right, I heard Mike say kind of under his breath, "Oh shit." He was seeing this too. That meant it was actually happening. All of a sudden, the ceiling cracked open and the fuckin' possum came crashing through like John McClane jumping off a roof with a hose tied around his waist in *Die Hard*. The possum hit the table with a thunderous crash and looked around. There were people screaming in Thai! I could see the shadow of a broom growing bigger against the wall. Immediately this cocksucker leapt off the table, and—you guessed it—made a bee line for me!

WHAT DID IT WANT!?

Before I could even push my chair back, a broom came crashing down about a foot away from me. There he stood, Chef Ong Bak, the Muay Thai Warrior. At least that's what he was to me. The impact of the bristles sent the possum running the other way and he went for the door. He was gone. At least for now.

More weeks had passed, and I hadn't seen the possum, but I did see one that had been run over on the highway exit toward our place. I wanted that to be it, the fallen-now-flattened fiend. I was finally safe from Florida's wildlife. Or so I thought.

One of the amenities of our place in Wild Wood Acres was it had its own washer and dryer set up in a small shed-like enclosure connected to our house. I'm a bit of a neat freak, and it would irritate me that every time I went to do our laundry, the top and front of the machines were always filthy from the elements. It constantly rained in Florida. Sometimes for days, and sometimes for five minutes at a time. I had taken to always wiping off the machines before I used them.

It was a weekday, after a torrential rainstorm that had lasted about two days. I grabbed the laundry basket and loaded it up. As I suspected, the washer and dryer were filthy. I grabbed a wipe and began cleaning them. I was bent over wiping off the front of the dryer when I heard it immediately to my left. A tap, tap, tapping sound. It wasn't loud but it was heavy enough for me to notice. I looked, and literally inches away from my nose was the biggest fucking spider I had ever seen. Oh, and that tapping I heard? That was each of its feet making its way up the wall. Holy. Shit.

Anyone who knows me knows that I have an extreme fear of bugs. I told Debi many times, "If eighteen men with torches, and heated dildos break into the house, I GOT this. If I see a bug, don't look for me because that shit is NOT my problem." My fear runs deep and, admittedly, has made me exaggerate the size of some insects that have come my way. I would say things like, "That waterbug is the size of a Cadillac," etc., but here I am looking directly at a huge hairy spider the size of a facehugger from *Alien*. This was no exaggeration. I screamed like a 1950s chick being chased by a monster in a creature feature. THIS THING WAS FUCKING MASSIVE.

Here's the hitch though; because of my past exaggerations no one would ever believe me about this thing's size. I did the only thing that I could think of to get proof – I ran into the house and grabbed our digital camera. I consider this to be one of the bravest things I've ever done. I mean I should get some sort of gold star for doing this.

With camera in hand, I went back outside and peeked into the laundry shed. By this time, this creature had made its way up the wall and was just chilling on a board by the ceiling.

Look at the size of this wretched fucking thing! The flash getting caught in its monstrous eyes!

I stood in the doorway and snapped two photos, and then I tore ass back inside. I rested my arms on the counter and looked at the screen. This fucking spider was SO BIG that the flash of the camera caught in its eyes! Can you even imagine my terror? I couldn't even stay in the house. I ran outside. Debi was pulling into the driveway just as I did the official "Holy-Shit-Am-I-Skeeved-Out" dance.

She said, "Aw how nice you've come to meet me."

I shrieked out my response, "FUCK THAT, THERE'S A MONSTER IN THE LAUNDRY AREA!"

I told her what had happened and once again she thought I was exaggerating. I even showed her the picture to which she responded, "Yeah, that looks a little big." A *little* big? This thing was enormous. Truly enormous. She went out back and I followed behind her shuffling from foot to foot. I half expected the hideous thing to be gone, and have this horrific event be chalked up to "Steve just being Steve."

She looked in the doorway, froze, and said. "Oh!"

VINDICATION!

"You see!? You see?!?"

"Yeah, really that's something," she said, adding "Get me the Raid."

"Raid!? RAID?!? HIT THAT FUCKING THING WITH A SHOVEL!"

This creature was big enough to fucking stab if you really wanted to. Still, I did what she said and got the Raid bug spray. With me standing a safe distance behind her, she aimed the can and started spraying. This absolutely unholy thing sprang from the wall to the laundry shelf where we kept the detergent. It immediately began knocking things around while it tried in vain to escape Debi's death mist. Finally, after like a minute it crumpled and died leaving one hell of a corpse. "It's dead," I heard her say from behind me, but I was already half in the house. On a mission, I grabbed the camera and marched to the management office. I threw open their door and put my camera on the desk to show the person manning the office.

"Listen to me and listen to me closely," I said like Dirty Harry growling out some important Make-My-Day-type shit. "You people you're gonna do one thing, and one thing only. Tomorrow morning, you're sending a maintenance crew to our place, and you're gonna tear down that fucking shed and build me a new one. You see, I'm not waiting around to find out if this thing has family. If you don't do this as a means to secure the safety of your tenants we will break our lease and move immediately." The person looked at me and didn't say a word. They shook their head, "yes," and I left.

I was able to learn what breed of spider this thing was. It's called a "Huntsman," and it is the exact same breed of arachnid which played the huge hero spider in *Arachnophobia*. Oh, and here's a few other tidbits about them... they're so big that they don't spin webs. They burrow and pounce on their prey, which includes birds and other small animals. Apparently, they're supposed to be harmless to humans, but you can't fool me, Wikipedia! It's right there in the name... Hunts Man. You and you're supposed "facts" can eat a big festering bag of dicks.

Florida life was a lot, but I knew deep down, if I was gonna make it in the film industry it wasn't the place I had to be. That place was California, so I was ready to trade in my prehistoric insects and possessed possums for the land of great weather, quaking earth, and a topography that's always on fire. Oh, and guess what? There's barely any water, so fuck putting the fires out and... I dunno... drinking! Let me tell you... the winos and rodents of yesteryear were looking better and better every day.

Be assured of one thing, dear reader: I am little more than the world's oldest kid in his fifties. My childhood sucked, so I'm trying to enjoy the more superfluous things I missed out on when I was a child now. Now, Debi? She knew this. Every so often she'd surprise me with some weird thingy that she knew I would LOVE from eBay. Oh eBay. I both love and hate you.

One day Deb bought me a roaring *Jurassic Park* cage. Basically, it was just a cardboard box that looked like a *Jurassic Park* dinosaur containment unit with a button on the front. When you pressed the button you would hear the roar of a T-Rex. How friggin' cool is that? To me, it was amazing. The littlest things mean a lot to me. I never had little things. Little surprises. Never afforded anything like that before.

The seller who had sold it to her ended up living directly down the street from me. It didn't make sense for them to put the item in the mail, so we decided to just meet up and make the exchange. One morning my phone rang…

"Hi, I'm looking for Steve. This is Tony and you guys bought something from me on eBay."

"Hey, yeah, man," I responded… "Feel free to bring it by. I'm home."

With that, we both hung up the phone and all I could think to myself was, "Wow. That dude's voice sounded REALLY familiar." I went out to my stoop and waited for him. Within minutes this dude turned the corner and began walking toward my place. He stepped up on my stoop and I stood as he handed me my prize…

"Hey, ummm… You're Tony… Tony Timpone from *Fangoria*, right?" I asked.

"That's right," he answered. "Are you a *Fango* fan?" Was I. Holy shit, was I ever. This man was one of my idols and he lived literally one block away from me and down the street. Tony, in true Tony fashion, was ultra gracious and incredibly friendly. We bonded instantly. I went to his house and met his lovely wife, Marguerite.

It wasn't long before we became friends. Again, holy shit. This was incredible. I was a kid, and this was the most important thing that had ever happened to me. I mean what are the odds? How lucky can one person be? I was on top of the world. He would take me to screenings with him and we'd have some rather long and thoroughly geeky conversations that were formative for me to say the very least.

Since we were neighbors who both worked in Manhattan, we'd often take the subway together. One time while speeding across the Manhattan Bridge, we had a conversation that would forever change my life.

This was the early days of the Internet and *Fangoria* had launched their own website. One of the many features that were considered cutting-edge back then was it had a message board.

For those of you too young to know what those were—first of all screw you and your damned youth—second, they were essentially a live online community where fans could get together and interact with each other in a digital forum where they could leave messages for one another and engage in many different types of discussions.

Tony said, "So, we have message boards on *Fangoria*, but we need someone who could moderate them to keep the BS to a minimum. Would you be interested?"

Interested? I was nearly jumping out of my skin and humping the air like an excited puppy. This was it, a chance to work for *Fang*-fuck-ing-*goria*! Somebody, pinch me. When I set up my account I chose "Uncle Creepy" as a screen name.

For those of you who don't know, the name Uncle Creepy was an homage to my favorite horror comic, *CREEPY*, from Warren Publications. Uncle Creepy was a character who, just like the Cryptkeeper from *Tales from the Crypt*, would introduce their macabre stories in print. I love him. It seemed like a great name and a great idea. Now, decades later in retrospect, if I had known the connotations that would come with the moniker, I may have been a wee-bit more selective in terms of choosing a screen name. It's too late now though. Most people know me as Creepy or U.C. Way more than the peeps who know me simply as Steve.

Uncle Creepy, had been born again. Quickly, I started to become a known entity on those message boards. I made friends there who I still have today. Dear friends like Joe Knetter, Jon Condit, Buz Wallick, Andrew Kasch, Morgan Elektra, the list goes on and on. It was getting to the point that when and if I were to show up at a *Fangoria* Weekend of Horrors, people began to recognize me. Some were even genuinely happy to meet me. I cannot even begin to describe to you how humbling that type of thing can be.

You never know when you're going to get to see someone again, so every person I met, I made sure that they felt like the only person who mattered. The people who come up to me... they're not fans. They are my peers. I'm no better than they are, and I never will be. This is a practice I still, to this day, employ. There will never be a time when I take anyone or anything for granted. All I ever wanted to do was make people happy.

Life was great... so great, in fact, that I knew it couldn't last. With my momentum building Tony began treating me a bit differently. I would go with him with new ideas, and he would shoot each and every one of them down. We were hardly ever hanging out anymore, and that really hurt my feelings. Being Uncle Creepy has never been important to me. Being someone's friend is what mattered. I loved Tony. I still LOVE Tony. Our relationship, however, had taken a turn.

Let me be clear... it was TONY TIMPONE who gave me my start, and no matter what happened, happens, or will happen, I will ALWAYS be grateful for that.

During my days at *Fangoria*, while I was the face of the company's message boards, it was my buddy Jon Condit who was behind the scenes making sure that they were running.

While there, Jon and I got to know and butt heads with a man named Joe Sena who was the backbone of the *Fango* website. He too felt Jon and I were becoming a little too big for our britches. What the fuck are britches anyway? Has anyone ever really worn them?

Anyway...

After a couple of years Tony and Joe introduced me to a group of people, whom I shall not name, who were getting set to try and launch a horror themed cable network and they wanted me to moderate their message boards. Let's just call them "The Ass Clowns." At the end of the day, I think this was Tony's way of nicely sending me off to the sunset. I was all in, and I would be taking Jon with me. He was my Tonto. I cannot stress enough how vital a role Jon played in my success. I may have been the game's master, but it was he who built the playground I was making a name for myself in.

Now these new people? The Ass Clowns? They dug me. They really dug me. Two of them were leading this new endeavor—Dick and Jackass. I started talking to them about some ideas I had for the *Fangoria* website. They encouraged me to run with them. Before I knew it, I was becoming the face of this new and exciting endeavor, and Jon had gone from helping me with message boards to running the whole damned website for them.

The site needed a horror news area, so I went out to the "then" best in the business. The guys from Creature-Corner.com, Johnny Butane and Ryan Rotten. Everyone had a cute name back them. Having a descriptive name on the Internet was like having a mullet in the '80s. They were everywhere. After lots of romancing both Johnny and Ryan joined the team. There was a lot of discussion as to what to call this news section. Ryan Rotten came up with several good names. The news area was dangerously close to being known as *The Shock Corridor*. Eventually though Butane came up with *Dread Central* and it stuck. Yep, it was he who named us.

Things were moving fast. The website was quickly gaining momentum. I had put together a staff of writers, some of whom I still work with. We were a team. A force to be reckoned with. It wasn't long before the world was getting excited, and everyone began knowing who and what that company was becoming.

Ryan... he's very much an incredible force of nature all his own. Ryan left *DC* to open his own site *Shock Till You Drop*. Now he's a producer for Blumhouse and I cannot stress how proud of him I am.

Butane and I, we became quite the team. I couldn't have asked for a better partner to have. There was just one problem... the years were passing and there was still no channel on the air.

What the actual fuck?

The people who ran the company gave me quite a bit of ownership in it, stock-wise. All they had to do was launch. Just... fucking... launch.

The company was at EVERY known horror convention there was, and I was flying all over the place, once again quickly putting both Debi and me into debt. Again, all this money trouble would have been cleared and paid back ASAP had the company just ended up doing what they were supposed to do.

Every con I would see fans asking when it was coming. I answered to the best of my ability what little the principals of the company had shared with me.

Online it was even worse. I began getting grilled day in and day out. People believed in this company. They were hungry for it. They believed everything I told them because I was just like them... a fan. I can say with absolute certainty that I believed this company was going to make it. I never felt I was lying to anyone or was trying to lead them astray.

There was just one thing... it became drastically clear in the end that I was the one being lied to. Red flag after red flag began waving. The main dude in charge, Dick, proved to be... well... let's just say he wasn't someone who any fan wanted to be at the helm of something that they loved.

One weekend we were at a convention. I think it was a Chiller Theater show in New Jersey. Both Dick and Jackass were there, alongside me, Deb, Condit, and Sean Clark. Sean had made himself a truly bitchin' custom [company name] workshirt that he made himself.

Dick walked up to him and just stared. You could literally see his inept wheels spinning in his head. "Tell me, Sean... that blood spatter there. What is the blood doing?"

"Well... it's uh... dripping," Sean replied.

"Yes," Dick continued, "but why? And why is it dripping in that direction?"

I remember thinking to myself, "You're, like, kidding, right?" He wasn't. He was genuinely perplexed as to why there was a blood spatter on a horror themed shirt. You really just can't make this kind of shit up.

Jackass was just as bad. He was the type of absolute poser who would put on guy-liner and black lipstick to attend the show. That wasn't him. Nobody bought this. If anything, it came off as insulting. This 40-something douche was anything but a Goth. Talk about patronizing!

One day, he in one hundred percent seriousness came to me and asked, "How about we have Sid Haig do a video chat with fans while he's taking a shit?" But... why? On what planet is this a good idea? I mean, I love Sid as much as anyone, but who in their right mind would want to spend time with the man, or any man for that matter, while they're taking a fuckin' shit?!

Dick also considered himself an incredible source of valuable website ideas. "We need a clock on the website," he said one time. I answered quietly and in a state of bemused disbelief, "Um... there's a clock on every computer screen, I'm fairly certain that people will be able to find out what time it is."

"Yes," he insisted, "But it could be like a gothic clock, like Big Ben or something! I think people would love that!"

Um. No, they wouldn't.

A week later he came to me and said, "Steve! I got it! I know what will set us apart from every other horror website out there."

I cringed and clenched my buttcheeks before asking, "What?"

He was SO fucking confident. "Horror fans shouldn't have to go anywhere else to get the information they want. We should have sports scores on the site." he yelled with the kind of enthusiasm usually reserved for cartoon characters.

Just when I thought it couldn't get any more fuckin' stupid, Dick tried to mandate the following rule for the website. "Instead of calling horror actors, actors, let's call them *axers*."

No. Just, no.

Please shoot me in the fucking face. How about you just concentrate on getting the fucking channel launched, will ya, mac? Thanks, I'll wait.

All the while, Jon, Johnny, and I had the arduous task of keeping this dude's nuttiness in check while hiding just how ridiculous this situation had become. It was a constant strain. A losing battle. It was like trying to keep the big dumb monster in the closet in *The Brain That Wouldn't Die*.

This pinhead would even send us emails in which he would refer to himself in the third person with attached checklists that asked, "What can I do to please my Dick (meaning his name, not his actual dick ya perverts) today?" No. That's not a typo. He actually wrote "please my" and his name. No, I ain't kidding. Not even exaggerating in the slightest bit. It doesn't get much more narcissistic than that, brothers and sisters. It really doesn't.

Things just kept getting worse, and truth be told, even more stupid. You see, Jackass, found his newfound "importance" intoxicating. He portrayed himself as the man who was going to "give horror fans exactly what they wanted." And people bought it, hook-line-and-sinker. This, of course, led to him eventually cheating on his wife, whom we all adored.

One night, after a convention we were all in a car. Debi was driving. I was in the passenger seat, and Knetter was in the back with Jackass. At this point Jackass was on the phone with who was to become "the other woman." He was trying to—I guess—impress her. His voice was low and just above a whisper. "Yeah," he said. "I'm in this limo with my friends. Well, they're more like my bodyguards. They're all dressed up in chains and stuff. They're a really rough looking bunch. When we get to the club we're going to, the people there will part to let us in. We never wait in line. People are too afraid to tell us no."

First off, we were driving back to the hotel, and second, this put us in a horrible position as, like I said, we loved his wife. I cannot imagine who would be buying his line of bullshit, but apparently this person was. He would go on to tell us after the call that she was a model.

It wasn't long before he got divorced and then got married at the Belagio in Las Vegas. We saw the wedding pictures. We also found out later that this chick was indeed a model. A *hand model*. Not joking. It wasn't long after this that Jackass and Dick had a falling out. I don't know the exact reasons, but, if I were a betting man, I'd say that it had something to do with the misappropriation of funds.

Years had passed and The Ass Clowns hadn't even come close to bringing their project to fruition. We had to give the public something and we had to do it FAST. Then I had an idea. I suggested we, at the very least, stream public domain horror movies and other flicks they could easily (read: cheaply or even freely) acquire to stream every Friday in an area on the site where people could chat together while watching the movie. This became known as "The Revenge of the Return of the Midnight Movie." Honestly, not a bad idea at all. It was even a bit ahead of its time, but unfortunately the technology just wasn't there yet.

One night in the "The Revenge of the Return of the Midnight Movie." chatroom, I said some off-color bullshit at about 3:00 a.m. It was only Jon Condit, me, and maybe one other person, a regular, there. The next morning, the world was about to change. Again. Because...

Seriously... Look at the size of this motherfucker...

Chapter 13
My Head with Fame!

I was fired.

Fired from a job I barely got paid for. Fired from a job that put me in over 20k worth of debt. Fired from a job over my answering machine. That's right... he left a message. I still have it. I even set it to music so I can listen to it from time to time when in need of a kick in the ass.

Here's the transcription which I've typed to the best of my ability as he was furiously shouting and barely coherent:

> "Steve, it is [Dick]! You'd better fucking call me today, motherfucker! You're gonna fucking pay for this shit, okay? You wanna fuckin' ignore me, when I tell you not to use references to drugs and sex and that shit in the fucking forum? On the... on the, uh... on the chatroom? Fuck me, Steve! You are *indecipherable fury and chubby-man-panting, complete with what I can only imagine was a shower of spite spittle* FUCK YOU! You're out of my fucking company! Fuck you, alright? You're fucking fired! That's it!"

Debi and I were listening to this from bed. By the time that this imbecile was done with his huffing and puffing, we looked at each other and just started laughing. I mean, what else could we do at this point?

Here's what nobody expected. Not even me. Within moments of me telling my staff I had been canned, every single person I had brought on to work with me on that company's website began tendering their resignation. Within an hour the entire writing staff quit. Then something else happened...word started spreading online and to say the fans supported us is an extremely gross understatement. Let me be clear... we just all left. Nobody had asked anyone to do anything! It was the first time that I could ever recall seeing an online revolt! A full-blown digital-based revolution. Even other horror sites like *Bloody Disgusting* were running news about what happened.

Fans were both rabid, livid, and EXTREMELY vocal. They were sending emails, private messages, posting everywhere they could online, and even created images and animated GIFs in support of *Dread Central*. To this very day, I'm sure I can speak with everyone involved when I say that was one of the most incredibly humbling experiences of not just our careers, but of our lives. On a personal level I can only say thank you. You've no idea what that kind of support meant to us, and I haven't forgotten a second of it. I will always cherish that. To think we had truly touched that many people... man, it was just an incredible moment to be alive.

The chaos and fervor never lost steam. It was going on hot and heavy for several weeks. I met with Jon Condit, Joshua "Johnny Butane" Siebalt, and our soon to be business manager, K.W. Low, and we collectively decided to do something. To take the staff who had been so very loyal and create something for all of us. There was no more corporate leash. There was no one spying on us. For the first time ever it was the inmates who were running the asylum, and it was glorious.

On July 4th, 2006, *Dread Central* declared its independence and opened its online doors. The forums were back, the news was constantly updated, and the movie reviews were pouring in! The staff was tremendous. In addition to Josh, Condit, myself, and of course Debi who was writing under the name The Woman in Black, we had David and Melissa Bostaph, Morgan Elektra, Scott A. Johnson, Bill "Splat" Johnson, Sean Clark, Justin Julian AKA Mr. Dark, Ryan "Plagiarize" Acheson, the enigma that remains the Foywonder, Andrew Kasch, Buz Wallick, and so many more. It was literally a dream team of talent, and I'm truly grateful to have spent time with each and every one of them. We will always be a family. Always.

But it was YOU guys, our readers, who were most important to us. A lot of people throw around the term, "By fans for fans," but when *Dread Central* launched, we were the working embodiment of that statement. I am so proud to be able to say that!

Dread Central's forums became an extended family. I've met so many people whom I consider to be genuine friends on there. That's where our most valuable feedback came from. Knowing what you guys wanted was integral to us being able to give it to you. You asked... you suggested... you got it.

Of course, we had more than our fair share of trolls who lived to cause us headaches. In true troll fashion, I'm sure they would like nothing more than for me to name them here. Guess what? My book, my rules. Eat a dick. Thanks, I'll wait. Moving on...

If I had to pick one thing for me that was probably my fondest memory of hanging out on DC's message boards, it's this...

One of the forums was created specifically for members to create and share their own original stories. There was this one dude whose screen name was TSMK (and a group of seemingly random numbers) and he wrote what I consider to be one of the greatest short stories ever written! Since it was posted on *Dread Central* and is no longer accessible to the public, I MUST SHARE IT! It is something that should be celebrated, remembered, and shared for generations to come. I cannot resist committing his master trilogy to print for the first time since those forums existed. Ladies and gentlemen, STEEL YOUR NERVES! Be ready to once again relive the greatest horror trilogy the world has ever seen. Completely uncut and thoroughly unedited, it's... *A TALE OF SUFFERING!*

A Tale of Suffering, Part 1

Getting ready school, I am 18 a senior in High School. I was pretty late so I did not have breakfast. When I made it to school I saw my friend Taylor, I go:

"Hey what's going on!" He goes,

"there is a huge Rave going on tonight." Than I ask him,

"where?"

He pulls out the flyer and shows it to me. I was like "Where did you get this?"

Taylor goes,

"I got it from online and passed it out to others in school."

Than I tell him,

"the pace it is taking at sounds familiar." Taylor than says,

"Manny do not worry everything is going to be fine!

Oh yeah do not forget your glow sticks."

I'm like "ok."

After school I ran straight home, had some snack, than took a shower and got my clothes on. After I got ready, I got in the car. The place Taylor told me that the rave was taking at was all hills and an abandoned boiler room. The place is called Suffer St. Well I made it, took twenty minutes to make it. I hear the DJ already blasting some Trance and Techno music. Than some came from behind and grabbed me!

I jumped! It was Taylor.

"Stupid fucking son of a bitch, don't ever do that again,"

I said. Taylor than says,

"Manny chill, it was a joke, come on let's get some beer."

I followed him to the beer cakes, checking out all the hot girls dancing and having fun. While the music was playing I heard someone scream.

BOILER ROOM

I saw a head get thrown in where people were dancing. Blood splattered all over a girl. She screamed so loud. I saw something my eyes could not believe. It started killing people by chopping their heads off, eating their brains, ripping of the girl's breasts! So my friend and me ran fast as we can to the boiler room. When I made to door I notice Taylor was missing. I screamed,

"Taylor!"

All of a sudden I see something coming down from

the sky. Blood getting splattered all over me, freaked out from it. I picked it up and it was Taylor's head. Not freaked out enough, Taylor's head told me

"GET OUT!"

Dropped the head and ran straight in the boiler room in disgust. The boiler had hot red lights like hell. Finding another way out of the boiler room, all of sudden I heard noises on the left. So I walked over there without making any noises, also seeing shadows move on the wall. When I made it over to the left, I saw four mangled people fighting over someone's body. I hear them moaning

"BRAIN!"

Taking apart the leg and spilling the blood on the floor, tossing the head around, when it fell to the ground the brain fell out and all four jumped attacking like hyenas. I could not take it anymore, so I walked away slowly.

I heard sounds so I tried making it to the corner and hiding. BANG! Something hit my head. I woke up, my head with pain. I noticed two guys and one girl. One of the guys ran over asking if I was all right. I ask him,

"Who are you and what happened?" Than he says,

"I'm John." Than he goes,

"I thought you where one of those things so I hit your head with a metal pipe."

He apologized, than I asked,

"what's the other two peoples name?" Then he says,

"the girl is Sarah other guy is Taylor."

I go

"WHAT? Taylor?" He says,
"yes!"
Taylor than comes over and asks, "are you ok Manny?"

TO BE CONTINUED...

A Tale of Suffering, Part 2

I go up to Taylor, "you were dead!" He says,
"Are you ok? John ho hard did you hit him?"
Than he pulls me up and tells me to, shake it off. I told them,
"We need to get out now before those things get us!"

So we start walking looking to see if there is a door to get out from. There were a whole bunch of lockers and a lot steam coming out from the pipes and it was very hot! It was very hot that Sarah's nipples were getting hard and that was turning me on. I turn around to say something to John and he was gone. I say than,

"where did John go?"
Sarah all nervous and can not talk, and than Taylor goes,
"I have no idea, he was right by behind." "We have to go find,"
I said. Than Sarah screams saying
"NO! Let's just find the way out his probably dead already,"
than Taylor says,
"She is probably right Manny." I than tell them ok.

We walked all the way to end of the boiler room and there was a door. It really looked fucked up. Than I here Sarah scream! I turn around and notice she was missing and also Taylor. So I start calling their names,

"Sarah! Taylor"

No answer from them. Than I hear a metallic dragging from the right, I turned around and I see a shadow of a body. It was moving slow and I hear it saying,

"BRAIN, I want BRAIN!"

When it came out of the shadows. It was Taylor he turned into one of those mangled looking people.

So I started running toward the door, when I got close to the door John's body fell hanging on a rope, blood dripped all over the door and his eyes gouged out. I turn around Taylor has already gotten close to me so I grabbed a pipe right be me and hit him. After I hit him, I got the pipe and pushed it down his throat. After killing him, I ran straight to door pushing John's hanging corpse of the way getting blood all over me. I made it outside.

The door I got out from was closer to my car so I start running toward it. I got into and started the car and got out of there as fast as I can. Driving pretty fast that I got on wrong lane so than I started slowing down. Than I heard a noise in the back seat, than Sarah grabs my head, so could not see where I was going so I lost control and hit into a tree. I woke up all of a sudden covered in my own blood. I got out of the car; Sarah pulled me back in and bites me right on neck. So I grab the pocketknife and stab her right in eyes. I than jump out of the car, seeing green acid like ooze coming out of her eyes and hear squeamish screaming.

I than ran home, when I made it my parents asked me,

"What happened?"

I told them

"nothing, I just got into an accident." Than they asked,

"what happened to the car?" I told them

"they had to tow it away it was completely totaled." After talking to my parents, they were happy that I was ok and nothing serious happened. So I cleaned myself up and went straight to bed, covered myself with my blanket.

MORNING

I woke up the next morning getting ready for school. I was not feeling really good. I was going down for breakfast, all of a sudden I felt a sudden pain in my hands, I looked at them and my veins were bulging and than my stomach started to hurt. I started getting dizzy trying to make it back to my room; I fell down half way in my room.

Five minutes my body woke up, and I had the taste for brain. When I walked to the kitchen I saw my parents and saying,

"BRAIN!"

My parents than said

"Stop screwing around and eat."

Than I grab my mom's head snap it off, taking her eyes out. Than I jump on my dad eating out his brain through his mouth. Than I fell on the floor and seeing what has happened to me, I got a knife and stabbed myself.

THE END

A Tale of Suffering, PART 3: THE END!

It was already night, there was thunder and rain. All of a sudden a lightning flashed and I woke up still covered in blood. Still the knife in my shoulder, I pulled it off. The whole kitchen covered in blood and body parts. I was freaked out, could not believe what I did. Trying to forget that any of this has happened I went to my room to sleep. Five minutes before I went to complete sleep I here the door knocking and the voice saying "OPEN THE DOOR! IT'S THE COPS!"

I ran downstairs and ran out from the backyard door. I ran to my school knowing it would be safe hiding over there. So there was an opening from the back to the basement of the school so I just went there and stayed in the basement until morning.

Back home, the cops broke in the door and witnessed the scene in the kitchen and lot of the cops started to throw up from the smell, also from the insects that were crawling on the body, through the mouth and eyes. The cops could not believe what they have witnessed. They brought in body bags to take the bodies. The cops were talking about what they have witnessed, and than one of the cop named Gary found something on the floor and showed it to the captain. Captain says,

Steve Barton

"This is a flyer to a rave."

So after putting the yellow tape around the house, Gary and the Captain went to the place where the rave happened. The other cops went back home.

The next morning, I heard a sound and woke up and noticed it was just the school bell. I opened the door and ran out. People were staring at me in a weird way, than I bumped into my Girlfriend when I was trying to get out of school. Her name is Jenny I knew here since Elementary school. I was like

"hi."

She than said

"What happened last night? I kept on calling you?" "I was doing my homework."

Than Jenny said "than what is this?"

I than noticed she had the flyer in her hands. I started sweating did not know what to say, than I started feeling a burning itching in the back of the neck. Than she asks, "are you ok? You look different all of a sudden, your ears look burned!" Jenny than says,

"you went to the RAVE!"

I all of sudden was starting to hear the heart beat, smelling very juicy, wanting to rip it out of her. She also asked,

"Where is Taylor?"

Since I could not control my desires I jumped her and kept on banging her head on the floor until it cracked and she kept on screaming,

"HELP!"

Than the security guard of the school came over and tried to stop me. I turned and growled at him than I ripped his head off and threw at Jenny. Jenny started screaming even more! Than everyone came out of there class, students, teachers and the principal. Half of the students threw up in there lockers when they notice the decapitated body. Right after, I ran out with my bloody hands from school.

I ran into the mountains, while I was there I noticed changes in me. My teeth where getting sharper, my skin where get more mangled up. Also I noticed that I was not only into brain I also like to eat a heart. I started eating bugs, a deer, and rats just anything. I was sure I became one of those things and would not really know what I would do next.

Back at school Gary and the Captain came to make the investigation of what took place at the school. They noticed the decapitated head and blood on the floor. Then they called in who ever witnessed the situation. Jenny walked in the room where the captain and Gary where sitting behind a desk. They started asking me questions; they first asked me if he was my Boyfriend and I told them yes. Then the captain asked,

"did he touch you in any weird way?" Jenny answered,

"He attacked me is that not weird enough?" Than Gary asked,

"did he ask for your BRAIN?" Jenny than says,

"WHAT?"

Than the captain says,

"Do not pay attention to him, now you can go."

While Jenny walked out the door slammed behind her. Then she heard them arguing, behind the door not understanding what they where saying. Noticing behind the blurry glass door that they fighting physically, than out of no were blood splattered all over the door. Jenny ran out of school screaming!

Jenny was running back home all of a sudden she stopped. She saw a tree with a body hanging with no skin and head removed. The head was put on the end of the branch and the eyes were taken out. The tree was covered in dark reddish blood. That made Jenny sick to her stomach and than ran faster to her house.

When Jenny made to her house she screamed, "Mom! Dad!"

Jenny slowly walked into her parent's room; she noticed there was puddle of blood on the floor. She followed the trail of blood to her parent's closet. Jenny slides the closet doors open. She screams after seeing her dad's body hanging from the hanger and gutted out. Jenny felt sick to her stomach after what she witnessed and than she turned to her parents bed. She noticed the bed covered in blood. She walked slowly to the bed, when she made to the bed she slowly pulled of the covers. She SCREAMED!

Her mother's body parts were laid around the bed.

Jenny ran out her parents' room to get into her room by the time she got near to her room, she heard noises coming from downstairs. So she ran faster, by the time she got closer someone pulled her in the bathroom. When she was going to scream the person covered her mouth.

"Do not worry it's me Steve your brother,"

Steve said. He was reassuring "you will be safe here."

A Tale of Suffering PART 3: THE END! Part 2

Steve opened the door a little bit to see what is going on. He saw the deformed looking things eating their Grandpa, playing with his insides. Then all of a sudden there was a change on his face as if he was satisfied what he saw, he grabbed the bat that was in behind the door and called his sister,

"Jenny."

She turns around and Steve hits her right on the head, knocked her out cold. The last words that came out from him were

"DUMB BITCH!"

Jenny woke up with a painful headache all confused and not remembering what the last thing that happened to her. Her vision was coming back; she was freaked when she noticed where she was. There bones everywhere, maggots feeding of the dead bodies, the room-smelling like shit from all of the dead bodies. Jenny got up and tried not to throw up, looking around to see for a way to get out of the dark room. Jenny finally saw red light, she noticed when she was getting closer to the room that it was getting hotter and hotter. When she got closer she also noticed the pipes and steam, she finally she entered the room, what she witnessed terrified her, seeing those things stretching of some ones face from the right cheek and the other one from the left cheek. Hearing the female body screaming gave her the shivers and made her sick. Jenny stepped out from the room walking backward slowly than she turned around and someone just grabbed her and pulled her into another room. Jenny was screaming,

"LET ME GO YOU SICK MOTHERFUCKER!"

Finally, when she was in the dark room that she got pulled in whatever it was pulling her was gone. Jenny got up to get out the room from where she was just pulled in, by the time she got their the door just got shut. Jenny screaming in the dark room

"LET ME GO SON OF A BITCH, I AM GOING TO KILL YOU, YOU DUMB FUCKING SHIT!"

Than the lights just turned on and Jenny notice that she was in some shit hole bathroom, the walls where white tiles covered in blood, she also noticed the toilet filled with shit, piss, blood and body parts. When she got up and turned around and witnessed a burned body pined on the wall like a crucifix gutted open, stomach hanging out. Jenny got closer and could not belief whose body it was.

Jenny started crying because the body she just saw was the body of Manny. Jenny could not take it any more; she just lost it and started hitting the wall, all of a sudden the door opened. Someone in a red robe with a hood walked in, Jenny turned around

"You sick FUCK!" Jenny said.

"Yes, I am sick a fuck,"

said the person in the red robe than he pulled off his hood and Jenny again was in even more shock because the person under the robe was her brother Steve.

Jenny could what she was seeing, she asked her brother

"why?"

That Steve answers,

"Why? Because I am not really your brother, your dad raped my mom she was a prostitute."

Jenny than said, "No you are lying."

"Sadly Jenny I am not" said Steve.

"Than tell me what are those things"

Jenny asked than Steve answered

"those are my specimens, I created them from the dead bodies who worked in this boiler who where killed from the explosion."

Jenny finally asked what happened to her boyfriend,

Steve answered again

"found him on the mountain all fucked sleeping on his own shit and the animal parts he had for food, than I got my specimens to bring him in and have him for dinner."

Than Jenny really got pissed and screamed "YOU MOTHERFUCKER!"

Than start running toward Steve to give him a beating, by the time she made it Steve pulled a knife and killed her. She fell down on her knees blood dripping in her hand and before she fell on her left side, she had one last to say to Steve

"See you in hell."

Steve called in one of his specimens, it was Gary and he told him to take Manny's and Jenny's out to burn it. Than Steve turned around and told Gary wait,

"I forgot on thing"

Steve said. Pulled out his gun and shot Gary straight in the head.

If that didn't bring a smile to your face you do not have a pulse. It's seriously one of my favorite things that I've ever read, and I genuinely mean that. English may not have been TSMK's first language, but his enthusiasm flows like a river. You have to admire it! It's friggin' genius!

As of this writing *DreadCentral.com* is eighteen years old and counting. Imagine that! In Internet years that's like 65-million-years-old.

Working on the site, I was lucky enough to become close personal friends with a lot of the icons in this industry. We won several awards and put out two compilations of indie short flicks with Jesse Baget's Ruthless Pictures entitled *ZombieWorld* and its spiritual sequel, *MonsterLand*. I'm seriously proud of those flicks and as a result, several of the filmmakers involved, all of whom are immensely talented, went on to make feature films. That is just so fuckin' cool, man.

It was during this time that I met filmmaker Daniel Farrands. You know, there are some people in your life that you immediately click with. Dan and I had INSTANT chemistry. Andrew Kasch had introduced us when Dan was serving as a co-director on the *Friday the 13th* documentary, *His Name Was Jason: 30 Years of Friday the 13th*. I gave what was possibly one of the best and funniest interviews of my life. Dan said to me afterward, "Don't be surprised if we don't use your entire interview in the film." He was semi-serious too. It was that good. There was just one problem...co-director Anthony Masi.

You see Masi wasn't a fan of the direction Dan had the film heading in. So, the two split ways. If you ask me, I think Anthony nixed most of my footage because I'm not, shall we say, cosmetically pleasing. Instead, most of his cut consists of an inordinate amount of screen-time for some guy from a TV show who was admittedly far prettier than I was. As a result, there's very little of me in the actual documentary, but the lion's share of my stuff can be found on Disc 2 of the DVD release, which is of course, out of print. Fans who did see it would spend a lot of time shouting the term "Homo-Erotic Shaving" at me, and also thanking me for my "Proud Freak" monologue. What was that? At the wrap-up of my interview with Dan, I said the following:

> "It's all about the kids, man. The people who grew up watching this are gonna show it to their kids. They're gonna build their kids' love for it...or at least I hope they do. The people who grew up watching this... Please don't turn into jackass parents who try to shield they're kids from it. You grew up just fine, let them make their own choices. Okay? Let them be who they are. If they want to be a horror fan, don't dissuade them. Feed them, dude. Give them these movies. Let them see how their father or their mother grew up. Let them see what they thought was entertainment. Let them judge for themselves. You know I read... God, I wish I could claim this as my quote. I read an interview with Rob Zombie, and one of the things he said in this

interview when he was asked 'Why horror movies are so popular?' He said to the interviewer, 'You know, in ten years...fifteen years...thirty years...I don't think anyone is gonna be talking about *Doctor Zhivago*, but I guarantee you that they're gonna be talking about *Dawn of the Dead*.' That's because it's in us. When you grew up, when you grew up loving this, it consumes you. It ends up lending itself to who you become, and you know what? That bullshit about people who watch horror movies turning into killers? That's such a load of crap. I know lawyers, doctors, nurses...I run a website. I have access to millions of people every day. They're just normal like you and me, but the one thing that they are, is almost kind of relieved to have a place where they can go where it's free of judgment. When you go see a *Friday the 13th* movie and you're in a theater, people there? These are your peers, man. These are the cool-ass cats that fuckin' get it. And you don't have to worry about if you're the strange one in the room. I think that... that feeling when you can just shed your skin and be yourself... That's what it's all about. I think horror movies are the only movies that can do that. We are the 'freaks of society' supposedly. Well, fuck you, I'm a proud freak."

I still echo that sentiment. I always will.

Dan eventually brought me onto the award-winning *A Nightmare on Elm Street* Documentary, *Never Sleep Again: The Elm Street Legacy*.

Clocking in at four hours long it still blows my mind that some people have actually sat through the entire thing in a single sitting. I am so proud of the work we did on that flick. It was a once in a lifetime gig. Dan directed it with Andrew Kasch, and Buz Wallick served as Director of Photography. For all intents and purposes, *Never Sleep Again*, probably never would have happened had *Dread Central* never come to be. All of these instances give that site such a pedigree. One that I'll always be proud to have been a part of.

Little did I know my tenure at *Dread Central* would also lead to the single greatest moment of my life. One that brought me 110 percent full circle.

Chapter 14
Night of the Living Dork

Of all the things I've been lucky enough to do and accomplish in my career working within the horror industry, the one I am most grateful for was the opportunity to not only meet but befriend a true living legend in our industry... George A. Romero. Simply put, the man is my idol, and even though we grew very close over the years, I would ALWAYS get the butterflies in my stomach every now and then.

While working at *Dread Central*, one of the people I got to know really well is the incomparable Chris Roe. Chris was THE man when it came to horror star representation back then, and we immediately became fast friends. Chris and I really "got" each other. His main client was the legend himself, Mr. George A. Romero, and it was time to meet and do my first ever interview with the dude who raised me without ever knowing it.

It was during the early 2000s at Horrorfind Convention Weekend in Maryland. I had an early interview scheduled with George. It was supposed to happen at 8:00 a.m. Needless to say I was beyond nervous. Who wouldn't be? At about 7:45 a.m. I started to make my way to George's room. Holy shit. This was REALLY about to happen. On the opposite side of the hall, I was walking down was the hotel's pool area. Standing there toweling off was one of my favorite horror stars, butt-ass naked. My mouth dropped. "What the actual fuck," is the only thing I remember thinking. But there he was totally naked, breakfast sausage swinging in the wind. Blocking out the errant genitalia, I shook my head and kept going. Further down the hall Chris was letting himself out of George's room and he noticed me approaching.

"Hey Steve," he said. "George is at a breakfast meeting that I have to get to. Just take his hotel key, let yourself in, and he'll be along right afterward." With that, Chris handed me the card key and kept moving.

I was standing there dumbfounded. In my hand I had GEORGE A. FUCKING ROMERO'S HOTEL ROOM KEY! This was before the era of smartphones so the only way I could properly document this moment was by calling every single person that I knew. The early morning hour did not matter to me. My friends and family NEEDED to know about this earth-moving occurrence. Each call went something along the lines of, "Dude... Guess what I have in my hand," and then I would go on ranting and blathering like an overly- excited madman. After making my final call it was time. I rubbed the card key between my fingers and slid it into the lock. The round light turned from red to green and I turned the door handle. I. Was. IN!

The first thing I noticed was his ashtray. It was brimming with already smoked cigarette butts. Beside it was a big comfy easy chair, and on the other side of that was a couch. Immediately I started doing the only thing I could think of doing... I sat in every seat. My ass was going to touch the same area as the ass of the mythical greatness that was George A. Romero. From there I entered his bedroom and I hugged both of his pillows. Finally, I entered his bathroom, lifted up the toilet seat (after sitting bare-assed on it, of course), and I took what could only be described as "The Hero Piss." You know, the kind where you just let your dick hang free while pissing so you can instead hold your hands upon your hips. Thankfully I have really good aim. I put the seat back into place, washed my hands, and sat down in the couch seat as close to the easy chair with the ashtray as possible. The wait had begun.

My heart was pounding. I could feel beads of sweat forming on my brow. This was a moment I NEVER thought would ever happen. This was the stuff of dreams and fantasy. After about fifteen or so minutes I heard movement by the door. I swear to you my heart stopped and shot immediately into my throat. I can STILL feel that sensation. The doorknob turned and in walked this absolute lanky giant. George stood tall at somewhere between 6' 3" and 6' 4." That's nearly a foot taller than me! I had no idea he was that tall. My intimidation level was at its absolute max. I was frozen in place. Then it happened. George took one look at me and smiled that magical smile of his, then said, "Hey, man! I'm George! Let's bullshit!" Almost immediately I was disarmed.

That's all it took. George had a way about him. He was just so warm and down to earth that I'm sure if he tried, he could melt an iceberg. They say never to meet your heroes, but here was mine, and we got along like gangbusters. We did the standard interview and afterward I told him my *Night of the Living Dead* story and he laughed his ass off and said, "Sorry, I got your ass kicked, man! Jesus Christ!" I then told him that I worked my first job just to save up enough money to buy the film on VHS and he stood up, grabbed his wallet and tried to give the money back to me. That was George. Of course I refused. This was probably one of the most magical times of my entire life. Every moment was precious. Little did I know the best was yet to come. George and I became close, and we'd email frequently. For some reason he used to call me Ramirez and I called him Whit Bissell. Mind you, there was no real reason for the name changes, it was just one of the many kooky things we did with each other. Every time he was on the road, I'd do whatever I could to go and hang out with him at a convention. It was actually at one of these shows that I first met Danielle Martin, who is now my wife. That's right, over 20 years ago I met the woman that I would end up marrying. Just thinking about that is kind of insane to me. In fact, not only did I meet her, but I also introduced her brother James to George. After a convention, George would always hang out with a select few folks and tell stories. I brought Jim up to George's hotel room to meet him and from what I understand he was there the rest of the evening until George called it a night.

It's funny how life works. Upon meeting Dani, I was sure of one thing—here was a woman so beautiful that I knew I'd never have a chance with her. She was completely out of my league. After all, she was the extremely hot ex-cheerleader, and I was the fat funny guy who liked horror movies. Need I say more? None of that mattered though, because at that time I was in a strong and very healthy relationship with Debi, and Dani was married. Beyond "She's outta my league," I didn't give her a second thought. However, we did remain friends throughout the rest of this sordid tale.

George and I grew closer. I would make sure he had something to drink and candy at every show. George would stay at his table until every single person who had waited in line got to meet him. That's just who and how he was. He spoke to every fan as if they were the most important person in the room and took the time to make sure that they would go home happy. He would remain at his table for sometimes two and three hours after a convention had closed, always with a smile on his face. It was remarkable to see, but then again, he was a truly remarkable man.

There are MANY stories I can tell from my time on the convention scene, and I will indeed tell some of them a bit later in this book. Some, however, will remain just mine. For now, though, let's fast-forward a bit.

It was in September of 2008 that the phone call I never dreamed would happen finally came.

I answered it.

"Yeah, Steve, it's George. I've got this new thing happening, and I know that there's no possible way that I could cast you as part of the living, so how would you like to come up and be a zombie for me?"

Let me be clear. If you are ever lucky enough to get a phone call like this or even an email, you do not say no. You pick up the phone, go on the computer, hire a team of carrier pigeons, erect a giant slingshot... you do whatever you have to do to get to the set and pray that you're one of the few lucky enough to "feed."

A Comedy of Tragedies

Weeks passed like years, but finally it was October, and my lucky fat ass was on the set.

In true excited fanboy holy-shit-is-this-really-happening form, I arrived before just about anyone else, and decided to use this time to get acquainted with my surroundings. I snapped I don't even have any clue how many photos there were and wandered about a blood-soaked barn. It was apparent that bad things happened in there due to the amount of blood on the ground. I was elated. After an hour or so George got to the set, and I hugged, kissed, and thanked him like you wouldn't believe. This was quickly becoming a dream come true. If you're lucky enough to have ever gotten the privilege to experience what could only be described as PURE JOY, then you know exactly what I'm talking about and exactly how I felt inside.

Pretty soon another familiar face showed up—Michael Felsher of Red Shirt Pictures was also to become a zombie for the master. Mike and I go way back, and just as he did on *Diary of the Dead*, he was already compiling materials for the DVD and Blu-ray of what would come to be known as *Survival of the Dead*. Mind you, at this point, the movie didn't even have a title. Mike and I would become inseparable during our time together on the shoot, and to prove it, we took the prerequisite "Facebook Picture!"

We were standing around talking when the call came.

They needed us in make-up.

Holy shit.

My first stop was wardrobe. After poking around a bit, there it was—a red plaid shirt. What fan out there hasn't wanted to be the ever-famous "Plaid Zombie" from *Dawn*? Couple the shirt with the fact that I am bald, and *boom*, I'm already halfway there. Since *Survival* was to be the second entry (just like *Dawn of the Dead* was) in a new *Dead* franchise, it seemed fitting that it had its own Plaid Zombie. Now dressed, off to the make-up chair I went.

I was greeted by three absolute madmen whom I love dearly. François Dagenais, Damon Bishop, and the man who would make me dead, Sean Sansom. When it comes to F/X, these guys are talent personified. The make-up trailer was like home, man. There were body parts everywhere, and Tool was blasting on the stereo. Life, or in this case death, was good.

I sat down in Sean's chair and was pretty blunt. "Listen, dude. I'm a good friend of George, but more so than that, this is my dream come true. I don't want to be gray-guy, and I especially don't want to be blood-smudge-guy. I'm bald; you can put shit anywhere you want on my head. Please torture me. Thanks." Sean laughed and got down to business.

About a half an hour later yours truly was fully zombified. Words cannot express my joy. I've never been happier. Within a few minutes it was time to head to set to do whatever anyone wanted. Before we got down to anything, though, it was my duty to do what dozens of my dead cohorts had done before me... get a picture with George while in full zombie regalia.

I shambled around, did some background stuff, and was fully content. Being a zombie for Romero was amazing. But for me what was even better was taking the time to see the man direct first-hand. It was like watching Picasso paint. George always knows exactly what he wants. This dude has a crystal-clear vision and when you're on set, whether you are a production assistant or the lead, all you want to do is give him your all, and he always takes a moment to let you know he's grateful for that.

The night ended, and I was floating. But little did I know what was just around the corner. George had a plan that I was not privy to.

Fast-forward a day or so, and I am back in the make-up chair with Sean, and he looks absolutely depressed. "Hey, Steve, I've got some bad news for you. We're slammed with making up dozens of zombies, so we have no time but to do just a little bit of color on you for this one." Yep. I was going to be gray-guy, but what the hell, man? I had the experience. At this point, even though I was a little let down, this was so much fun nothing was gonna nab me off my cloud.

Within minutes Sean started busting out all sorts of appliances and looked at me with this huge ass grin.

"I'm just fucking with you, man! You're getting the works tonight! You should have seen your face!" He, Damon, and Felsher, who was in the seat next to me being made-up, got a big laugh at my expense. Too funny.

Now I was curious, though. The works? For what? I'm totally happy being background guy. Would I actually get a bit of screen time? Was I gonna get a head shot?

Again... holy shit.

By the time Sean was done, I was completely and totally blown away by my make-up. This was it, man. Beyond what I could have imagined. I was hideous. It was glorious. Let the angels sing!

By this time Mike was dead and all messed up too, and together again we posed for the now prerequisite "DEAD Facebook Picture!"

We got to the set, and let me tell you, it was FREEZING out. The hot chocolate lady from the Honey Wagon was our only savior. Mike, bless his heart, was to be involved in a major scene, and I was so stoked for him. After all his years in the biz, he deserved the upcoming spotlight. Besides that, he makes a damned scary zombie, too. Hours passed, and we both did nothing. Finally, I was called to the scene.

From here on out there may be a couple of spoilers for those who haven't seen the film yet, but I'm gonna do my very best to avoid them. If you're uber-paranoid, just skip ahead to the end of this chapter.

They put me in a stable with dozens of other zombies including Mike, where we stood for what seemed like forever. Everyone's spirits were totally high, though, and as the hours ticked away, we all learned a valuable lesson: At 4:00 a.m. everything is a cock joke. Thankfully, no laughing zombies were caught on-screen. The scene was this: The lock is shot off the stable fence, allowing us to roam free and begin the killing. Once free, the moment I had been anticipating my whole life was here: George A. Romero was now directing me! "Come right into the camera, Steve. Hit your mark, then turn to the right, and keep walking," yelled George from the sideline in video village.

We did this like six times, each time with different things going on. The actors were shooting blanks at us from M16s and other assorted weapons. Stuntmen feigning headshots were dropping all around us. You can't imagine how LOUD the gunfire was. To say it was exhilarating is like the understatement of the century.

The scene wrapped, and everyone was ecstatic. About an hour passed, and Mike was getting ready for his big scene when over walked Romero.

"Okay, Steve. This is it," said George. "This is what?" I asked.

He looked at me, laughed, and said, "This is the main kill of the movie. The feast. I need you to come through that fence, establish yourself amongst the zombies, dig into the body, tear out the spine, and help rip the body in half."

All I could answer was, "Ummm … what?"

Then he added, "Oh, and by the way, we only have one body so that means we have one chance to get it right!"

And once more... Holy shit.

Turns out that I was going to be starring WITH Mike in the big scene. I had absolutely no clue this was going to happen. Yet, I suspect from everyone else's faces they did. To get to share this moment with my good friend and fellow zombie nerd Mike Felsher was the perfect way for this experience to end.

The call was in. We were to take our places. I started jumping in place and stretching. I was gearing up and was going to give this moment every ounce of energy that I had. George yelled, "You ready, Steve?"

I screamed, back, "NOW NOW! LET'S DO THIS FUCKING THING NOW!"

"Action!"

I landed on my spot perfectly on top of the actor. I had to weigh down the prosthetic body with my right elbow so it wouldn't pop up, dig in, find the spine, then tear with my left hand. There were two other zombies pulling the legs so that as soon as the body was broken, they could drag the appendages away. Mike was in front of me digging in from the other side. The actor was screaming! We wrestled with the innards of the dummy for a while until I located the spine. Once it was in hand, I started tugging on that thing for all it was worth. There was just one problem... no matter what any of us did or how hard we pulled; this body was NOT coming apart. I would later speak to François about this, and he told me that it was super reinforced to be very sturdy. They didn't want the body to break apart as easily as it had in other Romero zombie movies. This was information we could have used earlier! It was nerve-racking! We had only one shot, and this thing would not come apart. Adding to this problem, it was so friggin' cold on the set that the dummy body had actually frozen, and I mean frozen solid. No one wanted to let George down so we just went at it like you wouldn't believe. Finally, after about four minutes the body separated. "Steve, take a bite!" George yelled. I reared my head back and sunk my teeth in. Dream fulfilled.

When it was over, we stood up and everyone on the set applauded. We were covered in fake blood, and in my case real blood, too, as I was pulling so hard on that spine, my hands were cut. Immediately the blood literally started freezing on our hands, and that was an indescribable pain, but it didn't matter. We were all so happy. The crew came at us with hot towels, and that went a long way to relieving the freezing problem.

George came out to me and asked, "Holy shit, man! Are you okay?!"

I dropped to my knees in front of him, hugged his legs, and just kept repeating over and over again... "Thank you, thank you, thank you, thank you." I welled up immediately, and I'd be lying if I told you that I didn't get a little teary-eyed just now writing about this, the greatest moment of my entire life. From this moment on I was to be a part of George's legacy and he was going to become part of mine. Now the only thing to do was wait for the movie to be released.

The day came. First there would be a special world premiere screening at Fantastic Fest in Austin, Texas, and then another premiere in Los Angeles. I was in the crowd behind a velvet rope in Texas as George arrived. He got out of his car and began walking the carpet. As soon as he saw me, he grabbed my arm and pulled me from the crowd. In another dream scenario I could never have fathomed I was now walking the red carpet with George A. Romero.

Again, holy shit.

I can still see the cameras flashing. This was another moment that I'll never forget.

The movie played incredibly well. The crowd was hot, and there were lots of screams, laughter, and joy. My scene came up and people went fuckin' nuts. Weeks later at the Los Angeles premiere I met with George again before the show and hugged and kissed him. He reached over and grabbed one of the movie posters and signed it, "To Steve, Star of this film! Stay Scared, my friend. George A. Romero." There was not, and never will be, a greater honor than this, and I will cherish it until my dying day.

The first time I met George A. Romero.

A COMEDY OF TRAGEDIES

Right before riding the Spider-Man Ride at Universal Studios Orlando (Left to Right) Back: Joe Knetter, Sean Clark, George A. Romero, Suzanne Romero, Chris Roe, Eileen's husband Thomas. Front: Me, Debi Moore, Eileen Dietz. What a day!

Steve Barton

I thought it would be fitting for George to publicly announce his love for me while I simulated sucking his nipple. Because of course I did.

A COMEDY OF TRAGEDIES

Survival of the Dead—Behind-the-Scenes Hijinx

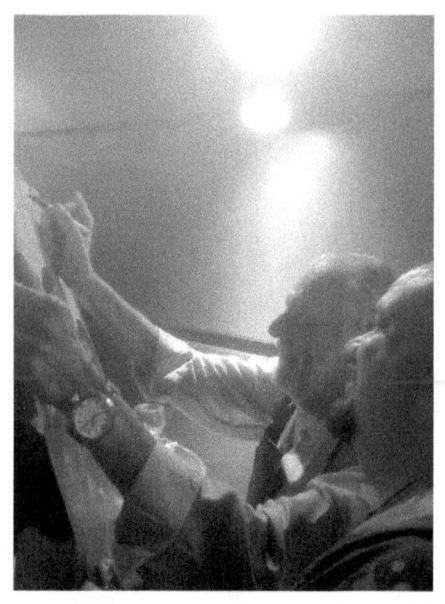

(Above) George declaring me star of Survival of the Dead (I needed photographic proof, damn it). (Below) Recording the commentary track in George's living room with his Muppet.

A Comedy of Tragedies

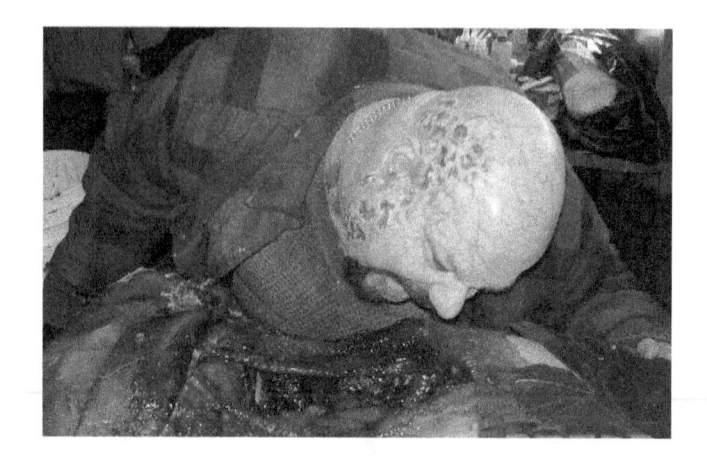

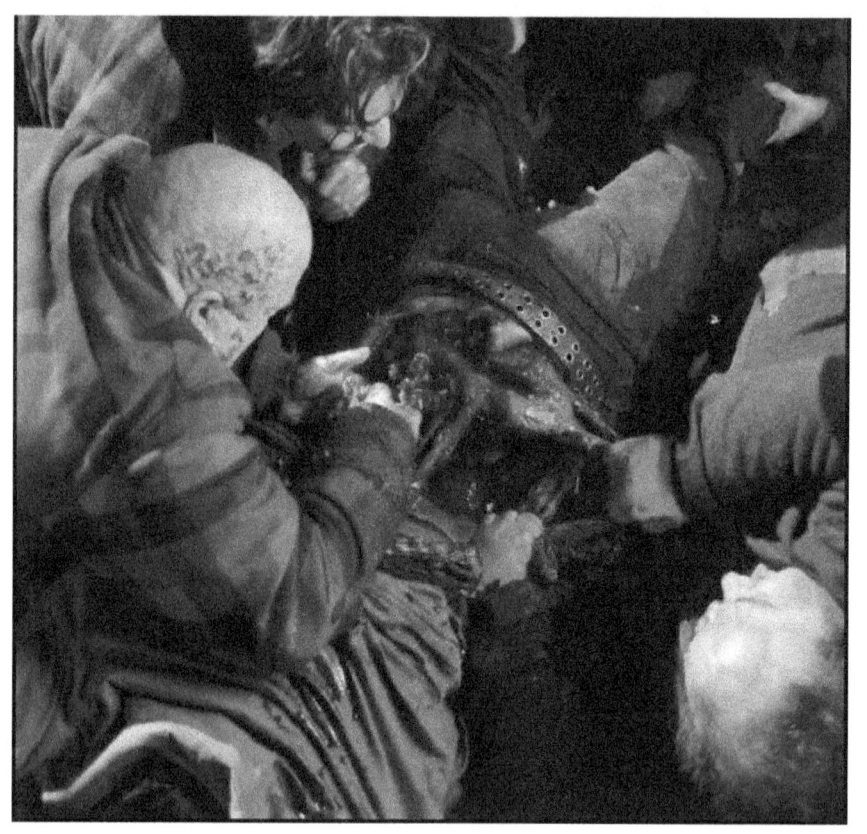

Behind the scenes of the biggest moment in my life!

A COMEDY OF TRAGEDIES

(Above) Walking the red carpet with George at the Survival of the Dead premiere at Fantastic Fest in Austin, Texas. (Below) George and I at the Los Angeles premiere of Survival of the Dead

175

Steve Barton

I recently had the opportunity to have the super-talented Stacy Lynn S recreate my make-up from Survival for an in-person signing at Chris Sembrot's legendary store, ScarePros in Levittown, PA. What's funny is I inadvertently paid homage to Bill Hinzman from Night without even thinking of it. Dani took this picture from inside our car.

A Comedy of Tragedies

My Undead Glamour Shot from Survival of the Dead.

George remains ever so cuddly. I miss him every damned day.

Chapter 15
It Just Tastes so Damned Good!

This period of time was one of the greatest in my life. Everything was clicking. *Dread Central* was making money and each month, sometimes each week, I was at a different show in a different state. Being on the road so much and doing horror conventions only strengthened my bonds with some of my idols who would go on to become great friends.

Adrienne Barbeau, Ashley Laurence, Andrew Divoff, Danielle Harris, Doug Bradley, Kyra Schon, Bill Moseley, Ari Lehman, Kane Hodder, Lou Gentile, Barbara Crampton, and another legend who would also go on to become—with George—one of my mentors, the wondrous Sid Haig. We all became kind of a road family. We'd see each other at least one weekend per month and over three days of an event we'd party until dawn each night. It was like *Carnivale*! The good times seemed endless.

The convention scene back then was not as... shall we say…"sanitized" as it is now. In a world where everyone has a camera on their phones and social media waves have caused a lot of destruction, the talent rarely hangs out anymore, and who could blame them? Gone are the room parties and the shenanigans which always ensued. God, there are SO MANY stories.

A Comedy of Tragedies

I remember one in particular that will always bring a smile to my face. It was at a Rock and Shock in Worcester, Massachusetts. The Shock portion of Rock and Shock took place at the DCU Center, and the Rock portion happened across the street at venue called The Palladium. After a long Friday night, Saturday seemed endless, but there was fun on the horizon. A couple named Dave and Kathy Wilbur always hosted the after con room parties. These two? They were GOLDEN! There'd be food, various—*ahem*—party favors, alcohol and good company behind closed doors. How in the world I ever got deemed cool enough to be at these parties will always be a mystery to me. Maybe it's Dave sitting high on my shoulder! My own personal Puerto Rican angel. One thing's for sure, I'm certainly not smart enough to have earned it all on my own.

Where was I? Oh, yeah! Saturday.

The show was coming to a close, when out of nowhere... and I do NOT know where this came from... someone handed Doug Bradley a megaphone.

Imagine, if you will, seeing Doug standing in front of his table, megaphone in hand, and in his English accent you hear him bellow... "Attention! You've all bought enough shit! Now go home!"

Apparently, Doug was as hungry to get to the party as the rest of us were. The whole con erupted with laughter. Finally, the show ended and myself, my then partner-in-crime, Joe Knetter, my girl Debi, and Joe's then wife Nicole headed to Dave and Kathy's room to begin the festivities.

The hotel we were all staying in and partying at LOVED US and we were allowed to make as much noise as we wanted without worry! One time they even gave us our own ballroom and outdoor gazebo. It was madness. This particular Saturday was long and busy. We were all starving. We knocked at the door and Kathy let us in. One by one, all the usual suspects began to file in. I looked toward the table, and I saw it... An entire tray of Buffalo Chicken Wings. It glowed like a beacon in the darkest night. I swear, if you looked juuu-uust right, you could see Jesus standing behind it, arms outstretched to his side, palms open.

"Hear is thy feast. Come unto me, my child, and fill thy growling tummy!"

Now, me? I'm a pretty picky eater. I mean, I love Buffalo Chicken Wings, but I only like the ones shaped like tiny drumettes. I don't like the "flats" as they're called. So, not wanting to eat all the type of wings that I liked to save some for everyone else, I took a plate, found five drumettes that caught my eye and placed them lovingly on my plastic dish. Just when I had put the final wing on my platter, Doug walked in. I put down my plate on the table and immediately walked over to him to share a quick laugh about the megaphone incident. We giggled back and forth, and I turned around to see the unthinkable. Kevin fucking Sorbo was standing near the serving table EATING MY FUCKING CHICKEN WINGS! The same ones I had lovingly picked out and put down for what had to have amounted to little more than ten seconds. I felt violated. I mean, sure, there was still a whole full tray of them, but those were MY wings! I chose THEM! Highly annoyed and without a second thought I yelled at him, "Yo, Hercules! Those were my wings and my plate! Did you think the food genie just came and prepared you a dish to swoop in and consume?! What the fuck, man?"

Mind you, I had never even met Sorbo before, so this was extra irritating to me.

He replied sheepishly, "Oh, I'm sorry," and tried to hand me back my plate. This somehow irritated me even more!

I said, "Dude! You got your sticky fingers all over that shit! I don't want them now!" I know that I probably came off like an overreacting dick here, but I was irate! After a few seconds or so, everyone started laughing at the absurdity of the situation and the rest of the evening went off without a hitch.

This night in particular was sheer madness. There's a lot that can be said about Sid Haig but believe me when I tell you this man was an absolute alchemist. At one point in the evening, he started making gumball martinis. I don't know how he concocted this creation, but it truly tasted and smelled like gumballs. One of my closest friends whom I miss dearly, paranormal investigator Lou Gentile and I, we're

A Comedy of Tragedies

guzzling them down and Sid was already refilling our glasses the second they seemed to slightly empty. Sid LOVED to get folks fucked up, and we loved him for it!

Lou said to me, "Hey Steve, I got some weed in my room. Take a walk with me."

Glasses in hand we strolled down the hall to his room. We put our drinks down, and Lou went rifling through his bag until he found his fat sack of greens. He grabbed his glass, and we immediately went back to the party room.

There was a lot of weed at this party, but this was also a period in time when NOBODY had medical marijuana. Nobody except for Michael J. Anderson. If you don't recognize that name, he played the backward-speaking Man From Another Place from the TV show, *Twin Peaks*. Michael took one hit off a pipe and said, "You just wait right here! I got something even better than this!"

Before we knew what was going on he came back in with a huge bag of medical grade pot that you could smell from across the room as soon as he opened the bag. From there he walked around sprinkling it on to waiting rolling papers and pipes. At that moment Michael had literally become the weed genie and we were all absolutely giddy! It was probably one of the most surreal moments of my entire life. There were so many pipes and joints being passed around that eventually Lou was handed one of each from both sides of our circle.

"I'M THE LUCKY GUY," Lou shouted with a heart-felt giggle!

We were all laughing to the point of tummy aches and tears when suddenly, WHAM! There was a loud purposeful knock at the door.

The door was opened, and we were greeted by a very angry Antoinette Gentile, Lou's wife.

"WHICH ONE OF YOU FUCKING IDIOTS GOT MY 7-YEAR-OLD DAUGHTER DRUNK?"

The room fell dead silent. You could hear a pin drop. Then we all heard it—the very distinct sound of a little girl cackling maniacally. This brought even more laughter, and eventually Ant started laughing too. Yes, I accidentally and stupidly left my Gumball

Martini in Lou's hotel room, where it was intercepted by a soon-to-be bouncing-off-of-the-walls kid named Samantha! Thankfully, the glass was mostly empty. I pride myself as being the first person to get one of Lou's daughters drunk.

The night went on and there were so many other things that happened. Most of which will remain with me, but at one point I did watch Doug Bradley drop a glass of whiskey, catch it, drop it again, and then catch it, and then drop it and, yes, then catch it. All without spilling a single drop. I remain highly impressed by this. Also, somewhere along the night we finally noticed that Joe was sitting there in nothing but a shirt and Spider-Man boxers.

"Dude, what happened to your pants?" I asked.

He responded simply with, "I don't know, Creepy. But I'm percolating!"

At this point one of the show's promoters, the lovely and stunning Gina Migliozzi got on her handheld radio and put out the word... "Attention! One of my people has lost his pants. If anyone finds them, please bring them to room..."

She was met only with laughter through the radio, and that laughter became quickly contagious. We all were percolating.

When not at conventions I was doing other cool things. Adam Green credits me with being the dude who created the *Hatchet* Army. That's very kind of him, but listen, I'm a fan. A fucking horror fan. OF COURSE I wanted unrated, gory-ass horror. That's like crediting me for being selfish! I'm for whatever gets us the red-stuff and with his *Hatchet* movies, Adam certainly spread more than his fair share of the red.

When it came time to do the inevitable *Hatchet II*, Adam wrote a scene for all his friends to be in. It's the one where Tony Todd's character of Reverend Zombie was asking for help from a bunch of hunters to go after Victor Crowley. Tony is an amazing actor. I'll never forget this story from the set Adam told me once.

"Adam, I need to ask you a question," Tony said. "My character, Reverend Zombie... does he have... powers?"

A Comedy of Tragedies

Adam answered, "What do you mean, does he have powers? You mean like supernatural powers?"

Immediately Tony answered, "Yes!" Tony was obviously excited by this possibility, but Adam told him that, Reverend Zombie did not have any supernatural powers.

Tony paused for a bit, thinking, and then said, "Well, is it all right if he thinks that he has supernatural powers?"

Adam told him that would be fine. That's the kind of actor Tony Todd is. There's a reason he's an icon. He gives everything to his roles and wants to know everything about his characters.

Back to the scene. It was simple. Tony was at the front of the room. As a means to ply the hunters, he had his associate hand out chocolate chip cookies. Once the hunters heard what he had to say, we were to get up and exit the scene thereby making us all look like pussies.

I don't know how much you know about movie making, but there's this thing called coverage. That's when a scene will play out while the camera films, and then the scene is played once again with the camera filming from a different angle. No big deal, right? Adam is a perfectionist. He wants what he wants, and he will take as many takes as possible to get it.

I was sitting next to Lloyd Kaufman of Troma fame for the scene. Adam asked me to look annoyed and angry which is, for all intents and purposes, my resting face, so that wasn't gonna be a problem. In my row I was the first to get a cookie, pop it in my mouth, and then pass the tray to Lloyd, and so on, and so forth. We did this about thirty fucking times and there were no drinks on the set. I had to have eaten at least twenty cookies. I don't know how many of you out there have ever eaten close to two dozen Chips Ahoy cookies without taking a drink, but I can assure you of this: After cookie ten it starts feeling like you're eating nothing but chocolate flavored sand. The annoyance on my face in the take that he ended up using? That shit was motherfuckin' genuine. All-in-all, it was an honor to have played my part in *Hatchet* history. I truly believe that Adam is one of the best filmmakers working in the business and I hope to see more from him soon. Just one thing... Hey, Adam! If you're reading this? How about giving me a role where I don't just run away from a challenge like a scared rabbit! I could have gone toe-to-toe with Crowley. I would have failed miserably to fight him, but at least I would have gone out with a non-cowardly bang.

I'd go on to appear in lots of other things, like multiple DVD/Blu-ray extras, The *E! True Hollywood Story* episode about cursed movies called "Cursed or Coincidence," the *Paranormal Activity* documentary film, *An Unknown Dimension*, and too much stuff to try and even list. I always joke with my friends that "I pop up every now and again like a scorching case of herpes." It was Dan Farrands, however, who allowed me to do something I'd always dreamed of... be in an *Amityville* movie. As a paranormal buff growing up in Brooklyn, New York, there were few things more exciting to me than *The Amityville Horror*. I mean for fuck's sake; the world's most supposedly haunted house was just a two-hour drive away. I'll never forget sitting in the school yard one night as a teenager and saying to my friends, "Dude. Let's go to the *Amityville Horror* house." We were either all high or drunk. Except for Kris though. He's straight edge and truth be told weird enough. That's why I love him so. Anyway, we hopped in the car and made the two-hour trek to Amityville. I'll never forget that feeling of excitement getting off the Amityville exit. There was just one problem—there was no sign reading "HAUNTED HOUSE THIS WAY." We had zero idea where the house was and, back then, the address wasn't readily available. We ended up driving around for a bit and then driving back home totally defeated.

I didn't let that stop me though. I kept on consuming everything that I could. When the dawn of the Internet came it began to get easier to find out anything. I've seen everything you can think of, from horrible DeFeo crime scene photos not released to the public, to the police files. I've become a bit of an *Amityville Horror* historian. Sometime later, when I was an adult, the house had been up for sale, and I posed as a buyer to get into it.

For the record, I "felt" nothing. It felt just like an ordinary home. Just being there, though. Wow.

A Comedy of Tragedies

Many years after that, Dan was making his movie, *The Amityville Murders*, which would tell the story of the DeFeo murders that served as the impetus for all of the haunted hoopla, and he asked me to be in it. Being on set was a joy. Dan had a house in California meticulously transformed into the *Amityville* house right down to the last bit of linoleum. Given the mob ties of the DeFeo family, I was to play a bag man—meaning I would hand over a bag full of money to Paul Ben-Victor, who was playing Ronnie DeFeo Sr. Little did I know, my role would be pivotal. The whole movie revolves around this bag of cash, and I show up again to hand it over to the late great Burt Young, who most of you will remember as Paulie from the *Rocky* movies. What a fuckin' honor.

The Amityville Murders is not only a good movie, but it's a treat for *Amityville* fans. It reunites Burt Young with his *Amityville II: The Possession* co-star Diane Franklin. Now I'm not saying the movie was good because I got to be in it. It just happens to be one of the few good entries in a franchise mired in bullshit. I was watching them film the birthday party scene in the backyard, when Dan told me to go and get into costume for my scene. My costume was simple... Black jacket, T-shirt, pants, and shoes. As I was walking down the steps to the area I was to get changed in, I rolled my ankle on a step. This wasn't an "Oh, thank god it wasn't a bad roll" either. This one FUCKING SUCKED. My foot had gone directly under my ankle, and my ankle had actually touched the ground. I was in agony, but no one saw it. I limped my way back to the area I was to get changed in. I was NOT about to let this injury stop me from being in this movie. No fuckin' way.

When I pulled off my shoes, I noticed that my ankle was already turning colors and swelling. I soldiered through. I got dressed and did my scene. Never limping. Never showing the slightest bit of pain. Later on, when it came time to do my second scene, Dan asked me to get in this classic car and drive away with Burt Young after giving him the bag. There was absolutely no way that I could do that. So, what did I do? I lied. I told Dan that I "didn't feel comfortable getting behind the wheel of a vintage vehicle, much less with a legend in the back seat. Through movie magic he found another way to shoot the shot without me actually driving. The entire time I was on set, all twelve plus hours of it, I never let anyone see me limp or let on that I was in pain. I wasn't gonna blow it. When I got home, I wasn't able to put any weight on my right foot at all. It was like that for two weeks. When I told Dan what had happened, he was shocked. He had no idea. We laugh about it now, saying that it was all part of the "Amityville Curse". I think I'm a curse magnet. Nevertheless, it was all worth it and the good times continues to roll right the fuck on!

Since this is my autobiography, I have to be honest. Or I could lie, but why start now? At times I can be painfully truthful. I spent a hell of a lot of time around people whom I grew up idolizing. I mean, of course there was George and Sid, but there's also Kyra Schon, Doug Bradley, Ashley Laurence, Eileen Deitz, Adrienne Barbeau, Andrew Divoff, Tony Todd, Kane Hodder, Caroline Williams, Derek Mears, Felissa Rose, Danielle Harris, and a slew of others. Sometimes I'd be sitting around with them, and we'd be bullshitting about something and one thought would continually enter my head… "What the hell am I doing here? I'm nowhere near close to being as cool as these folks." On top of that I certainly didn't have an exhaustive body of work behind me either.

I know it sounds cliché, but I was truly not worthy. Hell, I still don't think that I am. And yet, here I was. I always half-joked, "As soon as everyone realizes I'm actually an idiot, my whole shit is over." That's yet to happen and I doubt it ever will because I've learned so much. I'm still an idiot, but a well-informed one.

Because I was around so many conventions, events, and their respective after-parties I've seen some really strange shit. Now there will be times when I will not name names because I love these folks, and ludicrously enough, they love me back. I'd never violate anyone's trust because trust is the most important thing in the world to me. However, I'll do my best to spin a few amusing tales from the strange old days without getting some folks in trouble. All of these stories are rather short because I cannot get into much detail. As such, they didn't really fit in anywhere else. It made sense to condense them into one chapter where the timeline doesn't matter.

The editor of this torrid affair, one Scott Johnson, was privy to the *Survival of the Dead* premiere at Fantastic Fest in Austin, Texas. I had butterflies in my stomach the size of fucking Mothra. To calm me down he took me to a true Austin landmark, the Bat Bridge.

If you've never heard of the Bat Bridge trust me, you need to see this for yourself. Austin's Bat Bridge, formally known as the Ann W. Richards Congress Avenue Bridge, is a renowned attraction located in downtown Austin and it deserves every bit of the recognition it gets.

During the warmer months, typically from March to November, around 750,000 to 1.5 million bats roost beneath the bridge. When the sun goes down, they fly out in an amazing display of nature's beauty and deep guano. It's a shit show! Literally. I looked down after it was over and I realized, "Wow, I'm leaving footprints in bat shit!" How often does ANYONE get to say that? It's a living celebration of quickly amassing black poo pellets! When the bats take flight, you can be assaulted with them, sort of like the lord above has seen fit to batter you with machine-gun-like shit BBs that are being fired straight from a million flying assholes. Oh, the majesty!

After what amounted to a drive-by pooping, we headed back to the theater to see the movie. I was behind the press line with everyone else. A car pulled out and George emerged to deafening cheers. As he was getting set to walk the red carpet he saw me, and yelled "Steve, what the fuck are you doing over there? Get over here, man!" I ducked under the security rope and joined him. He immediately put his arm around me, and we turned to what I can only describe as seeing a million lights all going off at the same time. I have done some cool shit in my life, but walking a red carpet with George A. Romero and going into a theater to watch HIS new movie that I was in? Holy shit, that was magic. Just pure unadulterated madness. I don't even remember what happened next. Seriously.

My memory kicks back in once I was seated for the film. What a surreal fucking moment. There were all the people I had become friends with during the shoot, acting and moving around areas that I knew very well as I ogled every inch of them like the motherfucking fanboy I will always be.

I felt like I did before the world got its claws into me. Before the pollution of experience. This was a pure moment in which nothing else mattered. I was grinning from ear-to-ear the whole time. I truly wish that every one of you gets to experience joy like this. I was bouncing in my seat the whole time like an excited 3-year-old. My scene finally came on. Poor Scott. I literally beat the shit out of him during my excitement. As the body tore in half, the crowd absolutely erupted. It was deafening.

The afterparty was insane. The entire cast was there alongside mega stars like Robert Rodriguez, Quentin Tarantino, Simon Pegg, it was lunacy at its finest. I'll never forget the look on George's face that night. He was thoroughly happy and relieved. The movie had played exactly like he hoped. Upon coming out, *Survival of the Dead* was met with mixed reviews, and that's okay too. George's movies always take around 10 to 20 years to resonate with the audience.

When *Day of the Dead* was first released people hated it. Now it's just as beloved as *Dawn*. George was always ahead of his time when it came to "messaging."

He could predict the direction society would take like no other. In my honest opinion, I think *Survival* is his best movie since *Day*, and not just because I'm in it. I've always tried to professionally distance myself from everything that I've done to judge it fairly. Although, I'd be a fool to not admit that watching George make HIS movie, and seeing how thrilled he was while doing so, after having so many conversations with him beforehand about how "this was the movie [he] always wanted to make..." It's impossible for me to distance myself from his happiness. That just makes me love the film a bit more.

Sticking with George, one of my fondest memories of him is the time we got to go to Universal Studios Florida with him. We rode the Spider-Man ride together and if I try really hard, I'm pretty sure I can still hear him and his lovely wife, Suz, laughing. Fuck. How damned lucky am I? It just defies words. To be able to say I got to get to know,

A COMEDY OF TRAGEDIES

befriend and work with George, the man who created my absolute favorite film franchise, is one of the absolute highlights of my life.

Another of my favorite franchise's is *The Texas Chain Saw Massacre*. Like the *Halloween* franchise, the *TCM* movies are very much a choose-your-own-adventure-type affair. During my tenure at *Dread Central* we put on a convention called Texas Fear Fest, and it featured, at that time, a panel with every living actor who played Leatherface. The only one who had passed back then was Robert Jacks who played Leatherface in *The Texas Chainsaw Massacre: The Next Generation*, who had sadly already passed on. Everyone else was accounted for from Gunnar Hansen to Andrew Bryniarski. The afterparties from that event were absolutely crazed.

I'm not gonna lie, we had a lot of booze and a lot of weed. Very, very, VERY potent weed. One of the Leatherface actors was there and he was puffing away like a lunatic. At one point he dropped to his knees and began crawling around on all fours. I've no idea why, but once he was down, he stayed there. Everyone else was either so high or drunk that no one cared. Eventually he crawled over toward the door to the room and looked up at me and Knetter. Me and Joe looked at each other, shrugged, and opened the door. We were laughing our asses off. After a few minutes, like the concerned citizens we were, we decided that maybe we should go and check on him. You know, to make sure he got back to his room. Upon leaving the room we saw him. He was just standing by the exit staircase, staring up at the exit sign and marveling at what I can only guess was its warm red glow. Joe and I looked at each other, shrugged again, then went back to party more. It was just too strange for us to intercede. He was on his own, but he also happily made his way back to the convention the next day, so WIN! We all lived happily ever after.

Remember that Florida show that Sid, Joe, and I did the wedding at? (If the bride and groom are still reading this, you're STILL not married.) Well, that afterparty in Sid's room was EPIC. He had, I shit you not, a 126-proof bottle of this stuff called Arak. To this very day I have no idea what type of alcohol this was, nor do I care to. What I can tell you was that whenever my glass was empty, Sid took it and refilled it. This was probably the most fucked up I've ever been in my life. I remember four things from this evening.

1. At one point I noticed Cheeze-Itz on the bed. I grabbed them, started munching and apparently had stated, "You know! I'm pretty sure that Jesus baked these fuckers himself, godammit."
2. I remember trying to drink something other than Arak, grabbing ice from the bucket, and trying to put it into a glass. I missed completely, much to Sid's amusement, and my ice cubes went flying across the room. Immediately, Sid took this new glass and filled it with Arak.
3. Somehow or another I ended up in a 3-point stance that I could not get up from. I remember this only because of how hard I heard Sid laughing. I can still hear it.

Now, Debi, who was with me in the room, had never seen me this drunk, and she totally abandoned ship on me. That's why the *fourth* thing I remember is riding the hotel's elevator for twenty minutes up and down trying to find my hotel room. I knew the room number and the floor, but I couldn't see it. Thankfully, some fans got in eventually and helped me to my room. They told me about this the next day. I will NEVER touch Arak again.

Months later Sid invited me to do a set visit for a flick he was doing in Nevada called *Dark Moon Rising*. The flick had a great cast too, including Billy Drago, Maria Conchita Alonso, Lin Shaye, and lots more, so I was totally down for the job. Besides, Sid was really excited about this flick because it featured a scene in which he bites a werewolf and not the other way around. I was to conduct cast interviews. There was just one problem: the nights I was there, there were extreme sandstorms. One by one the stars filed in for quick ten-minute interviews. In all it took about an hour and a half to get everyone. That's a real long time for me, considering my mouth was open for a long while talking in a sandstorm. When I got back to the hotel, I was sick to my stomach. I went to the bathroom and threw up sand.

Motherfuckin' sand. This was WAY worse than any post drunken puking.

Speaking of getting drunk. One of my good friends is Tyler Mane who played Michael Myers in Rob Zombie's *Halloween* movies. One evening after a con we decided to go have dinner and drinks at the hotel bar. Tyler, aside from being an absolute gentleman, is also a wine connoisseur. The hotel we were staying at had Bourbon Barrel wine, which essentially means that the wine was aged in a barrel that was used to age bourbon before it. This creates an insane fusion of flavor and alcohol. Now I'm part Irish and that means I can pretty much eat and drink anyone under a table. I decided to go drink-for-drink with Tyler. We were there for hours. It was, I think, the middle of the night when we retired. I have no idea how many bottles of this wine we drank but it had to be in the double digits. That night, Debi helped me get back to the hotel. I remember asking her what time it was, and she said 3-something. I picked up the room phone to call room service. Once they answered I demanded that they bring me "chocolate soup." No, I do NOT know what chocolate soup is. All I know is that I wanted it. Moral of the story, don't ever try and go drink-for-drink with a 7-foot-tall human. Jesus Christ, I think I'm STILL a bit hungover. What an absolute tit-headed mistake.

Speaking of tit-heads, one time Joe and I went to, fuck, I think it was Arizona (it's been a while), to film something called *Monsterpiece Theater* for a director so green he had to be reminded to call "Action." He would try SO VERY HARD to make it sound like he knew what he was doing but failed miserably. One time he told the camera man he wanted an "Izzy Whizzy Shot." Everyone just stopped and stared at him completely bewildered. Thankfully he had an incredible assistant director in the late John Carl Buechler who basically directed everything I saw.

This anthology flick, which will most likely NEVER be seen because, again, tit-head had no idea what he was doing. He had an incredible cast including Tiffany Shepis, Kane Hodder, Leslie Easterbook, Ashley Bank, Kathleen Kinmont, and Caroline Williams. Joe and I were there to film a segment featuring Tiff and Kane called

"Moonlighting," about a kidnapped chick, a maniac, and a werewolf. We, as expected, were comic relief.

"Okay, man, what do you need us to do?" I asked the "director."

"I don't know, man, do anything," he answered.

Joe was like, "do we have any lines?"

The "director" responded, "just make it up." I kid you fuckin' not.

Being that we were in some sort of abandoned restaurant that had a bathroom, I said to Joe, "Hey! Let's have a jerk-off contest to see who cums faster!"

Joe laughed and Mr. Director, shouted, "I LOVE IT!"

So, there we were standing with our pants down around to urinals with a divider between them pretending we were jerking off. And, YES, you fucker, we were pretending. We heard the film crew fighting back laughs as we groaned and yowled during our mad dash to climax. During this moment Joe yelled, "Creepy, I'm dry" before putting his other hand over the divider for me to spit in it which I did. Joe and I always had that kind of timing with each other. We were like one person with a really fucked up mind. This moment roused unexpected laughter from everyone present, and we finished. Joe won. Once we heard, "Cut," we both broke up laughing. It was gonna be that kind of day. It was a brilliantly inappropriate moment.

Finally, Mr. Director decided that he figured out what he wanted us to do. "Okay, guys, I want a scene of you two driving and getting high in the car. Make believe you're stopped in traffic, when you notice that the car in front of you has an arm hanging out of the trunk."

"Okay," Joe said, "But we don't have any weed."

Director answered, "Don't worry, we'll just break-down a cigarette and roll it back up."

Hearing this I immediately chimed in, "Like hell you will. I'll get sick to my stomach if I try to smoke tobacco. Either you get us weed or we need to change the scene."

So, what do ya know? Within a half hour, weed somehow managed to get onset and Joe immediately began rolling. We were sitting in the back of somebody's car getting stoned for our shoot

A COMEDY OF TRAGEDIES

with the window down. Every now and then, completely unprompted, Kane would shove his black-gloved hand into the window opening holding a fistful of trail mix Joe and I would eat out of. This was both strange and thoroughly amazing.

Once we were high enough, and BOY were we high, we meandered over to our hero-car and got in. Buechler was in the backseat filming for sound with the windows up. I lit up a phatty. We literally improved for about thirty minutes smoking joint after joint. The shit we were saying was goddamned ludicrous, but in truth, I don't remember any of it. At one time Joe pulled down his driver side visor and two hotdogs, bun and all fell into his lap. Spattering his shirt with mustard and ketchup. I remember dipping my hotdog into the ketchup on his shirt and eating it. Again, pure Knetter and Creepy magic. The scene ended and we literally rolled out of the car. We were FUCKED.

Speaking of tit-heads... Fresh out of our scene in which Knetter and I smoked real weed in the never-to-be-seen Monsterpiece Theater

Buechler came out too. We forgot he was even there. He was contact-wrecked. Joe and I wandered off to some nearby hill, laid

193

down on a stuffed Ewok that was inside the car for some reason, and watched the clouds roll by.

After God knows how long, we heard Kane calling for us. We got up and went down to meet him. He was standing by a car.

"Did you know that I'm also a stunt driver?" he said matter-of-factly.

I answered, "Wow, man. That's cool!"

Kane laughed and said, "Get in, and put your seatbelts on."

We did and Kane fucking floored it and began doing donuts at a rate of speed in which I could swear was in excess of Mach three. Holy shit!

Now, completely sober, it was time for dinner. Me, Joe, Tiff, and Kane were all sitting around the table eating and laughing. Mr. Director comes over and asked to sit. We told him "No way! Go sit at the kiddie table." Which he did. Completely alone and thoroughly oblivious to… well… everything.

God, there are so very many stories like this. However, the rest of them, in order to make sense, I'd have to reveal identities and I can't do that. Besides, there's already a lot in here, and I gotta save something for the inevitable *A Comedy of Tragedies Book 2: Riding the Karma Train to Fuck You Town*.

Chapter 16
Irregular Guests, Fuckin' that Puppet, and Ass Aid

Another year had passed, and it was time once again for our favorite show, Rock and Shock. Days before I was on the phone with Sid when he called Gina on three-way and told her, "Gina! Hi, it's Sid. Listen, I'm gonna need a hotel room with a double boiler."

Her response, "Um. Okay?" Sid was gonna be making his "special" fudge. Yep. This weekend was gonna be motherfuckin' glorious.

Friday was killer. I wasn't through the door of the hotel for more than five minutes before someone put a drink in my hand. If you're wondering… my drink of choice is a Gin and Tonic. Please make a note of this as if you see me in a bar or some shit you can buy me one. I'm not one to argue about being given free booze.

So very many things happened during 2005, the most disturbing of which was the deadly Hurricane Katrina which devastated the lives of so many. In the world of horror, a young filmmaker named Darren Lynn Bousman had done the unthinkable. He created a worthy sequel to the original *Saw*. The movie shouldn't have worked, but Darren is crazy talented. This year's Rock and Shock was going to be his first convention appearance and it was time to meet you lovable sickos.

Gina told him I would be hosting his panel at the show and

Darren was happy. Because of *Dread Central* he had already known who I was. When I first saw him, he was noticeably uncomfortable. He was looking around with all the confidence of a paranoid man who's being followed around by some great unseen white-hot spotlight on his back. I knew this look well.

"Hey, man! Pleased to meet you! I'm Creepy. Let's bullshit!" Yep. The Romero Introduction approach has never let me down.

"Hey, I'm Darren. It's nice to meet you, man. Thanks for all the kind things you said about *Saw II*," he said, visibly relaxing a bit. "I don't really know what's going on here, or what I'm supposed to be doing."

I reassured him, "Don't worry, man, I got you. Just follow my lead, and then afterward...that's when the magic will happen!"

"Magic?" he asked. He had no idea what I had planned for him.

Darren's panel went great, and the crowd really warmed him up. It was the last of the day, and you know what that means. Yup, you guessed it. To coin a line from Rob Zombie's *House of 1000 Corpses*, "It's time to get drunk and do some fucked up shit."

I brought Darren with me to the holiest of holies...Sid Haig's hotel room. Sid had been putting his pre-requisitioned double boiler to good use. There were several plates of Sid's "Special Fudge." Vanilla, Peach, Chocolate, all meticulously designed to have you feeling no pain in no time flat. Darren had some and immediately he was "home." This was gonna be his life now and he was thrilled.

Once a more than adequate amount of fudge had been consumed to achieve the desired effect, it was time again for Dave and Kathy's room party. These parties would go on until the wee hours of the morning. Of course, the conversation became serious as the subject turned toward Hurricane Katrina. Sid was a lot of things—all of them fuckin' wonderful. All weekend long he had put a jar on his table so people could donate to the victims of the Hurricane. All proceeds were gonna go to the various charities that were helping the victims. There will never be another person like Sid. The man could go from lovable to absolutely frightening at the drop of a dime, but through it all he had the biggest heart anyone could ever be blessed enough to

A Comedy of Tragedies

have. There's not a second that goes by that I don't miss him. I expect that to last for the rest of my life. You better be holdin' me a spot on a cloud, you fuck!

Back to the hijinks.

My then partner-in-crime, Joe Knetter, and I were permanent fixtures at these parties. Why? We have no idea. Maybe because we were two giant bald idiots who looked scary and had warped senses of humor. In reality, I think it was because Sid liked us. Sid, Joe, and I were inseparable at shows. We became known as "The Terror Dome." A testament to our love of horror and our lovely bald heads and facial hair. We'd party together long into the night.

Like teenagers, we'd prank call people we either knew or people whose number we got outta the phone book. For you younger folks who don't know what the yellow and white pages were... #1: I hate you. #2: Fuck, I'm old. #3: It's how we got phone numbers before the time of the smart phone. Sid became infamous for his Beedee Beedee calls which he made after blocking his caller ID number. Essentially, he'd wake you up at 2:00 a.m. and just say "Beedee Beedee" into the phone and hang up. We all found this hilarious because it was so ridiculous. We were the very definition of ridiculous. If you're reading this and have received one of those calls, yep, that was us. Don't be angry. It meant that you were cool and that you were loved.

As a goof, the three of us started telling people we were starting a band together. The band's name? "Cuntgrinder." It was so ludicrous. So audacious. So "us." I was good with Photoshop, so I started making album covers. Then we found out that there was already a Swedish death metal band called Cuntgrinder and had to change it up. Our new name? Cuntroaster. Our debut album was called *CERTIFIED*, and it featured a roast beef sandwich as its cover. We had a live album called *RATTLE AND CUM*, and finally an EP of B-sides called *STILLBORN: THE STORK WORE BLACK*. It came time to do a tour poster so as a riff on the famous *Stand by Me* artwork, I announced our Middle East tour of Kazakhstan, Kyrgyzstan, Tajikistan, Turkmenistan, Uzbekistan, Afghanistan, and Pakistan. It would come to be known as *THE STAN BY ME* tour. Cuntroaster was to be a running gag along the lines of *This Is Spinal Tap*. Our end game was simple—we were gonna perform at the 2006 Rock and Shock Convention, and as we took the stage, we'd break up the band so we'd never have to play a single note. It was genius! It was getting quickly out of control. Before we knew it people started picking it up as a news story! A rock magazine in Bulgaria even did a news story about it. Man. We were FUCKIN' BIG in Bulgaria, dude. Then the phone call came…

"Steve! Yeah, it's Sid. Listen… we have to stop with the Cuntroaster stuff! It's snowballing too big, and people are asking questions! Even my agent called me about it!" And just like that, Cuntroaster was no more. We never even took the stage. You just can't make this shit up.

Oops. I guess I went off on a tangent there. Where was I? Oh, yeah.

The Rock and Shock Friday Night Room Party! During this period in time Joe, a soon to be prolific writer, used to do readings from one of his many books. The catch? He would do his reading pants-less while sitting on a makeshift toilet. Sometimes he would even get up and hand out brownies to the people in attendance. As weird as it was, Joe's stock was rising, and you know what that means… He needed an 8x10 to sell at appearances. Then it hit me like a bolt of heavenly lightning pinpointing the scalp of the waiting damned!

"Joe," I said. "I have an idea, man! Why don't you get your face tattooed on your ass, then we'll take a picture of your ass with your face on it, and then that can be your fucking 8x10!"

The whole room fell silent. Sid stood up, opened up his wallet and said, "I'm in for 100 bucks to make this happen!" Everyone there started laughing to the point of tears.

Joe stood up and said, "Fuck You, Creepy! Let's do it! I'm percolating, Creepy."

The die had been cast. Amongst ANY other group of people, this would have been dismissed and forgotten in an instant. However, we were NOT your ordinary group of people.

The next morning, Sid, had me going around to all of the celebrities' tables to kick in to get Knetter's face tattooed on his ass. Being that Rock and Shock had in-house tattoo artists inking at the event, we wouldn't even have to leave the show. Everyone kicked in. Doug Bradley. Bill Moseley. Lou Gentile. You name it. Within ten minutes we had raised over $700 to get the deed done. Joe took a deep breath and said, "Fuck it! Let's do it!" We found an artist who agreed to do it, and within seconds, Joe was laying there bare-assed getting his face tattooed on his bum in front of 100's of passersby and con-goers. It was just like I said... MOTHERFUCKIN' GLORIOUS!

From that day on Joe had the dubious honor of being the only dude who could sit on his own face every day, several times a day, and be totally comfortable. He could even grow out his ass hair to give himself a beard if he wanted to. The applications were *ahem* ENDLESS!

Before I go onto what happened on Night Two of Rock and Shock 2005, I'd be remiss if I didn't tell the following story as it relates to the shenanigans of that fateful Saturday afternoon. It was springtime and time for an annual show in Florida, which is now known as "Spooky Empire." It was being held at a J.W. Marriott, which, if you didn't know, is like a super elite hotel that's four stars or some shit. At least that's what I've been told as I have yet to ever stay in a fancy hotel. This was not a con-friendly hotel like the one we stayed at during Rock and Shock. The staff there hated us and everyone who was in attendance. This was a playground for the rich. Horror fans, in their eyes, were the lowest common denominator.

This is actually when I first started telling people that I thought of myself as "The Proud Representative of the Lowest Common Denominator."

Anyway, one of Sid's convention duties had become officiating weddings while dressed in full Captain Spaulding regalia. The hotel was reluctant to let us hold a wedding there but the show's promoter, Petey, convinced them it would be fine. I mean, it's a wedding! What could go wrong? Right? Enter the Terrordome!

The hotel's lobby was packed! There were several events happening, including your standard wedding receptions and some golf tournament thingy. A stage was set up in the bustling lobby and the time had come for the nuptials. That's when one of the hotel staff made their first big mistake… They handed me a live mic in front of an area filled with hundreds of horror fans.

"Ladies and Gentlemen," I said, "Thank you all for coming. The wedding will soon begin, but before we can get anyone hitched, I need to introduce the master of this ceremony! Put your hands together for CAPTAIN MOTHERFUCKIN' SPAULDING!"

The place erupted! I can still see the faces of the well-to-do covering their ears, their jaws agape! The look of shock on their faces! My god had someone just said the dreaded F-Word? You bet your fuckin' ass I did! And I was far from done! "Come on, you fucks! I can't hear you cocksuckers!" The horror crowd was happy and in a frenzy! Words alone cannot describe the abject horror on the faces of some of the people in this establishment. It remains unforgettable.

Sid took the stage, grabbed the mic and bellowed, "Howdy, folks! We're here to get the following two dumb fucks hitched, so without further ado, let's hear it for the bride and the groom!"

Again, the place went nuts! The bride and groom took the stage and Sid was just about to start when I stood up, walked over, and grabbed the mic from him. None of this was planned mind you. This is just how shit rolled. It came naturally.

"Captain, Captain, Captain… Wait a second. This is a fucking wedding, and every wedding needs a witness," I said. "Can I have Mr. Joe Knetter join us on the stage?" Knetter came up and I said to him, "Joe… please bare witness!"

As if on cue, Joe stood beside Sid, dropped his pants, and pulled down the back of his boxers so his ass was completely out. We are talking full moon, baby! With his ass tattoo of his face now facing the crowd and the soon- to-be-newlyweds, Sid began his ceremony!

All I remember is seeing people in the background darting back and forth, others leaving, heads shaking, and the looks of sheer outrage by the hotel's "regular guests." Here was the very definition of profane, including a half-naked man, stinking up the place. As soon as Sid, said the words, "I now pronounce you husband and wife, so make with the fuckin'!" the hotel's staff started piping Opera music over the PA. This was akin to them trying to spray air freshener in a shitter after a night of Mexican food and tequila. It just didn't work. The damage had been done. Petey and his show were permanently banned from the hotel, and our work there was done. The wedding took place on Sunday, the last day of the show. Most people who were there for it had already checked out. We, of course, weren't leaving until Monday. When we went back to the rooms they had been totally changed and spruced up. There were now silk bedspreads, body pillows, and small chocolates on the beds. This was a complete 180 from the room layouts the rest of the weekend. Yep. That's what this hotel thought of the horror fans spending money there. I'm glad we fucked up your Sunday and shocked the wealthy, snobby, and generally hoity toity. Screw 'em!

> Sidenote: I didn't divulge the names of the bride and groom married that weekend, mainly because I forgot and have drunk a lot of booze and smoked a lot of pot since then. If you're reading this—I hate to break it to ya—but Sid forgot to sign the marriage license so technically you're NOT married. Um... Surprise?

Now then! Back to Night Two of Rock and Shock 2005.

The deed was done. Joe had his face tattooed on his ass and we were all partying at the backroom of The Palladium where the "Rock" portion of Rock and Shock was held. Joe and me? We were FUCKED! His ass was out the whole night and all the celebs, and more were posing for pictures with it! (They shall remain nameless.) It was then that I saw it. In the corner of the bar was a life-sized blow-up skeleton. I was enamored. I HAD to have it. I approached, put my hands around its neck and claimed it. From that moment on I spent the rest of the night holding up my prize and telling people, "Ya see this? This is my puppet, and ya know what? I'm gonna fuck this puppet. I'm gonna fuck this puppet to death." It got to the point where people were yelling out randomly, "Creepy! You gonna fuck that puppet?" The answer was always "YOU'RE DAMNED RIGHT I'M GONNA FUCK THIS PUPPET," I then would hold it up in the air and EVERYONE would cheer! This was madness. I mean, it wasn't even a puppet, but that night... that night this was a puppet that was gonna get fucked.

After The Palladium party Joe and I took "The Puppet" back to the hotel. Before you ask, no. I did not fuck the puppet, nor did I have any intention of doing so. What we DID do though was take it and spread chocolate all over where its ass was as if it were freshly plunged shit. We then left it in the hall outside our door and watched through the peephole as people laughed at this... um... curious site? Then it hit me again... ANOTHER idea! Dave and Kathy were still at The Palladium, and we had the room next to theirs. Joe and I snuck into their room as best as two drunks could and put The Puppet in their wardrobe. The idea was the next day, they'd open the closet, and it would scare them. Dunno if that ever happened or not. Minutes later Joe and I were out like lights. Sleep came quickly and deeply.

The next morning EVERYONE was so hungover and out of it. Joe and I were hanging at Sid's table. I swear this dude had a line no matter what time of day it was. People would line up to meet him and rightly so. He's a legend. He'll ALWAYS be a legend. To us though... he was so much more. Despite Sid's heartier than usual constitution, you could tell even he was feeling it. What had we done? Asses were tattooed. Puppets were fucked. It was so surreal. I remember Joe and I watching Sid sign his first few autographs. It was like a hungover assembly line. Greet. Sign. Move on. There was no chit chat. We started laughing.

Sid, looked up at us with a tired smile and said, "What the fuck are you two nitwits laughing at?"

Joe said, "Your autographs, man. The last three that you signed, you did so with a dead sharpie. You literally signed nothing."

Sid looked to his left and there were three fans all with nonexistent autographs just staring at each other and us, completely confused. We all just looked at each other and started cracking up. Yep. It was gonna be THAT kind of a day.

A Comedy of Tragedies

That afternoon Gina came over to Joe and I. "Guys," she said. "Um... the skeleton from the Palladium..."

"Yeah, yeah! The puppet," I answered.

"Yeah, the Puppet. It's kind of like The Palladium's mascot. We need it back. It's been our mascot for years." A mask of horror fell over my face. This was our favorite convention, run by people who lovingly put up with no end of shit from us, and we have misplaced the only thing they cared about! The one thing we should not have done!

I played it cool. "Oh, no worries. We left it in Dave and Kathy's room. I'll just swing by and get it!" Gina gave a very relieved smile and went about her business.

Shit.

Immediately I called Dave on his cell.

"Oh, yeah! We saw it this morning and laughed. That was just chocolate on its ass, right?"

After assuring Dave it was just chocolate, I asked him where the puppet was. He said they'd left it in the hotel room for the maid, and that they'd already checked out.

Shit. Shit.

I went running back to the hotel and spoke with the manager, who by this time knew us and wasn't at all surprised by the oddness of my dilemma. He said he would go and talk to the cleaning staff. A few minutes passed and he came back as white as a sheet.

"The room was cleaned already, and the woman who cleaned it threw it out as trash." Then he told us that she was now in the incinerator room getting ready to burn the trash!

Shit. Shit. Shit!

Thankfully, she had a radio on her, and he called her immediately. They spoke over the radio to one another and all I remember is the manager yelling, "NO BASURA! NO BASURA!" After a few minutes he told us that he "thinks" he saved it! Moments later I looked to my left and saw this tiny Mexican woman running up the hallway in what I swear was slow motion. In her arms, like Mary holding Christ

203

in "The Pietà" was a now limp and rapidly deflating puppet we all started high-fiving. It was like a movie. Un-be-fuckin-leivable.

Gina got "The Puppet" back and all was right in the world. We went back to Sid's table.

"How's the donations for Katrina doing?"

"Terrible," he answered. "This fuckin' jar has been there since Friday and we made like, what? Thirty-two dollars?" Yep. People suck. But there was a bright side. Given that we raised over $700 bucks in minutes for Joe's ass tattoo, there was money left over. We had already decided anything made over the cost of Joe's most infamous ASSet go to charity. The tattoo only cost $200, so we put the other $500 into Sid's Katrina jar and named the entire endeavor Ass Aid. This weekend has since gone on to be the stuff of convention legend, and to this day, no show-going experience will ever measure up to the exalted joy and sheer lunacy of this one. It will remain in all of our hearts forever. Just like Joe's face... sitting proudly... on his ass.

Things were great for a long while. Sid married the love of his life in his girl Suzie, and Joe and I were invited to his wedding with our own then "significant others." It was a glorious day. Everyone was there. We laughed. We danced. We enjoyed each other. Sid and Suzy weren't going on a honeymoon any time soon, so he invited us to hang out at their place the next day.

We got there and Sid was by the stove cooking up some of his "special brownies," and you could literally smell the sweet scent of Mary Jane the second we got to the door. He looked at us, smiled, and pointed. There on the counter was a veritable mountain of edibles. Were they strong? FUCK were they strong! We all started laughing and eating them immediately. The time was 3:00 p.m. Around 10:00 p.m., I snapped out of whatever haze I was in and looked around. There we were, the six of us, all staring, mouths agape, watching the Sony Blu-ray Screensaver bouncing around the totality of Sid's big screen TV. I said only one thing... "Yo!" which was met with boundless laughter. We didn't know how long we were sitting there, what we were trying to watch, or when we even went into the living room for that matter. The only thing we knew was that we were high as fuck and hungry.

There was a Carl's Jr., down the street from Sid's and we all wanted food and milkshakes. On the way to the car Joe and I stopped and got some M&Ms. We literally couldn't wait just another few minutes for food. After gobbling them up, we got in the car and made the two block or so drive to fast food goodness. We pulled into the drive-through and sat there for like five minutes until we realized we had to drive up to the window. There was just one hitch. We drove into the drive-through backward and needed to go in reverse to get our order.

We secured our snacks and had to back out of the drive-through to turn our car correctly into the street. While doing so, a cop pulled into the drive-through and slowed down. They were staring at us.

I rolled down the window and said, "Sorry, we came in the wrong way!" They were probably hungry too, and they just laughed and waved. Joe and I were shitting our pants, but it all ended up okay.

On the way back to Sid's we stopped and got some more M&Ms because we couldn't wait to get back into the house to eat. This was an amazing time. The best time. A time I will always look back at fondly. That's the real bitch about the good times. They don't last forever, but thankfully their memories do.

Of all the things that *Dread Central* was responsible for, my relationship with George and Sid will always be my greatest gift. The two of them taught me so much and we had a ton of insanely great times. These stories are just the tip of the iceberg.

CHAPTER 17
WHAT A TANGLED WORLD-WIDE-WEB WE WEAVE

When *Dread Central* started it took on a life of its own. Myself, Jon Condit, Johnny Butane, and K.W. Low were the work horses of it. Butane did the news, Condit the backend of the site giving us a digital playground to play around in, and K.W. handled the business aspects. Along the way we took on a staff. Not a writing staff, but a staff comprised of fans who just wanted to share their enthusiasm for horror and what we loved. What a motley crew! Johnny Butane, Ryan Turek (now of Blumhouse fame), Sean Clark (who's gone on to do simply amazing things despite wearing a blood spattered work shirt with no sense of "direction"), Justin "Mr. Dark" Julian, Buz Wallick, Andrew Kasch, Matt Fini, the indomitable Foywonder, Scott A. Johnson, Paul "Nomad" Nicholasi... those were just a few of the names involved, and we loved each other. Me? I became the face of the company and the chief writer of reviews. I don't know how I became the face. I wouldn't have picked me to be the face of anything, but it was what it was. To this very day I don't think anyone—including myself at the time—really knew or realized the pressures of being "the face" of something. It was taxing to say the least, but someone had to do it.

Eventually Turek set out on his own, and personal issues caught up with Butane. Once he left, it was up to me to learn how to write the news, and learn I did. I was used to giving my opinions and reviewing horror films, but the news was a different beast. I was never taught how to write, so to me it was kind of a joke that all of a sudden, I became the head writer. I was now face, critic, and editor-in-chief.

Let me be very honest about something... If you think that there is money to be made by having an online news outlet, let me stop you right there. There wasn't. Do you know what there was plenty of, though? Work! My average day consisted of waking up at 4:00 a.m., updating the website, going to work at 10:00 a.m. at a local Gamestop, then coming home at 4:00 p.m. to update the website again until about midnight, and then doing that all over again. I did this for seven fucking years. Most of the money we made went to the writers who helped keep things cooking while I was doing my retail stint. Anyone who works on ANYTHING deserves to be paid. It was 7-8 years before *Dread Central* started making any real money. Up until then I was literally living at poverty level. I just had invested so much in this whole crazy thing, that I had to see it through. Once we finally—and thankfully—hit our stride, I was able to quit Gamestop. It was like Christmas! I could now just do *Dread Central* full-time and so we expanded our staff to some of the most well-respected writers in the business, namely John Squires and Sean Decker. These two folks are nothing short of rockstars in the world of horror journalism, and I'd LOVE nothing more than to work with them again.

One day, man. One day.

The way that *Dread Central* made money was simple... advertising. For example—if Warner Brothers had a horror movie that they wanted to promote, they would come to sites like ours to buy ads. We were their pipeline to the public. However, technology constantly changes and keeping up with it is a chore in and of itself. It was long before the death-knell of many dot-com sites came in the form of two frightening words... social media.

Now, instead of working with the websites, studios would hire people to run their social media accounts for a couple of weeks and that's where they invested all of their ad budgets. At one time *Dread Central* had a worldwide staff of nearly 20 people and we were making really good money. Then it dried up at what seemed like warp speed. We had a choice. We went from making thousands of dollars a month to literally about $700. This just wasn't sustainable. Either close up shop or sell.

My favorite thing about *Dread Central* was that we were ALWAYS independently owned. We never had a parent company, and we succeeded on our own steam. The thought of someone stepping in and taking over was scary. We devised a last-ditch effort. At the time, *Dread Central* was doing around over a million hits per day, so we turned to Patreon and launched a "Save Dread Central" campaign. The plan was simple… for just $1 per month, all users could get the site completely ad free. No pop-ups. No banner ads. NOTHING. Just $1 per month. Pretty much the entire horror industry rallied around us including legends like John Carpenter, but in the end hardly anyone wanted to leave a dollar on the table just once a month for a place they visited every day.

The writing was on the wall, and I was heartbroken.

Enter Epic Pictures Group, run by Patrick Ewald and some schmuck who's name I'll only refer to as Shake-and-Bake, because he's an absolute snake oil salesmen who'd feel right at home working at any used car lot in the world. Patrick is a gentleman and a businessman. Shake-and-Bake was a narcissistic moron who thought that he was the smartest person in the room. Patrick let Shake-and-Bake handle the deal with us and was purely the money man. He and K.W. worked out the details of the sale, and upon the deal being signed, K.W. was out.

Shake-and-Bake promised us the world. To start, both Condit and I would be making salaries of 35k a year. That's STILL below poverty level, but he also promised a 5k a year raise, and a paid vacation. Epic was gonna take care of everything, including getting us a dedicated sales team to make sure our ad revenue picked back up. Shake-and-Bake insisted he wanted to have no involvement in the day-to-day running of the site content-wise, and was only buying our name and voice, both of which brought his company credibility. The idea was simple—keep doing what we're doing, and they get to use the *Dread Central* name as a home video label for their horror releases. This sure sounded great on paper, and the option of flipping burgers somewhere just didn't appeal to me.

None of these promises ever materialized. Not a single one.

About a year went by before the realization came that Shake-and-Bake wanted a "Yes-Man." I am a lot of things, but a "Yes-man?" Ehhh... not so much. If I think that something is wrong, I am gonna say something. That's who I am. It's how I am. That will never change. Shake-and-Bake was a shrewd snake-in-the-grass. He knew that he HAD to get rid of me so that he could assume his ultimate final form of Douchbag the Great and Powerful.

He had a plan. Drive a wedge between Condit and I by making me out to be a problem child. Condit, whom I loved like a brother, sadly fell for it hook-line-and-sinker. How? Why? Well, being that I was the face of the company, Condit always felt that he didn't get the credit that he deserved. Jon was an introvert at that time. I begged him and pleaded with him to come out of his shell. To be the face. Hell, that would have even taken some of the pressure off me. He never did. I would ALWAYS tell countless people that Jon was the backbone of the company and a true hero. To me, he was all of those things, but it didn't matter how much I praised him or anything else. He felt the way that he felt, and there was nothing that I could do about it. Shake-and-Bake used that and immediately began preying upon Jon's feelings and ego.

Shake-and-Bake set me up to fail. He took away my writing privileges and wanted me to sell ads. That's like having Babe Ruth on your baseball team, but instead of giving him a bat so that he could do what he does best, you handed him a mop. It didn't matter that at the time I was 40-something years old and didn't possess that tool in my toolkit. Selling ads is a very particular skillset. I just didn't have that. Shake-and-Bake's logic was, "Everyone likes you." Yeah, um... Part of the reason why everyone liked me was because they didn't have to worry about me trying to sell them anything! Because I'm well-liked, doesn't mean that I can perform as a sales agent. This fell on absolutely deaf ears. It was, again, me being the problem child who didn't want to pull his weight in the company.

I went from being full partner in the website to feeling like an inept towel boy. In essence, he gaslit me. Shake-and-Bake would also do things like sending self-help books entitled *What Got You Here Won't Get You There*. He even had lackeys. One in particular was his absolute snobbish nitwit of an accountant talking down to me. There was never any penalty for disrespect. I was no one. Shake-and-Bake would tell me how irrelevant I had become on a daily basis, and that no one cares what I had to say. I was broken and totally beaten down.

When you have someone telling you that you suck every single day you start to believe it.

Well, I listened to this man tell me how much I sucked for a year straight. The one person who I depended on and loved, whose back I ALWAYS had—my ride or die—Condit was totally on his side because Shake-and-Bake would praise him incessantly, giving him the validation he so hungered for. It didn't matter if it was genuine. Condit just couldn't see it. I even said to him one time, "Jon, I really feel like you don't have my back anymore."

His response? "I have the company's back."

Things were about to get worse for me. A LOT worse.

Under Epic Picture Group I was assigned the task of picking the first movies to be released under *Dread Central*'s home video label. This made complete and perfect sense. I sifted through an endless amount of movies made by folks who probably shouldn't be making movies. In short, just because you can give someone sauce, cheese, and dough doesn't mean that they can make you a delicious pizza, know what I mean? I ended up picking two movies, one that was submitted (the Kane Hodder documentary *To Hell and Back*) and another that was poised to set the horror world on fire.

In 2016, Rob Zombie released a movie called *31*. A quote of mine from my review was used on the film's artwork. This brings me to Damien Leone. Damien is a ridiculously talented filmmaker whose unwillingness to compromise his vision reminded me a lot of the likes of George A. Romero. That's a high compliment and I do NOT give it lightly.

Damien had seen my quote on the cover of *31* and immediately shot me an email. He told me he had made a feature version of one of his shorts, *Terrifier*, which had appeared in collection of short films, the 2013 anthology film, *All Hallows' Eve*. Even though I was inundated with shit to watch, I had remembered and loved the character of Art the Clown, so I told him that I'd watch it and give him a quote. This story has been confirmed by Damien a bunch of times in interviews. Keep that in mind because it will come into play later.

I watched 2016's *Terrifier*, and by the time it had ended I was blown away. I then watched it several more times until I was positive that it was every bit as good as I had thought that it was. Once satisfied, I called Damien back.

"Dude, what are you doing with this?" I asked.

"Nothing. I'm having a really hard time getting it out there." he replied.

He was having lots of difficulty selling the movie. The folks he had been speaking to had wanted him to—among other things—edit the film, etc. He and his team were on the cusp of self-distribution.

I said to him, "Please don't do ANYTHING else with it until you hear from me," and hung up the phone.

This was it. This was the title I was looking for. *Terrifier* represented, in a nutshell, everything that I was looking for to kick off the *Dread Central* label. I called Shake-and-Bake and told him the great news. I had found the movie we needed, and distribution rights were STILL available. There was just one problem...

Everyone else at Epic hated it.

Because things like *Stephen King's It* were a fan-beloved box office darling, I was told stuff like, "The world already has a killer clown movie," and I fought back immediately. This was something altogether different. I was NOT about to take "no" for an answer. Eventually, and probably to just shut me the fuck up, they relented and acquired the film for release.

In Shake-and-Bake's eyes, I HAD to be wrong. There's no way

that I could possibly know what I'm talking about. After the film's acquisition, which he deemed "one of the stupidest acquisitions he had ever made," I was removed from my duties of picking movies for the *Dread Central* label. Now, that job was to go to Robert Galluzzo. To make matters worse, my voice was all but completely silenced on *Dread Central* as Shake-and-Bake brought in Jonathan Barkan to take over my everyday duties "to free up my time to do other things." After all, "I was an executive," and I had to start behaving as such. You know, by doing things like attending masturbatory weekly meetings where everything I said was overridden, and forced to sell ads.

These meetings were fucking ridiculous. During them everyone would pat themselves on the back for coming up with ideas that would never be implemented, so in essence they were pointless. I would, pardon the pun, dread these things. Then a godsend happened. I had a horrible flood in my house. In the flood I ended up losing about 2k dollars' worth of stuff. Irreplaceable stuff. That hurt, but ya know what? Being that construction had to begin in my house, I was no longer required to be at the meetings as there was too much noise on my end and I couldn't hear them.

In all honesty the repairs only took a week or so, but fuck that! These people, Condit included, were doing nothing but looking down their noses at me and telling me how much I sucked. I dragged the construction stint out for a month. How you ask? Simple— YouTube! I would get on my computer, head to YouTube, find a construction video and play its volume at full blast the duration of the call until they pretty much either begged me to leave or understood that I couldn't hear them anyway and I left on my own accord. FUCK 'EM! This was a small victory. One that they would make me pay for.

Things just got worse and worse. I was being mentally battered every day. Shake-and-Bake was doing this to force me out, but I would not go. I wouldn't give them satisfaction. I don't think Patrick had any idea what was going on. I hold no ill-will toward him, but Shake-and-Bake? He could have stepped on a landmine in front of me and I would have done the Cabbage Patch dance with his charred

A Comedy of Tragedies

and smoking entrails. Happily. As a matter of fact, I still would. Have I written "fuck him" yet? Okay, just making sure. Oh, and while I'm at it… suck my dick.

I remember once we were gearing up to cover the South by Southwest film festival. Shake-and-Bake wanted *Dread Central* to have a HUGE media presence there. When asked my opinion I said, "That's a waste of money. People only care about one thing when it comes to film festivals… reading the reviews." Of course, I was "wrong" and was "just being difficult to work with as always." Shake-and-Bake's proposed coverage was gonna cost a few thousand dollars between the tent and the video coverage he had wanted Condit and Barkan to man. Whatever. I mean, why listen to me? I've only been doing this for eighteen years. What could I possibly know?

During this time, I was tasked to update the site while the rest of the "team" was at South By. It felt so good. I was finally updating the site like I normally would. That lasted an hour. Shake-and-Bake called me and instructed me that he only wanted me to write about what *Dread Central* was covering and doing at the festival. I answered, "But that's not news. What about the other stuff that's happening? We're a news site. People should be able to get the news from us when it happens."

His answer? "Bank the news."

How fuckin' ludicrous was that? "Bank the news?" For what? Later? I told him, "You can't bank the news. News is no longer news once it is covered by every other website in existence. And just why do you think all the other sites are covering it? BECAUSE IT'S NEWS!"

Then this nitwit tells me, "You know, Steve, I'm a producer. I know a thing or two about making and delivering successful content."

To which I replied, "Okay, so tell me what you know about running a website?" Silence. He hung up the phone. I was flabbergasted. Fuckin' gobsmacked. Then I noticed it… He had Condit take down all of the work I had done that day and replaced it with various videos that were uploaded to the *Dread Central* YouTube page. These videos are still there. Just search *"Dread Central SXSW."* In the years since this coverage ran on YouTube and the *Dread Central* homepage only two of the several videos from South by Southwest have cracked a 1000 views. Again, what do I know?

Morons.

After tons more arguing, it came time to release *Terrifier* to the masses. How'd that happen? Well, Galluzzo hated the movie too, stating that, "It's the worst thing I've ever seen." He was even going around and posting on other websites shit like, "Hey, don't blame me when you see how awful this movie is. It's honestly horrible. I would never have picked it." When I saw that I called him.

"Rob, I don't care that you don't like this movie, but it's not your job to like it. It's your job to promote it to the best of your ability." Of course, he didn't, but I can't really blame him for that, as he had Shake-and-Bake watching every move that he made. I was getting all sorts of static about *Terrifier*. Shake-And-Bake would constantly needle me about it. He would say things like, "In order to release it we have to edit out some of the more troublesome parts of it."

My answer was ALWAYS the same - "If you edit a single frame of *Terrifier* it's no longer *Terrifier*. It's one of a thousand movies. What makes this movie good is its edge. Its shock value. Its balls! That's what will make it successful." Then they wanted to retitle the film to *#Terrifier* so that at least it would be before the letter "A" at Redbox. Then he'd press me about Damien and his production partner Phil Falcone regarding some other stupid shit, which eventually led to the first and only time Damien and I ever shouted at each other. We weren't shouting out of anger though. It was just sheer frustration on both of our parts. It felt like he and I were the only ones who saw the potential in this movie, and at that time we probably were.

Things got so bad and heated with Epic that at one point in one of our meetings I said to everyone in attendance, "If *Terrifier* does NOT perform EXACTLY as I think that it's going to, I will resign, and you can have my part of the company."

I put everything I had, all eighteen years of my work, on the line for that movie. NO ONE CAN EVER DENY THAT. Shake-and-Bake, of course, took me up on my offer. After all, this was probably the only sure-fire and most painless way to get rid of me.

The film premiered to pretty much zero visibility in a handful of theaters with barely any promotion, even on *Dread Central*'s own website. How the fuck could there not be *Terrifier* ads on *Dread Central*? It truly boggled my mind. Again, I was heartbroken.

"I was wrong. I sucked. They told me so." In short, the movie was dumped.

However, what they DID do right was get the movie on Netflix. It wasn't long before fans began to find it and embrace it. Murals of Art the Clown were popping up all over the world. Sales were through the roof for Epic. It became one of their best all-time sellers, if not THE BEST. More on that later.

I remember one time I was at the Texas Frightmare Weekend event a couple of months after *Terrifier*'s release. Everywhere I looked I saw *Terrifier* T-shirts and various bits of merch. I called Damien and asked, "Dude, do we have merch?"

He said, "Fuck, no," with a laugh.

"Then I think we have something here," I answered. "We really fucking have something." The fans, man! Words alone cannot describe how much I love and appreciate you all. You guys were making your own homemade *Terrifier* merch. That totally blew our minds. This was my validation, and it felt SO fuckin' good.

A couple of months later, it came to my attention that Shake-and-Bake and his lackeys engaged in some activity in my name that I did NOT approve of. I had had enough. I called Condit, who was complicit in all of this, and told him, "Tomorrow morning we're driving up to Epic's offices." It was a long ride. I didn't say a word to him. I got there and immediately Shake-and-Bake tried hugging me.

"Whoah," I said putting out my hand. "Are you kidding me? I'm not hugging you!"

I went into the meeting. Everyone was there. Shake-and-Bake, Condit, Shake-and-Bake's lackeys, and Patrick, who to this very day is the ONLY ONE who said "Thank you for bringing us *Terrifier*. You really know the fanbase, and it's appreciated."

I sat down. "Before I begin, I'd like to give everyone here a chance to get out whatever is on their minds. I want to listen. I want to hear it." I knew what was going to be said, and more importantly, I knew it was bullshit. Patrick said nothing as I honestly believe that he had zero idea how far out of control things had gotten. When Shake-And-Bake was done with his drivel I asked, "Is that it? Good." I stood up and said, "[Shake-and-Bake] you like to think that you're the smartest person in the room. Well, you need to understand something... that depends on who the fuck you are in the room with." I looked around. "I may not be book smart. Hell, I'm a high school dropout with a GED, but you had better believe when it comes to street smarts, I am the smartest motherfucker in this or any room. As such I know when I'm getting fucked, and you [Shake-and-Bake] are fucking me. And you..." pointing to Condit "let it all happen. You, more than anyone, should be ashamed of yourself." Back to Shake-and-Bake, "You are nothing more than your average fucking used car salesman and a complete and total fucking asshole." He took every word silently. I then let them know it was my intention to resign and have nothing more to do with the company. This was one of the hardest things that I've ever had to do, and I did so with furious tears in my eyes.

For legal reasons I cannot give you all the details of departure from *Dread Central*, but I assure you that for every one reason I can give you, there are 10,000 more I cannot. One major reason was that they never gave me the credit I deserved, even though they had no problem using my name to "take credit." Funnily enough, Shake-And-Bake was let go by Epic just a short-while after my departure. I do not know the reasons for this, and I can only speculate. They coasted on what I had built for quite some time, even though they were hemorrhaging readers.

All I can do is shake my head. I don't go to *Dread Central* anymore. To be honest it still very much hurts seeing what they've done with my baby. The last time I was there, I couldn't even figure out how to navigate the site. I now get my horror news from *Bloody Disgusting*. You should too. There's a reason why they have always been #1. I'm just happy and grateful I could compete to the point in which *Dread Central* became #2.

As for Condit... When Debi and I first moved to San Diego from Florida, within a month the entire state of California was on fire. The fires were just a couple of miles from our place. Jon's mom, Beverly, whom I will ALWAYS love dearly, took in me, Debi, and our five(!) cats, while we waited to see if everything we had just brought there from the other side of the country, would be lost in the fires.

Beverly did not have to take us in at all. I mention this because her act of selfless kindness had become very pivotal at the end of my relationship with her son. Beverly Condit passed away due to complications from a stroke in 2014, long before all of the shit with Epic went down. One of the last things I said to Condit after all of the betrayal and hurt was this—"You know, Jon, if I ever went public with the EXACT reason (which will remain unnamed) why I left *Dread Central*, the court of public opinion would burn down the site immediately, and you along with it. The only reason I'm not going to do that is because of your mother. Her act of kindness is the only reason you will have whatever you have in life. You had better thank her. Every night. My act of reciprocal kindness to her will be to 'not be the reason why her son is left with nothing.'" I've spoken to Jon a few times since then. I wish him well.

I built *Dread Central* to be a place where I and others who were labeled "freaks" by society would have some place to belong, and it was taken away from me. As you can see from reading this very book, everything I've ever had that I loved and cared about was ripped violently out of my life. Still, this is not a "woe is me" portion of this tale. Wonderful things had come from *Dread Central*. Things I will ALWAYS be grateful for, and NO ONE can take these memories away. Besides, I unwittingly had a huge hand in bringing the world what the fans would come to call the next great horror icon. How many people can say that? *Terrifier* would become my swan song from *Dread Central*, and you know what? I wouldn't have it any other way.

Mic fucking drop.

Chapter 18
The War on Common Sense and Curses from Beyond

Dread Central was over for me. Now what? Being Uncle Creepy was the only thing I knew. The only thing I was good at. Everything in my life was at an end of sorts. I spent eighteen years adhering to the same old routine, and now there was no reason to wake up in the morning. To say that I was depressed at this point in my life is an understatement.

Even the moniker of Uncle Creepy was beginning to give me a headache of sorts. No, not because of the aforementioned connotations that had come along with the name. In truth the name Uncle Creepy has brought me nothing but goodness and joy. Except this one time.

On Twitter (or X or whatever the fuck it's called by the time that you read this... you know, where intelligent conversation goes to die? Yeah that! Anyway...) I started getting messages to @UncleCreepy from some woman talking to me about being her husband. At first, I played along, because, well, I still enjoy being a bit of a dick at times, but she was getting a bit carried away. I finally said, "Lady, I'm sorry to tell you this but I'm not your husband. Sorry! You are messaging the wrong account."

She flipped the fuck out, man. As it turns out she was mistakenly writing me thinking that I was her husband, Ian "Uncle Creepy" McCall. Who the fuck is that you ask? Some Mixed Martial Arts fighter who got the name from his niece. She demanded that I surrender the name and the account immediately, because her husband was a renowned sports figure. Me? I don't watch sports, or sports ball, or anything like it. I only watch scripted sports like WWE. I never heard of this cat, and there's no way that I would have. I told her no and to get the fuck outta here. Of course, her hubby joined in on the kerfuffle and now I was in a full-blown Twitter war with an MMA fighter over the name Uncle Creepy of all things.

Only. Fucking. Me.

Of course, I told him "no" and to do something along the lines of "swing from my nuts like a happy monkey."

Things may have been bad, but I've always kept my sense of humor.

Eventually the excitement died down and he went away. I've no clue if he's still fighting. I would like to thank him for this impromptu but very welcome distraction from my dilemma. Even though I'm much bigger than him, he's a fucking MMA fighter and I'm an untrained street dude who would most likely be twisted into some kind of large fleshy pretzel by a professional athlete. With that now over with, I was left to face the music and the song I was dancing to was cleverly entitled, "You're a Nervous Wreck and Spiraling Out of Control."

During the *Dread Central* debacle, I had ballooned up to 367 pounds. I'm a stress eater and holy fuck, was I stressed. I looked in the mirror one day when I was at my fattest and didn't even recognize me. I had these huge dark circles around my eyes. Even my fuckin' lips were fat. It was horrendous. It was sad. I began to cry. It had dawned on me that I was eating myself to death. Because of my father's alcoholism, I had stayed away from drinking and hard drugs. I never wanna find out how much of his recessive addiction gene I have. But while I was avoiding those addictions, I had ended up picking up a new one: eating. I was completely addicted to food. I wasn't eating because I was hungry. It was literally like me getting my fix. There was no doubt about it. I was dying. Holy shit, my pallbearers would have hated me. That fuckin' casket would have weighed at least five-hundred pounds.

Now, I didn't know at this point just what I had to live for, but I didn't want to die. I couldn't. Well, that would let Dave down. I firmly believed that since he didn't get to live out his best life because of some piece of shit in the Middle East whose death I celebrate mentally every second of every day, I had to live mine. Letting him down is something I swore that I wouldn't do. So, I decided to take action and launch what would become the #WarOnGirth.

I had tried every single diet you could imagine. None of it worked. Listen, I'm Italian. If your diet says I can't eat pizza, then fuck it, I'm out. So, I decided to start slowly by counting calories. I downloaded a free app on my phone called My Fitness Pal and got a Fitbit. I was so fucking fat that I would be completely exhausted just walking from the couch to the bathroom. My waist size was 56. I was walking around with the weight of a whole other person on my frame. It was insanity.

How My Fitness Pal works is simple—you put in your age, your height, and your weight. From there you put in how much you want to lose and how quickly that you want to lose it. The app then calculates how many calories per day you need to stay within to get the job done. The only thing I had to do was log every bit of food I ate from their database, which consisted of every food and restaurant menu you could think of, and it would count the calories that I had consumed thereby allowing me to keep track. In theory and practice, this allowed me to eat pizza while dieting! Ha-fuckin-zah!

Once I had the calories thing down, I decided to hold myself publicly accountable by posting weekly progress reports on my social media platforms. I was gonna do this. I had to change. I had to live. After dropping a few pounds, I decided that I had to start exercising. The Fitbit connected to My Fitness Pal, and it would deduct all the calories I had burned off from my daily caloric intake. I didn't even have to do that math!

I don't think that I have mentioned this before, but I have a severe case of artithmophobia. There's something about numbers that makes my brain short circuit. The frustration of this has literally brought me to tears several times, and I'm not ashamed to say that. The fact that, combined, these two devices would do that numbers part of the #WarOnGirth was and is FUCKING GLORIOUS!

When it comes to exercise, I fucking HATE it. I have an aversion to it. Nothing about it brings me joy. Besides that, I could barely even move without huffing and puffing. I decided to start walking. First it was a block. Then two. Then three. Then a mile. Then two miles. At the height of my #WarOnGirth I was walking about ten miles per day or more. My calorie allotment was 2,200 per day, but I decided to stay at around fifteen-hundred per day. That may sound drastic, but these were drastic times. I did this every day for about a year and a half. Through dedication and hard work, I dropped 167lbs and was a size 36 waist while eating my two favorite things: pizza and Chinese food.

I looked great... in clothes anyway. What was going on under my clothes was NOT okay, but my dick looked SO much bigger. It was like, "Hello, old friend!" I had cock real estate to spare.

Oh, what a time to be alive, and alive I am. As of this writing I have gained back about thirty or so pounds, but I'm bound and determined to get back into what I consider to be fighting shape. More importantly, I know how to do it, because I know what works for me. Make no mistake, I will get it done. Everyone kept asking me, "What's your secret?" It's so painfully simple... eat and move. Eat only when you're hungry but don't deny yourself your cravings. Just be reasonable about them. That's really it. That being said... I am NOT saying ANYONE should do what I did, the way that I did it. I'm a lunatic. It probably wasn't the healthiest or safest way to lose weight. This is just a classic example of me being me, and how I chose to do things.

I probably could have easily kept the weight off too, but little did I know that a global pandemic was on its way that would force me to mainly stay in the house.

During this time, I would bring stuff to neighbors in my area who couldn't and shouldn't leave the house whenever I could. Any excuse to get my steps in, but still. I was basically sitting on my ass again like the rest of the world. I'll get more into that next.

Also, during this time, with *Dread Central* now in my rearview mirror, I launched a new site and podcast called *Brainwaves Horror and Paranormal Talk Radio*. Knetter and I would host the show every Wednesday, with Jonathan Barkan doing the Horror News, and Justin Julian, a.k.a. Mr. Dark, doing the Paranormal News. The first hour of the podcast/internet radio show would be the news, and the second hour was gonna be the special guest interviews. Everyone, from horror luminaries to ghost hunters, to people who had experienced genuine hauntings, were guests. *Brainwaves: Horror and Paranormal* is currently available on Spotify. Truthfully speaking, I have zero idea how it got there because I didn't upload any of the episodes. I think it was either my show's then producer, the extremely talented Amy Martin, or it was the work of two genuine heroes I have the pleasure of knowing, David and Tiffany Hahn.

Doing the show was a blast. During it, one of the bright spots became Mr. Dark's segments. However, it wasn't just because of him. His wife Jennifer would constantly chime in and bust his chops while we were on the air. Some of that banter would go on to become one of the highlights of every episode. There was no one like Jenn. She was the best. She was also kind of spooky. Let me explain.

> NOTE: As you may have been able to guess by now, I've lived a really weird life. It was about to both get weirder and even start to make sense. I swear to you, as unlikely as this sounds, none of the following is in ANY WAY made-up and to the best of my memory is all 100 percent accurate.

It was 1:35 a.m. when the phone rang. Nothing good ever comes from phone calls in the middle of the night, but this? This was VERY unexpected. I answered because I was—of course—still awake and have never adhered to what could be considered a "normal" sleep schedule. I answered.

"Steve?"

"Jenn?"

"Yeah."

"What's up is everything okay? Are you okay? Is Justin okay?"

This was extremely unusual, and I felt the pit of my stomach drop, and drop hard.

"Everyone's fine," she said, "But I have to talk to you." After a long pause she said, "I don't usually tell anyone this, because I don't want anyone to think that I'm crazy, but... I am a sensitive. I see things."

I was absolutely perplexed and a little more than unnerved. Was she telling me that she was a psychic medium? A clairvoyant? I had no clue, and truthfully if this was ANY other friend calling me and saying this stuff, I would have told them to go scratch their ass. However, Jenn was a solid person. Bullshitting was not in her. It honestly just wasn't.

"I have to ask you a few questions, okay?"

"Sure," I replied.

"Okay. Good. Your mom. Did she speak Italian?" What. The. Fuck.

"Yes. She did," I answered. "That's a bizarre question to ask someone at nearly 2 in the morning. Why?"

"I'm sorry it's so late. I mean, I know it's okay because you're up anyway, but still. So, when you were young... Um... did you do something you weren't supposed to do? Like take part in some kind of ceremony?"

"Jenn," I said, "the only thing that I can think of even remotely like that was when my friends and I fucked around with a Ouija board in the school yard right before my mom died."

It should be noted that I had never told Jenn, or ANYONE for that matter, this story. The only folks who knew it were there. This memoir is actually the first time I've ever written about it, and I rarely speak of it publicly.

"That's it! That has to be it," she said excitedly with a genuine "I KNEW IT" kind of tone. "That wasn't a normal Ouija game, was it?

Like, you did it differently? Was it a special board? A homemade one? Or did, like, someone make you use it differently?"

What. The. Fuck. Times Two.

There was absolutely positively no way at all that she could have known that. I was utterly dumbfounded.

"Jenn," I asked cautiously, "what are you saying?"

"That night... the way it was done... you woke up *something*. Something is very unhappy with you. In fact, it's pretty pissed off. It's been following you around ever since. It makes bad things happen to you. It wants you to suffer for disturbing it. Your aura. I can see it. It's black and reddish and there's all sorts of things pulling on it. I think it's whatever you woke up."

"Are you saying I'm cursed?" I asked, half-joking.

Her reply was a stone cold sober, "Yes."

What. The. Fuck. Times Infinity.

"Now, listen to me carefully," she said sternly. "This thing, whatever it is, it doesn't want to be around you as much as you don't want to be around it. But it cannot leave. It has to be put to rest somehow. I don't even know how or why I know that, but I just do."

I was completely confused. "But what does this have to do with my mom and her speaking Italian?" What Jenn said next chilled me to the bone.

"Every night for the last several nights I keep having this weird dream," she said. "It's this Italian woman. She's not old. Maybe middle-aged." (My mom died in her fifties.) "She is crying and praying over you. I see you, and she's over your shoulder. I don't really understand what she's saying, but it's something like 'por favor, owitta my feelio,' or something like that. It's hard to say, and that's probably wrong. I just know that it sounds Italian. This woman... It has to be your mom. Something is definitely wrong and she's crying for you. She seems so desperate. That's why I said to hell with it. I had to call and tell you... even if you think I'm nuts."

I didn't think she was nuts. Anyone else, TOTALLY NUTS, but not Jenn. I didn't know what to say. Finding out that you've been cursed nearly your whole life isn't something that's easily processable. That only thing I could say was a timid, "What do I do?"

"Well, I don't know," she said with a laugh. "I just know that this isn't something that I can help you with beyond warning you." She paused. I was absolutely silent. "You know a lot of people. Is there someone who works in these areas that you think that you can trust?"

I've done a LOT of paranormal investigating in my time. More than most. That's right... at this point I was a *bona fide* forty-something-year-old male who ran around in the dark looking for ghosts. Because, you know, I'm an adult and stuff. I know a lot of the greats. I was trained by Lou Gentile, who taught me a very important lesson. "Steve," he said, "You can have all the gadgets in the world helping you find these things, but your best piece of equipment will always be your body." Lou was right. Dead right. More on that later. Back to this story.

The first thought that came into my mind was to call Zak Bagans from *Ghost Adventures*. Zak is a good friend, and we get along famously. Mainly because I don't ask him about paranormal stuff, and he doesn't ask me about horror movies. Win/win. I consider Zak to be the real deal as he is VERY GOOD at what he does. Some may balk at that, and some may even think him an actor of sorts, but what you see on TV is a persona. Zak takes the paranormal world very seriously and is actually a very thoughtful and sweet dude who will literally give the shirt off his back to help someone. That's the Zak that I know and trust. Still, I didn't think he would be the right fit to help me. My mindset was this... I need extreme help and I needed it fast.

I'm lucky to have people who I can call that deal with these kinds of things, and for this particular situation, I knew that the best person to ask advice from would be Amy Allan, former host of *The Dead Files*. Via her show, Amy's job was to get help for people who were in ridiculously bad paranormal situations. My problem more than fit that bill. I called her and explained what was going on. I gave her no in-depth details, just the five-hundred-foot perspective. She gave me the phone number of a curandero. What's that you ask? GOOD QUESTION!

A *curandero*—or as was the case here—*curandera* if female, is a traditional healer or shaman in many Latin American and Hispanic cultures. Since the impetus for this would-be-curse debacle was that chubby Latin guy, Neal who was into Santeria, Amy figured that this was exactly the type of person whom I needed to go to for help. Curanderos are believed to possess spiritual and medicinal knowledge passed down through generations, and they often play a significant role in the healthcare and spiritual well-being of their communities. My spiritual well-being had apparently been under attack for decades and I was desperate to get rid of this thing, if indeed it was there. Like I said earlier, I am a skeptic, but I'll certainly hedge my bets if it can help my situation. Everything Jenn had told me had me shook and shook well. I called the *curandera*, who will remain nameless. As soon as she answered her phone I was ready to tell my story, guns blazing. However, I wouldn't get a chance to do that. As soon as I started introducing myself, she cut me off. "I was expecting your call," she said. "You were referred to me by Amy, yes?" she asked.

"Yeah," I replied. "You see what happened was..."

She interrupted again. "No, no, no," she said.

"I don't want you to tell me a single thing. Now that we've spoken, what I need to do is get in touch with my spiritual guides. They will tell me the rest. I have your phone number now. I will call you back in a few days."

With that she hung up the phone and I was left there, kinda slack-jawed.

Days passed like weeks. About four days later I received my call back at around two o'clock in the afternoon.

"Stephen," she said. "I'm ready to speak now." And, boy, did she lay it on me. She was telling me things that there's no way she could have known. Take that for what it's worth. I didn't tell Amy about anything in-depth at all, and the *curandera* certainly didn't know

Jenn. None of this was online anywhere, and I have never spoken about it.

"This person who you did the ritual with," she said.

"Neal," I answered. "He suggested we do a Ouija board session. I thought it was for fun."

"These things are NEVER for fun," she said, somewhat admonishing me for my ignorance. "There's intent behind them. You're opening a line of communication with the other side, and you do NOT know who or what is going to answer you. It's rarely who you're expecting to speak with. Your friend was young and didn't know what he was doing beyond his minimal knowledge. I believe what he was trying to do was bank your soul and the souls of everyone there."

"What?!?" was the only thing that I could think of to say. "Bank souls? What does that even mean?"

She went on to explain, "This person... I believe that they had a mal intent. He was exposing you and your friends to a ritual so that he could take a little of each of your souls away to be kept for whomever he is serving. He was creating a soul bank, so that when he passes over, he'd be treated well and held in reverence for amassing a high number of souls for his master."

Now, let me be clear... I did NOT have any idea just what to expect from this phone call and situation, but this is SO far out of the realm of anything that I could have even unexpectedly heard or have been told it's not even funny. I mean, I thought Shake-and-Bake was a fuckin' bastard for stupidly saying I should "bank the news," but fuckin' Neal... this was some next level fuckery!

"Now you can tell me everything that happened." And so, I did. Every word of it, down to the last syllable. It felt like removing three tons off my shoulders. She took it all in, but then I paused for nearly a minute. There was nothing but silence.

"Why did you stop? Is that everything," she asked.

I was uneasy and she was reading me like a book. My darkest fear was coming to be realized, and I was about to say it out loud for the first and only time in my life. My heart was beating seven thousand miles an hour. I said the only thing I didn't ever want to say out loud and held my breath while waiting for the answer.

"Did I cause my mother's death?"

"No," she said. "Your mother's death had nothing to do with this. This was a totally different."

"But what about the thing Neal said he saw in my house? The one that wouldn't go away until it got something from me?" I asked. I had to ask. I had to be sure.

"He was scared of it. Maybe it was giving him its disapproval."

I began to not just cry, but sob.

"It's okay," she said. "But now you have work to do. This has been going on too long. This spirit that's with you... it wants so badly to go back to sleep, but it cannot so long as it's attached to you."

She told me that I needed to take an egg and put it in a container with water and a little lemon juice. From there I was to take the container and put it under my bed where I sleep, directly under my head. It was to remain there for no longer than one week. After the week had passed, I was to recite a prayer of sorts she had given me over a candle. Once that was done, I was to take the egg and bury it in the soil by my home. While I was burying it, I was to apologize for disturbing this spirit's sleep and it would finally, again, be at rest. I followed her instructions to the letter. I then smudged my house with sage.

Did I feel any different? I did. I felt... I dunno... lighter? I called Jenn and told her everything that happened. She was a little miffed that I engaged in a ritual without telling her, but it seemed okay. She said she'd call me in a couple of days, which she did.

"I can see your aura now," she told me upon calling. "It's beautiful. It's bright, whatever was there is gone." Holy shit what a relief.

Needless to say, I'll never touch a Ouija board ever again. Maybe there's something to it and maybe there's not. One thing is certain though... I do not want to find out. One thing was still nagging me. That thing Jenn said that my mother was saying during her dream, *"por favor, owitta my feelio."* Well, I Googled it. It is Italian, and Jenn had poorly translated it because she didn't speak the language. The actual words are *"Per favore, aiuta mio figlio,"* which translates from Italian to English as, "Please help my son." If that doesn't send a chill down your spine, I don't know what will.

Jennifer Julian passed away in a hospital a year later. I'll keep the details of her passing to myself as a means of respecting her and Justin's privacy. I miss you Jenn. Thank you. A million times thank you.

Things began really turning around for me. It seemed as if the curse, if there was one, was broken. Little did I know, however, that the globe itself was about to be cursed in a far more frightening way.

This brings us to the obligatory...

Chapter 19
Chapter COVID 19

Watch TV, play *Animal Crossing*, Eat, watch TV, play *Animal Crossing*, eat, watch TV, play *Animal*

Crossing, eat, watch TV, play *Animal Crossing*, eat, watch TV, play *Animal Crossing*, eat, watch TV, play *Animal Crossing*, eat, watch TV, play *Animal Crossing*, eat, watch TV, play *Animal Crossing*, eat, watch TV, play *Animal Crossing*, eat, watch TV, play *Animal Crossing*, eat, watch TV, play *Animal Crossing*, eat, watch TV, play *Animal Crossing*, eat, watch TV, play *Animal Crossing*, eat, watch TV, play *Animal Crossing*, eat, watch TV, play *Animal Crossing*, eat, watch TV, play *Animal Crossing*, eat, watch TV, play *Animal Crossing*, eat, watch TV, play *Animal Crossing*, eat.

Get the picture? Good. That was pretty much the majority of my year. It was during this time that my twenty-year relationship with Debi hit the rocks. If nothing got resolved after being locked in a house with her for a year, nothing was gonna get resolved. This was also the time when Danielle and I started talking. It wasn't a romantic thing. That didn't come until MUCH later. We were both in relationships that had gone sour, and each of us was at our wit's end. We became kind of like each other's psychiatrists. COVID-19 hit us both hard.

Out of respect for Debi, who is an awesome person, whom I loved dearly, and will always love in some capacity, I'm not going into details. You'd only be getting one side of the story, and that's just not fair to her. Know this—which I fully admit—I walked out of our relationship the way that a coward would. I'm ashamed to say that to a certain degree, but I am also certain that it was the only way for it to be final. Not just for me, but for both of us. I still feel a certain degree of guilt over it, and I probably always will. She didn't deserve the way that I left in the slightest. However, I more than had my reasons for doing what I did. You never truly know what goes on behind closed doors, and frankly that's none of your business either. We were both to blame for it. I've learned to make peace with that. Debi is one of the strongest people I know. If anyone would rebound in a positive way, it would be her. She's that smart, and that good of a person.

In any event, I basically threw a hand grenade on my life, and it was time for me to leave the West Coast and do something that I swore that I would NEVER do…go back home.

Chapter 20
Part V - A New Beginning

"Dani. I need pizza."

Having been away from New York for over 20 years, that was the first thing I had texted Danielle before getting on the plane. It was long overdue. Fresh, hot, East Coast pizza was on the horizon. It was impossible not to salivate just thinking about it. Couple that with the stress of the last few days, and the fact that I hadn't eaten ANYTHING that morning, and I was ravenous. The five-hour flight to Philadelphia seemed endless. With me, I had enough clothes for two weeks and all of my video game systems. That was it. The rest of my stuff was to arrive in two weeks. No furniture, mind you, just my insane amount of collectibles and the rest of my clothing.

I was nervous as fuck. My mind was all over the place. Even though we had always kept in touch, I hadn't seen Dani in over a decade. In that time she had several children, and I had—well—everything you just read about, along with my aforementioned clothes, video game systems, and enough mental baggage to overflow several planes, a small village in Guam, and at least two shoeboxes. Maybe three. The flight landed and there she was... She was gorgeous. I could literally smell her from several feet away. It WAS gonna be exactly what I had dreamed of... a hot, cheesy slice of pizza that was fresh outta the oven. I ate this slice like an award-winning porn star... I cupped the crust, felated the folded shaft, and it slid down my throat. It was so good that I got up and hugged the server.

As for Dani, she informed me later that she was pacing back and forth like a caged animal, nervous as hell, and not knowing what to expect. Life with me, though? It's impossible to pinpoint what to expect. There's always some strange adventure around the corner. Sometimes it's a good one, and other times, not so much.

The wait for the movers to bring me my stuff from the West Coast was nerve-racking. I had countless things, massive collectibles, the remainder of my clothing, and personal items that were absolutely irreplaceable, such as things from both George and Sid. My whole life was on a moving truck.

The two weeks passed, and it hadn't arrived. The weeks turned into months. My calls to the movers were falling mainly on deaf ears.

Finally, after wearing the same fourteen outfits for nearly two months, my stuff got here. The movers, cocksuckers that they were, went on to charge me another $200 to actually bring the stuff from the street to my front door and into my basement. They were more than happy to unload at the curb if I didn't want to pay up. At this time, what was I gonna do? I had to pay their convenience fee, and they knew it. I didn't have much, and all-in-all it had taken them less than twenty-five minutes to move all my stuff into the house.

I was about to begin unpacking when I realized that they had given me someone else's 55" flatscreen TV. Like I said, I didn't bring any furniture with me. This TV definitely wasn't mine. I ran outside to catch them; they were in the truck and about to pull away. "Wait," I yelled, and the driver rolled down his window. "You gave me someone else's TV." The driver looked at me and said, I shit you not, "So? Keep it!" and he drove away.

What the actual fuck?! If they were so careless and flippant with whoever's TV this was, this did not bode well for my stuff. Nope. Not at all. Little did I know the extent of the shittiness that was on the horizon.

Within minutes I realized that the movers had literally smashed nearly everything that I owned. Part of what I paid them for was to pack my stuff into boxes and then move it across the country. They packed my stuff all right... in the most careless way possible. They even went so far as to use my clothing as packing material. Looking back at this day makes me physically ill. They had, to the best of my knowledge, wrecked over $50k worth of my belongings including my clothing. I called them immediately, but it didn't take long for me to realize that I was screwed. Even worse, not only was I now dealing with the loss of my stuff, but I felt terrible about whoever this TV belonged to. Then I came across another box full of someone's family photos. Was the TV theirs? Was this stuff from two other families? My mind was swimming. I exhausted every avenue that I could think of to find these people. A friend of mine, Renee Maler, even hooked me up with a TV news program to spread a simple message: "Hey! I have your stuff! Let me give it back to you!"

I tried for six months. I spoke to reporters, churchgoers, you name it. Every other day I was posting some of the pictures of this family to my social media feeds in hopes that someone would recognize them. No stone was left unturned. In the end I came up empty, and finally had to resign myself to the fact that whoever these people were, they got screwed too. There was nothing that could be done about it.

Apparently moving companies do shit like this all the time, as no one regulates them, but I didn't have the money to hire one of the bigger moving companies. This was a chance I took, and I paid dearly for it. At this point I barely had any money in the bank and things were looking dire. Thankfully, another good friend of mine, Sue Procko, who I had worked with over the years, started a Go Fund Me. It raked in a few thousand dollars, and that helped me get back on my feet. I will always be grateful to Sue, and everyone who kicked in. I'll never forget that kindness. Ever.

Months passed and Dani and I had fallen in love. This was incredible, and also the perfect living example of Beauty and the Beast. I knew one thing about Danielle from the moment I met her: here was a girl that was TOTALLY out of my league. She's gorgeous from head-to-toe, and we both had the same exact same ridiculous sense of humor. She's tough, quick-witted, and hilarious. In other words, she's me—only way better looking with breasts and a vagina. Oh, and that butt. That glorious butt. Nom, nom, nom, nom.

Things continued to look up relationship-wise, but I was also scared shitless. Holy hell, did I have my work cut out for me, though. You see, Dani's family, like my ex's, were pretty well off. Her dad is a lawyer, her mom is someone you do NOT mess with, one of her brothers was an ex-Marine, and the other is a fucking archaeologist. The words, "You're not good enough for my daughter," had been ringing in my ears for a very long time, and now they were back EXTRA LOUD and CRYSTAL CLEAR.

There were SO many different nightmare scenarios running through my head, along with the usual circus of crap.

"Family, meet Steve. I know him mainly from online. Oh, and he's also better known to everyone as Uncle Creepy. He doesn't have what you would call stability in his professional life, nor does he have a normal job. He makes his money in the Horror industry. Don't worry though! You can totally trust him with me, and my daughter. What could go wrong?"

As it turns out... Nothing. Somebody pinch me! Dani's family not only gave me the benefit out of the doubt, but they welcomed me with cautious but open arms. I cannot even begin to convey to you what this continues to mean to me. As you can tell from these pages, my family life was vile at worst and unusual at best. This was a whole new world, and one that I was desperately yearning for without ever even knowing it.

BONUS: I now have enough "actual" family members to go on *Family Feud*. That may sound ridiculous to you, but to me it's the coolest thing EVER. Let me be frank about something. I'm not a kid person. When it came to Dani, it was like "add water, have a family." In total she had four children, Lexi, Estevan, Kaela, and Bridget. Kaela has since tragically passed on. When I came into the picture, Lexi had a family with kids of her own, Estevan was struggling with and searching for how he would fit into this world and has since become an excellent hard-working dad whom I am very proud of.

The only one still at home for a couple of more years was Bridget who was sixteen at the time of my arrival.

Guess what? I was now not only a stepdad, but also a stepgrandpa! Who the fuck would have ever of thought this would have happened. Not me, that's for sure. I said to B (which is what we call Bridget for short), "Listen, I don't know fuck all about being a stepfather. But I do know that I can be your friend." That was really all I could offer her. It took a while for us to click. I wasn't used to dealing with a teenaged personality, and she didn't understand that there's never any hidden meaning regarding what I would tell her. I'm as black-and-white as they come. I say what I mean, and I mean what I say. Once we found common ground, I grew to love her and treat her like she was my own. There are no lengths I would not go to for her or Dani. They spent the majority of their lives with men who, for one reason or another, proved to be... shall we say... irresponsible. I wanted to prove to both of them, and the rest of their family, that it didn't have to be that way. That I could be depended on, and if given a chance, I could do this. Guiding B as best as I could for a couple of years was a mostly wonderful experience, and one that I'm happy I got to have. As of this writing B's now a college student at the New School in Manhattan and living in New York City. As for my now-step-grand kids, they call me Uncle Grandpa and I love them dearly.

BONUS PART DEUX: I can give them back at the end of the day!

I'm a city boy. I don't do the woods. I like rural areas, but I've seen enough horror movies to know that this motherfucker does not go tramping around in forests. Before we got together, Danielle would tell me how much she loved camping and expressed to me that she really wanted to take me on a camping trip. I'm a diva. I need a place to poop and a shower in the morning. I made that clear to her. She agreed.

We decided to go camping. It was me, Dani, her Brother Jim, his wife Jenn, our friend (also named Jenn), her cousin Sarah, and the man who would become like a brother to me, Sarah's boyfriend Brian. They found a place with both bathrooms and showers, so I was in. During one of our planning phone calls, Brian said he was bringing a generator. I said, "Cool, I'll bring a blender." This was met with everyone in the fucking world laughing at me. I was like, what the fuck?

"Who brings a blender camping?" Dani asked laughingly during this ruckus.

"Dude," I explained. "It's summertime and if I'm going to be lost in the fucking woods somewhere, I wanna be shit-faced. I'm making strawberry margaritas!" Even more laughter. I stuck to my guns though, and let me tell you, when it was ninety-five fucking degrees outside NO ONE... NOT A SINGLE ONE of them was complaining about having a nice frosty blended margarita. They went like hot cakes.

Fucking. Hate. Camping.

The woods are weird man. Even weirder than I expected. Other than the random wildlife, it was a special kind of quiet. I remember wandering around a dirt path with Dani and shouting into the woods as loud as I could ... "TELL ME WHERE YOU ARE, JOSH!" several times just to hear it echo back to me. Hey, I'm a big *Blair Witch Project* fan. How could I not? What, you didn't like it? Fuck you, it's a good movie and this is my book. Friggin' movie snob.

Later that night, our friend Jenn (not Jim's wife) got a call from her pal, Kristen, who had come into a litter of abandoned baby raccoons during her day job as a pest control contractor who also does wildlife rehab. Kristen was home but wanted to come meet Jenn and her pals in the woods.

"Can I bring the baby raccoons?" she asked.

You're damned right. We said "yes" immediately. I love animals. I love animals more than people. They're literally like little angels brought to keep us company in this godforsaken world. They love you unconditionally no matter what kind of an asshole you were acting like. The prospect of playing with and feeding baby raccoons made my heart sing.

These things were impossibly cute and made the most adorable noises. I reveled in every lovely second of this moment. This wasn't an evil possum or giant fucking manhunting spider. This was a moment I could only have dreamed of. I didn't want to let them go, but hey. All good things come to an end.

This little visitor made camping a much more fun experience.

Why am I telling this story? Is it interesting? Funny?
Consequential? I don't think so.
However...
Months later Dani and I were watching a game show called *America Says*. On it, they give you a subject and you have to come up with one of the several answers relating to the subject. The subject

came up, "Best things to bring camping." Don't you know BLENDER was on there? Immediately, I began taunting Dani and then calling every fucking one of them who were there and laughing at me. I'm committing this story to print as a means to spite them all for eternity by waving my balls in their general direction. Hu-fucking-zah! TAKE THAT!

My stunning, amazing wife, Dani.

A Comedy of Tragedies

How could I NOT marry this woman, and what the hell is she doing with me?

STEVE BARTON

Danielle looking STUNNING on our Honeymoon

A Comedy of Tragedies

I still have a hard time rationalizing that Dani is with me. It just blows my mind, man.

Chapter 21
I Did it All For the Spooky! The Spooky!

The paranormal has always been a huge part of my life. I've been fascinated with ghost stories from as far back as I can remember. As a child, I did a lot of reading and would frequent the local library to take out anything they had involving ghosts, the supernatural, or anything related to them. My life would literally stop when TV shows like *In Search Of* would start broadcasting. This was an addiction. I'd spend hours and sometimes days pouring over stories of actual hauntings like *The Entity* and *The Amityville Horror*. I'd stay up late into the wee morning hours listen to the great Art Bell on the radio. Whatever and wherever it was, I consumed it.

This addiction would last my entire life and come to a head at the very first Rock and Shock in 2004 when I met paranormal investigator Lou Gentile. We already talked about him a bit ago, but there was just no one like this guy. There probably never will be. Lou claimed to be able to able to capture EVP's (which stands for Electronic Voice Phenomenon, for those of you not in the know) anywhere, and he proved this to me time and time again. The second that Lou and I met, we both knew instantly that we'd be fast friends, and we truly bonded. We were both weirdos, with a totally warped sense of humor.

Let me be clear, when it comes to most things, I'm a died in the wool skeptic. Though I studied the paranormal incessantly, I had never seen a ghost or anything like that. For me to even raise an inquisitive eyebrow, a capture has to be super-compelling. Orbs and such, which became paranormally *en vogue*, did nothing for me. About 95 percent of the time, these visual anomalies proved to be little more than dust particles that were floating in the air. I was on a hunt for the real deal and needed to see and hear shit that I couldn't explain. Lou provided that in spades. He would take out his digital recorder anywhere and speak. Beckoning to "anything" around him. Sooner or later, he would get a response, and most times it was an intelligent response; like an answer to an innocuous question such as, "What's your favorite color?" He really was amazing, and what he did was baffling.

As I stated earlier, the rock portion of Rock and Shock took place at a venue across the street from the Worcester's DCU Center called The Palladium which, again, was run by Gina Migliozzi. Gina had told Lou about some strange goings-on at The Palladium over the years, and Lou offered to do a spur-of-the-moment investigation that evening. Joining him would be Gina, myself, Knetter, and several other people in the horror industry who will remain nameless. There were chairs arranged in a circle on the stage and that's where we all were headed, led of course, by Lou. We all took our seats.

"We're gonna do an EVP session first to see if we can come up with anything," Lou said, his voice booming and echoing through the large empty venue. He began.

"We're here to speak with anyone who may still be here at this theater. We come in nothing but respect, and we mean you no harm. We would like you to answer us, if you can. We'd appreciate that. We'd also appreciate it if you did not follow anyone here home. You respect us, and we'll respect you."

You could hear a pin drop. Lou continued.

"What I am going to do is place this recorder in the center of our circle. No one will be able to touch it or manipulate it in ANY WAY. Once the recorder has been placed, I will ask a question. We will wait thirty seconds, and then the person to my left will ask a question. This will go on until everyone in our circle has had a chance to ask their questions. In between each question we need to maintain absolute silence. Is that clear?"

We all agreed. Lou walked to the center of our circle, raised the recorder to his mouth, hit the button and said, "Beginning of EVP Session 1, The Palladium in Worcester Massachusetts," and placed the recorder on the floor before retaking his seat.

The questions were completely random. Things like, "Who's the President? Do you know what year it is? What's your favorite color? Who's your favorite baseball team?" Then Lou asked his final question which completely confused me. "Have you ever lived," he asked. What the hell could that mean? I would definitely have to ask him later. Once we were done, Lou stood up, walked to the recorder to pick it up, and said, "End of EVP Session 1, The Palladium, Worcester Massachusetts." Lou asked us, "How many of you saw the red light on my recorder blink during the quiet time in between questions?" We all had. "That's because this recorder is voice activated and will only record when something is audible," he explained. "The red light is an indication that it was picking up sound. I can already tell you guys without even listening that we captured something. Now let's see what it is."

It should be noted that The Palladium was built during the '20s and opened its doors on November 24, 1928, as The Plymouth Theater. The building underwent a name change to become E.M. Loew's Center for the Performing Arts on April 14, 1980, before officially becoming The Palladium by 1990. Suffice it to say, many plays, shows, and performances had taken place there, leaving behind a ton of energy, happy, sad, and otherwise.

Lou began playback. At first we'd only hear what I can only describe as a barking of white noise, sort of like what you'd hear between stations when tuning-in a radio dial. But then the answers started coming. Lou wouldn't tell us what he thought was being said. He'd ask us what we heard after every question.

"Do you know what year it is?"

"1951," responded a very clear yet whispering voice.

"What's your favorite color?"

"Blue," said a disembodied but clearly female voice.

"Who's your favorite baseball team?"

"Red Socks," a throaty voice answered. This one really had us whooping and hollering for a while. I mean we were in fucking Massachusetts for Christ's sake! It was just remarkable. We sat there discussing what we had heard for a few minutes when I saw the silhouette of a man walking down the aisle and moving into one of the rows to take a seat. Like he was there to watch us.

"Gina," I asked, "Who else is in here?"

"No one," she answered. "I locked the door behind us when we came in. It's just us." I told everyone what I just saw, and I was and remain adamant that I actually saw someone. The shape of the person was black and absolutely solid. I was positive. The entire time I was staring at the location where I'd spotted the silhouette. Gina got up and turned the venue lights on using a nearby switch. The entire venue was now lit, and there was absolutely no one in the spot which I could swear that I'd seen them. To this day this remains absolutely unexplainable, but I'm POSITIVE about what I saw. There's nothing else to call it but a full-body apparition, and that sounds completely fucking nuts. Not even a full day had passed knowing Lou, and I had what I consider to be an authentic paranormal experience.

After this, Lou led us around the building and upstairs where Gina said a lot of her staff "doesn't like going." Admittedly, it was very creepy up there. We sat together in this one room in complete darkness. I was stymied by what had happened a few minutes ago and it was all that I could think about. Lou was doing his thing. One of the people we were with, an actor, started having a very hard time.

"I see something. It's darker than dark, and I don't like how it's making me feel." She was nearly in tears.

Lou said, "Alright, it's time to go," and we immediately headed back down the stairs.

I didn't see anything up there, but there was a strange feeling present, to say the least. It's like the atmosphere itself was different.

We were all, to a certain degree, shook by what happened. Especially the actor and I. We went back to the hotel we were staying, and I got Lou alone.

"Hey, man. I need to talk to you," I said to him.

"I kinda figured you were gonna say that," Lou answered. "I saw it on your face back at The Palladium. Was that your first genuine paranormal experience?"

"With spirits, yes," I said. "I mean I've seen some strange shit in my life, but that was different. It was as real as you or I."

Lou laughed, "Ha! I busted your fuckin' ghost cherry!" We both had a chuckle at that.

"I do have a question though. When you asked, 'Have you ever lived,' what did that mean?"

Lou looked at me for a moment. I could see he was thinking about how to answer. "I asked that, because there are both human spirits, and inhuman spirits," he finally said. "These inhuman things can be demons, devils, or even fucking angels for all I know. I like knowing who or what I'm dealing with at a location. That is, of course, if they're even telling the fucking truth."

I'm aware of how unbelievable that last bit sounds to a rational person. I was also very much aware Lou believed every single thing that he was saying, and to him, this was gospel. I was convinced beyond a shadow of a doubt that Mr. Lou Gentile was indeed the genuine article.

Lou and I shared many escapades together. Spooky just followed him. One morning at a Chiller Theater show in New Jersey, Lou, Sid, Susie, myself, and Debi gathered to have breakfast. The waiter brought over our water glasses and sat them down. We were in mid-conversation when one of the water glasses slid by itself from one side of the table to the other, stopping in front of Lou. Everyone just stopped talking. We all saw it.

Lou said with a smile, "Did you fucking see that? That was cool!"

I mean what the actual fuck? Another time, he came downstairs after showering once a show was over and he sat next to me. I could see something was wrong.

"What's up," I asked.

"I was just attacked in my room. In the shower," he answered.

"What?!?," I exclaimed. "Get the fuck out of here!"

"Come with me," he said. We went into the bathroom downstairs at the venue together. I looked around and told him we were alone. He lifted up his shirt and showed me his back. On it were three extremely long scratch marks that were deep enough to draw blood, which stretched from just under his neck down to, and onto, his ass. There's no way he could have done that to himself. He was alone that weekend too. There was no one staying with him at all. I had no idea what to make of any of this.

Lou's friendship is one that I cherished. He taught me everything that I know about paranormal investigation. Including how to use my body as an instrument to detect the presence of something that's not supposed to be there. This is magnified because I'm also an empath. Lou helped me to realize that too.

For those who have no idea what that is, an empath can feel, discern, understand, and even share the emotions of another person. For instance, I lived in Los Angeles for a few weeks. The homeless problem there is startlingly bad. Entire streets I'd walk down would be lined with tents filled with people just trying to survive. These streets would fill me with despair each time I walked them. It would take a while to shake that off.

Because of my ability to key-in to the feelings of others, when I walk into a supposedly haunted location, I can pick up on any energy that was left behind. It feels like walking through the ocean, and my body has to exert extra energy just to move through it normally. It's almost like wearing a weighted body suit. Something is just "off" about everything. That's really the only way I can describe it.

Years later, Lou was later diagnosed with cancer. They found it after he went in for an operation on his back. We were all shocked. I went to visit him in the hospital.

"They removed a tumor the size of a football from my fuckin' belly," he said with a laugh. Yep. He never stopped joking. Never stopped being Lou.

"Yo. Are those Snowcaps," I asked pointing at a nearby box of candy. Lou nodded, and I grabbed them and jumped into his bed next to him. "You ain't going anywhere you fucker. You got this!"

We both laughed. I believed this wholeheartedly. Lou was a robust individual and a tough sonofabitch.

The next couple of years were going to be difficult ones, but I was bound and determined to keep Lou fighting by keeping his spirits up. Every night we'd get on Xbox Live together, and play games along with my brother, and my buddies Kris and Tim. Lou would be high as a kite! He'd start rattling off rap lyrics out of nowhere, like, "Interior crocodile alligator. I drive a Chevrolet movie theater..." and we would laugh and laugh and laugh. I cherish those memories. Even when it became apparent that he would not be winning this fight, we all rallied behind him to keep him smiling as best as we could. Lou had become one of my best friends, and it was an honor to have known him for as long as I did, and to have helped him to laugh in his last few years on earth. He died exactly one day after my birthday on June 28th, 2009. I'm pretty sure he didn't want to die on my birthday, so he hung in there to make sure my day wouldn't be associated with sadness.

I miss you, man. So much.

As indicated, the paranormal had become a big part of my life, and now years later I was with Dani, and she loves it just as much as I do. You see she's an empath too. She and I can pick up on things way before anyone else does. It happens literally all the time. Sometimes we can even finish each other's sentences. To be able to share that with someone who understands it is incredible. It also makes it exceedingly difficult to hide anything from each other, but that's okay too. You shouldn't hide anything from the one that you love, unless it's some sort of playful surprise.

I have a good friend named Sean Austin who is the protégé of another friend of mine, Ralph Sarchie. Sarchie is the ex-New York City Police officer-turned-paranormal investigator who was played by Eric Bana in the Scott Derrickson film *Deliver Us From Evil*. Sean worked with Ralph on a TV show called *The Demon Files* on Destina-

A Comedy of Tragedies

tion America. We all became friends while press was being done for the show. Now that I was back on the East coast, I was local to Sean.

One day he called me and said he'd be in my area because he was shooting a documentary on a neighborhood that was haunted.

"Did you say the whole neighborhood is haunted?"

He confirmed, and Dani and I made plans to join him and his partners in the investigation. I mean a haunted house is one thing, but a whole neighborhood? I couldn't be more "in."

We got lunch first and then drove to the location. Sean was going to interview the owner of a home who was getting ready to sell it because she couldn't deal with the weirdness there anymore.

While they were talking, I asked, "Can I walk the house?" The owner gave me permission. Dani stayed downstairs and I went up. I walked into each room. One bedroom had a connecting bathroom, nothing at all set me off. I walked down to a bedroom across the hall. Nothing. Then I walked into the second bathroom. It was like getting hit in the face with a bag of sludge. The energy in this room was 100 times heavier than anywhere else. I needed to step out of it. I noticed a door to my left that was closed, and I left it that way. I yelled down to the first floor, "Dani, can you come upstairs?" She did. I asked her to walk the rooms and let me know what she feels. Instinctively she walked the rooms the same exact way that I did. I don't know why or even how this happened, but it did. She visited every single room in the exact order that I had. By the time she got to the second bathroom she said, "Oh my. This isn't good. This isn't good at all. Holy shit." This was all the confirmation I needed about what I was feeling, and we both went downstairs.

I went up to Sean and the owner and I asked, "What happened upstairs?"

The owner informed me that there was a girl who lived there that tried to commit suicide in the bathroom. That's what we were feeling. There's no question about that. You see, there are two types of hauntings: **intelligent**—meaning you can interact with whatever is there, and **residual**—meaning you can feel the energies left behind by whatever or whomever was there. This was 100 percent residual, and it was goddamned strong. The locked room was that same girl's bedroom. We went in and did an EVP session. Sean ran it, and he got immediate responses. This was pretty cool. Even cooler that I shared this experience with Dani.

Once we were finished there, we then went to the house next door. While Sean was talking to its owner, Dani and I walked the house. I felt zero there, except for something being kind of off in one of the bathrooms. Dani was in the same boat. She felt nothing anywhere except for that one area that I did. However, we both agreed it didn't feel paranormal. We went back in and listened to the owner's interview. She had indicated that she was epileptic and had her worst seizure ever while in the garage. She also went on to tell Sean that her cat had almost died in that very same garage. Interesting. She went on to reveal that she had some work done in one of the bathrooms. The light fixtures had been changed and she hasn't felt right in there since.

A common trope of hauntings is that, if you mess with a spirit's environment, they will become active and sometimes hostile. Ghosts, like most people, aren't very fond of change. Since both Dani and I felt something was off in the bathroom I asked one of Sean's assistants if they had an Electro Magnetic Field meter, which is a common tool used for ghost hunting. They did.

I took the EMF meter into the bathroom.

Every area has an electromagnetic field, and the base line reading of a normal area is zero-point-five milligauss. Around electrical outlets it can be higher, but that's normal given that their function is to provide electricity.

The meter spiked to a two-point-zero in the bathroom by one of the overhead lights.

"Is this the area you had worked on? Where you had the new light fixtures put in," I asked the owner. She confirmed that by saying, "yes." Interesting.

From there we went into the garage with the EMF meter. I walked directly up to the fuse box, and it registered a bit higher than it had in the bathroom, but this is normal, considering what it is. The whole room was checked. There was NOTHING unusual at all, except for the garage door opener. When the meter was waved in front of that, the reading was so high that it sent the meter's screen into an error. It literally redlined it and shorted out. We reset it and tried again with the same results.

"Did you say you were epileptic and had your worst seizure in here?" She confirmed that was the case. Danielle explained to her that high EMF fields can trigger seizures in people with epilepsy. This was BEYOND a high reading. Also, if her cat fell asleep on top of the car under the garage door opener, that too could have been the reason for its sickness.

I looked at the owner dead in the face and said, "Lady, you don't need paranormal investigators. You need an electrician!"

We all laughed. Lou would have been proud. You can see some of these events in the paranormal series *Darkness in Suburbia* on the Scare Network. I don't know how much of these events made it in.

For me, this was more proof that Dani and I were meant to be together. Everything about us clicked. Her crazy plays well with my crazy. We began having a tradition of sorts—every Sunday we go get bagels at Westmont Bagels down the street from us. One morning we were sitting across from each other, when I grabbed a toothpick and scraped up a healthy dollop of cream cheese. I then took two potato chips and inserted them into the aforementioned dollop, and it looked like a bee. I pointed it at her and made a buzzing sound and then stopped. She looked at me wide-eyed and laughing. At that moment I said, "So, what do you think about getting married and such?" Her eyes welled with tears, and she said, "YES!" I was shocked. I didn't have a ring. Nothing about this should have worked. I was brandishing a fuckin' cream cheese bee at her, and she actually said "yes!" This strange occurrence has come to be known officially as The Cream Cheese Bee Incident??™.

See fellas? Save your cash! Fuck rings!

Months later the day had finally come. October 5th, 2023. We decided to get married in our home with just a few people. We're planning on having a big party later in 2024, but this gathering was gonna be as intimate as intimate gets. It was us, the person marrying us, our friend Brandon Brooks, our neighbors Alex and Jenny, and Antoinette Gentile, Lou's wife, and her family including the daughter whom I got piss drunk on gumball martinis! It's funny how life comes full circle. Lou had been cremated, and I asked Ant to bring his ashes. She didn't, but she said she had definitely thought about it!

The ceremony was grand. I had my TV on with Spotify open playing our road trip playlist. It's basically all grunge and shit featuring Korn, Nirvana, Pearl Jam, Rob Zombie, etcetera.

It got to the point in the ceremony when I was gonna make my vows. I could feel my throat getting choked up, like I was trying to swallow a softball. The tears were about to break. I began, and mid-sentence, we all heard it. Somehow the playlist ended, and the music became loud. Fucking Blaring LOUD!

"AMAZING GRACE… HOW SWEET THE SOUND…"

I tried to ignore it and continue, but I just couldn't.

"Can somebody PLEASE change the music? I mean what the fuck?!"

Everyone laughed. How could this happen? No one changed the music, and no one certainly would ever put on the one song played at every fucking funeral in the history of the goddamned world. This literally this would ONLY happen to us. I like to think that the prank interruption was both Lou and Dave letting me know that they were there. That fills me with joy beyond words. The rest of the ceremony went off without a hitch and Danielle is now a Barton!

#poordanielle

Chapter 22
Terrifier Too

As I indicated before, one of the only good things *Dread Central* did for *Terrifier* was to put it on Netflix with some truly killer artwork. It was scary, eye catching, and truth be told… PERFECT! Other than that, though… I personally felt that *Dread Central* had treated both Damien and the film poorly. Since I got Damien and Phil involved with Shake-and-Bake in the first place, I took the onus of that. In my eyes, that situation and the way that they were treated, as fucked as it was, was partly my fault. I own up to shit. That's part of who I am. A vital part.

Damien and I spoke sometime later, and he told me they were ready to do a sequel. "Dude," I said. "I have to be involved in this." Not just because with *Dread Central* gone I literally had nothing, but because the *Terrifier* story had become entwined with both of our stories. The gang launched a Kickstarter for *Terrifier 2* and it shattered and exceeded its goal in just a few hours. This was amazing. Everyone was elated. At this point in time, I was clear across the other side of the country. Damien's team, of which there are about nine people, were gonna shoot the movie and do all the heavy lifting in terms of getting the physical product done. I told Damien that I "would do anything that they needed on *Part 2* for free." I didn't want to be paid because I felt I owed them for the debacle that had occurred with *Dread Central*.

Before the release of the movie, I had gotten him music from Powerman 5000, hooked him up with a couple of possible actors for roles (which they didn't get, but came close), and consulted on a couple of points that he wasn't sure about, including the post-credit scene and where it should go. Damien trusted my opinion as much as I trusted his.

Terrifier 2 is a movie that breaks literally every conventional horror rule. It's over 2 hours, features a mass shooting, is one of the single most sadistic and violent films ever created brimming with glorious practical effects work, and introduces fantasy elements not present in the first movie. Damien made this movie for fans of the first one. He was hoping the new slant would attract new viewers too, so he took a gamble.

This movie is a total throwback to the days of splatter goodness. It's exactly the kind of movie that's frowned upon by studios and the public at large. Especially in these overly sensitive times. This was for horror fans and whether you liked the movie or not, the love for the genre is apparent in every single frame and second of the film. The effects work is masterful, especially the bedroom scene, but it should be noted that there is an unsung hero in the mix—visual effects artist Josh Petrino. Simply put, if you didn't notice his work, that's the highest compliment anyone could pay him. Josh is a true master at what he does and is beyond humble and talented. Josh's work was integral on many of *Terrifier 2*'s biggest set pieces and he deserves way more credit than he ever gets.

The movie took about three years to finish "thanks" (that's sarcasm, kids) in part to COVID-19 and some other factors. By the time it was completed I was back on the East coast. The film was being shopped overseas and creating kind of a buzz. Again though, no one wanted to lay out a reasonable amount of money for acquisition and Damien and Phil were rightly sticking to their guns this time.

It was midway through one of my morning hikes when I got a call from Brad Miska of *Bloody Disgusting*, Cinedigm, and Screambox. "Steve. What do I have to do to secure distribution for *Terrifier 2*?" Brad called me because he knew I was responsible for plucking the original film from obscurity and now I was serving as a producer of *Part 2*. I knew the troubles Damien was having. I knew the kinds of offers they were getting too as Damien told me all of this. If worse came to worse, as with the first movie, they were fully ready to self-distribute.

I said to Brad, "Dude. This is kind of a big ask. I think that they were screwed already by one website, and now you want me to ask them to entertain an offer from another?" Brad understood that, but I could tell he wasn't fucking around. He wanted this movie as bad as I wanted the first one. I appreciated and respected that. "Here's what you do," I said. "I'll let them know about this, and you guys can set up a call. When you speak with them, make them a legitimate offer. This is a franchise now and one that could very well end up making some decent money given its cult following. Do NOT insult them and above and beyond anything be fuckin' transparent."

That's exactly what Brad did after I put them all together. It was about three or four in the afternoon two or three weeks later. I was sitting on the couch with Dani when my phone rang. It was Damien and I put him on speaker. "Steve," he said. "We are talking to *Bloody Disgusting* and one other company. Both are making good offers, but I'd rather go with *Bloody*. They're just a few [sum will remain anonymous] shy of what we're looking for."

I asked him what he needed to make the deal happen and he told me. "Give me ten minutes," I said, feeling pretty confident that I could make this happen.

"Go to work, babe," Dani said. I got on the phone with Brad and was blunt with him. I relayed exactly what and how much it would take to make the deal happen.

He called his people, and then me. "They agreed," Brad said excitedly.

"Good, I'll call Damien and let him know."

That's exactly to the letter how the distribution deal got closed.

They had their meeting, signed contracts and *boom*. Finished. *Terrifier 2* was in the hands of people who actually knew what they were doing. Even cooler, they liked the movie and wanted to give the movie a theatrical run. This was literally the polar opposite of the experience we had with *Dread Central*.

At one point Damien told me that they were asking about the possibility of him cutting together an R-rated version for the theatrical run. Upon hearing this I became alarmed. Everything was going so well! This was NOT gonna be the *Dread Central* mess all over again. No fucking way. With Damien's permission I wrote one of the executives handling *Terrifier 2*'s distribution with Damien CC'ed, and told them simply… "The only people who are going to go see *Terrifier 2* are the fans of the original. If they hear that the film is gonna be rated R for its theatrical release, but will then hit home video and streaming uncut, they will wait for the latter. Releasing an R-rated cut of the movie is a bad idea, and you're setting yourself up to fail."

A few days later the decision was made to go uncut. I want to stress this Brad Miska, *Bloody Disgusting*, and Cinedigm are heroes. They took a chance on this movie literally no one else was willing to take.

Sometime later we were all hanging out after hours at New Jersey Horror Con. We were sitting around a table outside of the Showboat hotel: it was me, Danielle, Damien, and producer Mike Leavy.

"This fucking guy," Damien said regarding me. "He did it again. Just when we were about to self-distribute, he came in and scored us a deal." We started laughing. Damien went on "'You're setting yourself up to fail,' when I read that I fell in love with him all over again," he said to Leavy. It felt amazing. Not because I was being acknowledged for doing something good, but because I felt inside that I had made up for whatever headaches *Dread Central* had caused them. We were even, and at the end of the day, no matter what *Dread Central* had done, it was just a means to an end to get to this moment. "Your name will forever be associated with these movies. You know that, right?" Damien said to me with his arm around my shoulder. I didn't want this night or this moment to end. I belonged. I was alive. I had found a place where I belonged.

Before the release of the film, I began hitting all of my social media platforms hard. Harder than I ever had for anything. I made sure the made-up word *"Terrifier"* was on the lips and minds of horror fans everywhere. Every post that I made was *Terrifier*-related. Every time interest waned slightly or began to quiet down, I found a new angle to keep it going. This was a grass-roots-advertising clinic the likes of which the world had never seen. I used every single ounce of my platform, experience, and credibility to make sure there was constant buzz. I pulled out every trick in my bag, and even came up with some new ones. The movie premiered at FrightFest in the UK and was met with incredible reactions. I hunted every one of them down and tweeted, posted, retweeted, and reposted them. It was everywhere. My pacing was well-timed and absolutely ferocious.

The time had come for the film to open in US theaters. Cinedigm were supposed to get us a Friday, and Saturday night release, with some theaters even showing us on Sundays. We were only playing once or maybe twice each of those nights in their respective theaters. Monday morning... the word came. *Terrifier 2* had brought in over a million at the domestic box office and was the film that knocked *Top Gun: Maverick* out of the top 10.

The odds of this happening were pretty much nil. Especially since it was playing only once or twice a day. A miracle had happened. We were all emotional. Elated. This little flick had done the impossible. Little did we know, that was just the beginning. We got booked for another weekend. Then another. Then another. The buzz was EVERYWHERE: the *Howard Stern Show*, Jerry O'Connell was talking about it on the morning show *The Talk*, one of the Buffalo Bills had taken to the field during a game wearing custom *Terrifier*-themed cleats, even WWE announcer Corey Graves gave us a shout-out on *Monday Night Raw*, coining the term, "That was Art the Clown ugly."

Art the Clown was everywhere. Stephen King had mentioned on Twitter that he wanted to see it. Stephen fucking King! I immediately reached out to his manager and got him a screener. Mr. King was kind enough to give us a quote. Wow. Holy fucking shit. *Stephen King!* This entire time I went on a social media blitz that fans were reposting and retweeting everywhere. It was amazing. We were riding the lightning. Then, people started puking during the movie. Some thought that this was a marketing ploy, but we weren't even smart enough to think of something like that. But puking they were. This only intensified the coverage. Jerry O'Connell said on *The Talk* that "the marketing team behind this movie are brilliant." Yeah, hi. That was me, *Bloody Disgusting*, a few members of the cast and crew, alongside the fans. That was the marketing team, because there just wasn't a budget for one.

During all of this favorable chaos Cinedigm brought in a marketing team to handle it, but there was nothing for them to do. I basically did it all. The one thing that they did do was a faux ad campaign called "Mothers Against *Terrifier 2*." When I first saw it, I thought it was legit. It was during a phone call with Brad that he told me some ad firm was behind it. My response was immediate: "Are you nuts?! If people find out this campaign is fake, it will take away from all the cool things that were happening that were organic and insanely wonderful. Any little bit of inauthenticity would literally negate them." He thought about it and agreed. You simply cannot buy the type of fervor that was happening within the horror circle. It just has to happen. I put a stop to that campaign immediately when I told people that while it was a cool idea and we wish it would have been real, it was fake. That's a pretty unprecedented move, but everything about this whole shebang was unprecedented. The fan base, like I knew that it would, appreciated the honesty and embraced us even tighter. Everyone was winning—especially horror fans.

One day during this chaos Brad mentioned to me that because of the length of our theatrical run and a few other factors, "we technically qualified to submit *Terrifier 2* for an Oscar."

"Submit that shit right the fuck now!" I answered, grinning ear-to-ear. Originally, *Bloody* took a relatively serious slant to announce that the movie was being submitted to the Oscars. I took one look at the story before they posted it and said, "No. This isn't the way we announce this. This makes us sound like we believe we have a chance. We know full well that we don't stand a chance of actually winning. The slant of the story NEEDS to be *'Bloody Disgusting* Submits *Terrifier 2* for an Oscar Because it's Too Funny Not To!'" My reasoning was simple: "If we can make just one of those folks on the Academy sit through even five minutes of *Terrifier 2*, that's a win and a goddamned HILARIOUS one at that." I rewrote pretty much the entire article for them in a more humorous self-aware voice and they published it. As I surmised the fans ate it up and immediately got behind it. This whole trip was the kind of lightning in a bottle few people get to experience, and it ended with me setting up a screening of both *Terrifier* and *Terrifier 2* with Kevin Smith at his SMODCASTLE Cinemas. This was actually happening. It wasn't some fairy tale.

The day of the SMODCASTLE Double-Feature had arrived. I got there early with Danielle, Josh Petrino, and Brandon Brooks. I was about to introduce myself to Kevin when he saw me smiled wide and shouted "Uncle Creepy," before giving me a massive hug. What kind of a weird fucking world was I living in that Kevin Smith actually knew who I was? This was insanity. The double-feature ended, and it was time for the Q&A. Kevin brought me up to the stage with words that STILL to this very moment humble me.

"The producer of tonight's epics, ladies and gentlemen. I got to meet him earlier, and fuckin' he introduced himself with his nom de plume and what not, and I gave him a big hug. It was like meeting a goddamned celebrity because he is one. Welcome Uncle Creepy himself, Steve Barton, man! Get up here goddamn it!"

AGAIN—what kind of a weird fucking world was I living in that Kevin Smith not only knew who I was, but called me a "goddamned celebrity?" I am forever grateful to Danielle for getting this on camera. In some of my darkest times I've watched it, and it lets me know that I am on the path that I'm supposed to be on. This whole experience proved to be my ultimate validation and vindication. My whole life I was put down, written off, and told I was nothing. Everyone was wrong about me. I did know who I was and what I was doing. As the poster reads… "Who's Laughing Now?"

Lots of people ask me what I think the success of *Terrifier 2* could be attributed to. The most vital part of the equation is that the team made a good movie. The rest, I feel it was a *right place, right time* scenario. The world had just gone through a really shitty few years what with COVID, and its effects. Millions of people worldwide had passed on because of this vile virus. We were all fit to be tied. Everywhere you looked there was just more bad news. Information was everywhere and stuck on OVERLOAD. Even our forms of entertainment had become overly preachy. People just wanted to have a good time. *Terrifier 2*'s only message was, "sit back and take the ride." Have fun! It's okay to laugh, scream, and cheer. It was escapism at its finest. This whole ride was something else, man.

Even though the movie had come and gone I stayed active on social media platforms. I made sure everyone kept talking about it relentlessly. Damien told me at the afterparty for *Terrifier 2*'s New York City premiere that the third *Terrifier* was gonna be a Christmas movie. What a brilliant way to keep it fresh, and interesting. I knew I had to find ways to keep interest hard and heavy, and I did.

One of the challenges the guys were facing was they weren't doing the bigger conventions like MonsterMania which is run by the WONDERFUL Dave Hagan, who has been a friend since my *Dread Central* days. I spoke to Dave about this quite a few times for several weeks. One day he texted me something along the lines of

> Okay. I got the guys coming to Monster-Mania. Normally, I wouldn't be doing this, but I'm doing this for you.

I showed Damien his text. I was proud of this. Monster-Mania isn't an easy show to get into but given its location it was PERFECT for being the *Terrifier* squad's home base.

From there everyone was being asked to make convention appearances. Everyone, but Phil Falcone. This bothered me because as I have said in past and probably every interview I've ever done, "These movies don't exist without Phil Falcone." He did an insane amount of work on these movies from finding money, to building

A Comedy of Tragedies

sets, to even learning how to do special effects from Damien so that he could help with that too.

Phil would always say to me, "These shows. They don't want the producers." That may be true to some extent, but Phil, without question, deserved to be there.

I told him that I intended to start doing shows because I've had a thirty-year career, but before "I had anyone accept me, I wanted to push to get him into the shows first." Especially because he gives whatever he makes to the Veterans' charities, and that is without question a great cause. I knew when the time came for me to do convention appearances it would be relatively easy. I'm a living Romero Zombie for crying out loud! I started making calls and sending emails, and sooner rather than later Phil started making his first convention appearances for *Terrifier* and *Terrifier 2*—his first official one being at Days of the Dead. I knew after he did a couple that he wouldn't need me to keep pushing for him. It would be a given. The honor of appearing was well-deserved. Phil is the heart and soul of these movies. I've said that 10,000 times and I mean it with every ounce of my conviction.

The days and months ticked on, and I kept my now year and a half long *Terrifier* ad campaign successfully going. Little did I know come November of 2023 things would begin to fall apart for me.

It started with a phone call from my niece, Franny, who is my eldest brother Tommy's daughter. "Uncle Stevie. It's my dad. He's dying."

Chapter 23
Turbulence 3: Heavy Mental

My brother Tommy is hard to talk about because every time that I do, he fills me with equal amounts of sorrow and rage. Let me explain. In his youth Tommy was a bass player with charisma to spare. His claim to fame is that he played bass on the classic disco song, "In the Bush" by Musique. Growing up during the 70's in New York's five boroughs, that song was EVERYWHERE. He went on to marry a great woman named Francesca and together they had my niece, whom I call Franny. Later on, in life Tommy would get divorced, remarry, have more kids, get divorced again, rinse wash and repeat.

When my dad died, Tommy decided to leave New York to go and live off-the-grid in Las Vegas. That's where Franny lives, and to my knowledge he never stayed in touch with his other wives or kids. I always wondered about this decision but at least he had some family in Vegas. Tommy probably didn't want his other ex's to be able to find him and force him to pay child support, etc. Sadly, he was exactly the type of person who would do such a thing. Tommy's time living off-the-grid was tumultuous to say the least, but his tale is not mine to tell. Over the years we'd speak sort of regularly but eventually he'd always end up getting drunk and then saying that he was gonna kill me. I didn't do anything to him to get that kind of reaction,

A Comedy of Tragedies

but I don't think that he liked the fact that both Robert and I were doing fine, without any of the problems he had. That's the thing with people who lived shitty lives. Misery loves company, so they try making your life shittier. After the last time he threatened me, I decided I was done with him. We didn't speak again for a long while.

The first time I had seen Tommy in over a year was when Franny's mom passed away due to COVID-19. Franny was having a Zoom get-together for the people who couldn't make it to Vegas. Tommy came on the screen and truth be told I was horrified. He was gaunt, and clean shaven. He looked kind of like Boris Karloff in *The Mummy*, and I'm not at all saying that to be funny. Franny, who as of this writing is battling lung cancer, wasn't doing well at all. Tommy spoke on camera, and he just seemed very "off." It pained me to see him this way. In my eyes he was my big, strong, and extremely virile older brother. I didn't know who this was that I was looking at, and I was so incredibly sad when I realized it was really him. This is the classic example of what hard-living can do to a person.

After a month or so he called me. I answered and we reconciled. He said to me, "You know, little brother, you're the only Barton out of all of us to put our family on the map. Thank you for that. I love you." I loved him too. More than I care to realize. Fast-forward a couple of years to Franny's "He's dying" phone call.

Franny told me that essentially, he was suffering from every possible thing that could go wrong. From COVID, to sepsis, to neuropathy, to possible cancer, to "you name it." I honestly didn't know what to say or do. I told Franny that I would be there for her to support her and make phone calls when she needed to. That's exactly what I did.

Telling Rob that Tommy was dying wasn't easy. When Rob heard this, he got very angry. "You know, man, If he just would have acted like a normal person and lived a normal life, instead of being off-the-fuckin-grid, none of this would be happening to him." Rob was absolutely right. He insisted that he get involved in Tommy and Franny's affairs, but I told him not to. I would take care of this. You see, Rob, whom I love dearly, doesn't handle loss very well, and even though he means well and has a heart of absolute gold, he would most likely drive Franny crazier than she already was. Besides that, he and Franny hadn't stayed in touch or spoken for around forty years. This was not the time to come into her life, I was as sure of this as I'm sure that I have a nose on my face.

Neither me nor Rob had spoken to our sister, Camille, since my dad died. Truth be told I didn't want to. She is a conniving and manipulative bitch who married into money and thought she was better than everyone else. I swallowed my pride and sent her a message on Facebook. It read simply, *Hey, it's Steve. Tommy is dying. If you want to say goodbye to him, now is the time to do so.*

Tommy was the only one of us who had kept in touch with Camille. Should she have written me back I would have given her Franny's number as well as the number for the hospital Tommy was at. She never did. Weeks went by and I found her children on Facebook, so I messaged them too. *Hi. We have never met or spoken but I'm your Uncle. Can you please tell your mom that Tommy, her eldest brother, is dying, and now is the time to say goodbye if she wants to.*

Again, dead silence. Tommy's condition was rapidly worsening. He had become incoherent with only a few moments of lucidity each day. Franny called me and told me, "Uncle Stevie, he keeps saying that he broke the family, and he wants to fix it. Do you know what he's talking about?"

I didn't. Not a clue. "Franny," I said, "unfortunately you're dealing with the rantings of a dying man. I'm sure not even he knows what he's talking about." I mean, that had to be it, right?

A couple of days later Franny texted me and told me that Camille had sent her a typed letter in the regular mail with no return address. The letter had basically said that when my dad died, she "laid out around 18K in expenses." If Franny was "looking for money, [she] was barking up the wrong tree." Yep, just as slimy and cowardly as I imagined she would be. Yet, something seemed off about her letter and it wasn't just her overt bitchiness. I asked Franny to send me pictures of it. It was bothering me. REALLY bothering me. Then I realized what it was—for the first time in my entire life I was actually

A Comedy of Tragedies

paying attention to math. Her "supposed" expenses—which were itemized from when my grandmother had died to when my father died—did indeed totally out to about 18k. Huh. Interesting. Until this letter I was unaware of any of this.

Kris is my oldest friend and sounding board. He knows everything about me and my family. I called him to inform him of my sister's latest round of unsurprising twatiness, and he said, "18k! I'm surprised she didn't take that out of yours and Rob's split of the house." It was as if a lightbulb had gone off in my head. When my dad's house was sold, Tommy and Camille had told Rob and I that "with all of my dad's expenses there would only be 40k left that we would split four ways."

"You know what you should do, Steve," Kris said out of nowhere, "You should go on Zillow and look up your house's sales history. Just to see." I didn't even know that such a thing was possible. I did it and there it was; in the '90s when my father died, my house was sold for $220,000. Let's say Camille took 20k out of that to cover her expenses. Then Tommy, Rob, and I were given 10k each. That would still leave $170,000. My dad was a lot of things, but I am certain that he was not $170,000 in debt. That would have been kinda noticeable in our everyday lives. Plus, that leftover amount is not even taking into consideration my dad's bank account, his insurance, his pension, etc.

It hit me like a fucking ton of bricks. It was extremely likely that both Tommy and Camille split that money and then quickly left the picture. Tommy to Vegas, and her to whatever Cunthaven she had found for herself. Rob and I were in our twenties and stupid. We wouldn't have known any better and would never have thought them capable of doing such a thing. Knowing what I know now, though? Not only were they capable but given their quick exit from the scene after my dad's demise, it all makes perfect sense.

What the fuck was I supposed to do with this information now? Tommy was dying. Maybe that's what he was talking about when he said that "he broke our family." What was I gonna do, yell at him? Besides that, as much sense as this scenario makes to me—and in my bones I feel like that's exactly what happened—this was all speculation. In truth, I'll never know. The one thing I did know for sure was that I was thankful. Why? Because I learned to live with so little. I learned to scrape by and save, and be thankful for whatever I had. If I had been given the privilege of a monetary cushion, then maybe I wouldn't have ended up where I am right now. Maybe I wouldn't be who I am right now. I like me. I like where I am. I wouldn't trade it for anything, and I certainly wouldn't go back and change a single thing. I grew up hard and it made me stronger. That's a win.

It wasn't long after that when Tommy passed away. As mad as I am at him, he'll always be my brother, and I will always love him. As for Camille though…

After his passing I was hurting. I learned how to deal with the deaths of my parents and close friends, but this was my brother. This was different. He would always be "young" and strong to me. In agony, I once again turned to the horror genre for comfort.

This was around the time that *Terrifier 2* was slated for a theatrical rerelease. Fans were elated! Word had broken that there would be a teaser trailer for *Terrifier 3* shown after the movie. Even cooler, everyone who went was supposed to get a collectible *T3* poster. About a week or so prior to the rerelease, a few fans wrote to me privately. A few die hards couldn't make it to the rerelease because of some issues ranging from:

1. It wasn't showing near them.
2. No money.
3. Family sickness.

I felt terrible. They just wanted to know if the teaser trailer would eventually make its way online or if the poster would be for sale at some point. I didn't know the answer, but I did know one thing… I was gonna make it my business to get their posters. I wrote Cinedigm to see if they could send me a few. They said that they would, but ultimately didn't. That's okay though… I was not about to be deterred.

Dani and I got into our car on opening day and drove to several

A Comedy of Tragedies

theaters around our area. Some of them were all out of posters, but three had some left over. I couldn't just walk in and take several posters so I walked in, introduced myself, told them what the situation was, and they said I could take a few. They asked me to sign a few for the theater staff and I obliged. A few theater goers were just coming out of the theaters and recognized me, so I signed theirs too. After collecting enough posters for the folks who wrote me that couldn't get them... for whatever reason... we went home.

Immediately I contacted them and got all of their addresses. They were so shocked and thankful. It warmed my heart. It STILL does. They offered to pay for shipping, but I was not about to let that happen. I did this because I wanted to. I value the fans. Without them none of us exist. Period.

The next day I went to the UPS store and shipped them all out. They asked if they could thank me publicly online, but I asked them not to. I do not need and was not looking for praise. I was only trying to do right by a fanbase who never let me, or at that time "us" (meaning the *Terrifier* crew) down. The fans whom I did this for shall remain nameless as I respect their privacy, but should they want to come forward after reading this they are more than welcome to do so. Again... Thank YOU all for being exactly who each and every one of you are.

I started healing. Feeling a bit more like myself. Little did I know that another punch was coming from a very unexpected place. After my brother died and about a week or so before Thanksgiving of 2023, I got what amounted to a "Dear John" letter from none other than Phil Falcone.

In a nutshell, Phil expressed to me that he had felt that I had taken credit for the work other people had done. He went on to say that since I wasn't on set for the making of *Terrifier 2*, I didn't deserve to be doing the amount of publicity that I was or getting the recognition that had come along with it. He said I wasn't a "person of title," and insinuated that I was given my executive producer credit as a courtesy (read: pity) credit. As a result, we would effective immediately be parting ways.

My jaw was on the fuckin' floor. Never once have I EVER said I was on set for the making of the movie. I used words like "we" or "us" because I was part of the team. At least I believed that I was. This was never about vanity for me. It was about the horror genre kicking ass. I was incensed, outraged, and more than anything, heartbroken.

I wrote Phil back and told him how I felt. I tried to explain to him that what they were seeing was a two-year long marketing campaign. Of course, people wanted to interview me, I've been at it for decades, and have done TONS of other things. I have never in my life taken credit for anything I did not do, and I always give credit to whomever had earned it. Hell, it's hard enough getting to me to take credit for the stuff that I *DID* do. There's nothing to be gained from being dishonest. After over 30 years in the business without screwing anyone over or lying to anyone, I did not need to start doing so now. Sure, lies and hyperbole can be used as shortcuts, but I've never seen a shortcut lead to anywhere that's worth being.

There's a reason why I'm one of the most respected and trusted names in the horror genre, one that I've worked my entire career to be able to tout...

I got to where I am because I've EARNED my spot the right way. The way that both Sid and George taught me to. No shortcuts. All while being the fucking Jack of all Traumas! Not many people can say that.

I would have preferred a simple discussion instead of a letter that laid out that I was never thought of as part of the team, and that all of my contributions were not appreciated. Phil replied that he was "comfortable" with his decision. I didn't see this coming. I know in my heart I did everything right and for the right reasons.

The very next week after this all went down, I was presented with a Vanguard Award for all the work I've done during my career at the Vampires of New Jersey Con. Of course, Art the Clown was prominently on it. I didn't make a speech. Inside I was like "You've got to be fuckin' kidding me." Instead, I held it proudly above my head and did not say a single word. I tell ya, folks, you just can't make this shit up.

I honestly do not think any of this was done out of malice. While I vehemently disagree with his views, it was ultimately Phil's decision.

March 8, 2024.

I've been sitting with this latest disappointment for months. My original plan was to leave this chapter right there at the previous paragraph. You see, I didn't want to give anyone the satisfaction of knowing how badly this had hurt me and the damage it has done. The establishment of the *Terrifier* brand was a labor of love for us all, and I'm truly grateful for its success, and the ride that I got to take.

However, lately I find myself at times severely depressed. I'm just not thinking straight. Since November I keep playing all of the events over and over in my head. It's been very bad, and extremely hard on me. I will always be happy to have been one of the people who had put the *Terrifier* franchise on the map. You can make the greatest movie in the world, but if no one knows about it, it just doesn't matter. I busted my ass to make sure that *Terrifier* was ingrained into the collective horror-psyche, and I will always be proud of what I did. Everywhere I look Art the Clown is celebrated, and I celebrate being a part of his infamy.

However, this experience has affected me emotionally, mentally, monetarily, in every facet of my life. So here I am. Back to living check-to-check. Barely scraping by. Sometimes it's hard not to feel like I'm at best treading water, and at worst—drowning.

I've been both shellshocked and down for months. I gained back over 40lbs of the weight I lost because I have been stress eating. I feel ugly. While insanely proud of my accomplishments, almost every time I see or hear anything about *Terrifier* or Art the Clown, my stomach churns into knots, and I become physically nauseated. The people who currently know about this keep telling me, "you'll pull through." I know they're right. I know that I will. I'm just tired of always having to pull through. My arms are exhausted from constantly swinging at shadows.

It's been killing me keeping this all to myself. Why haven't I said something? Why haven't I tried to burn it all down? Because I sincerely don't want them to fail. *Terrifier's* continued success is what's best for the genre, and I love horror more than ANYTHING—other than my family of course. I remain proud of the people who made *Terrifier*, and the role I played in getting it out there. No words or disappointments will ever change that.

Personally, though? It's really hard for me to explain how I feel. Hence the ups and downs of this chapter. It's a fucking hurricane of emotion, and no matter how much I try and get off this pendulum, it keeps rapidly swinging from good to bad. For the past thirty years I've been hearing shit like, "You're just dreaming. You're never gonna make it." With all of the events of last year I felt as if I had proved everyone wrong. That felt amazing. And you know what? I DID prove them wrong. *Now* though? I'm right back to where I started. Square One. I've had the rug pulled out from under me so many times that I can't help but feel like a failure, even though I do not believe that I am.

Maybe that's why I've been keeping this all so close to my chest... Fear. I can't bear the thought of looking at and into the eyes of folks who've told me that I've "inspired them" with my success story, only to know that I've been knocked down... again. However, that bell hasn't rung just yet. I'm still very much in the fight. At the end of the day, this is a true Hollywood story, and the fact of the matter is they do not always have a happy ending. That's okay too.

Despite all of my confusion, darkness, and mixed feelings there is one thing that I am absolutely certain of—*I am someone*. The truth is, I helped to change every one of their lives. Hell, I've changed dozens of lives, and I have never, not a single time asked anyone for anything.

Sorry, world, I am and will always be...

"A person of title."

A Comedy of Tragedies

Me getting a Vanguard Award at the Vampires of New Jersey Convention literally days after Phil shit-canned me for doing my job too well. Ya just can't make this stuff up. A comedy of tragedies, indeed.

STEVE BARTON

Better days.

Kevin Smith called me a "goddamned celebrity." I still can't believe that happened.

Chapter 24
That's Another One for the Fire

And there it is. The final twist in this twister. The stinger. Jason emerging from the water to pull down his victim. Carrie reaching up out of the grave. Ren chewing on a bar of soap as part of his "Space Madness." Well, maybe not that last one. I do love me some *Ren and Stimpy*, though.

Some of you, maybe even all of you, are probably surprised how that last bit turned out. I was too… at least momentarily. This is life, man. Everything happens for a reason. I firmly believe that. Besides, if we lived in a world rife with predictability we'd be little more than lemmings marching toward the eventual cliff drop-off.

This is the roller coaster. At fifty-years old—in a single year, I helped to make horror history, got married, buried my brother, and was then unceremoniously thrown off the project I shepherded to success from the beginning for essentially being good at what I do. I've been in this business for about thirty years now, and I'm not one cent richer than I was when I started. How many more punches can one person take without staying down for the count?

In my case—an innumerable amount. This is what I do, and I do it because I love it. I'm only truly alive when I'm furthering my passions. If that makes me a fool, then gimme a jester's hat complete with tiny bells and hand me a slide whistle. I will blow that shit happily for the rest of the day without ever complaining. I may not be monetarily wealthy, and I'm fine with the fact that I may never be. There are no guarantees. However, when it comes to the heart, I'm one of the wealthiest motherfuckers to ever walk the earth. Setbacks fuel me. I've learned to thrive on the chaos and simply put… I will not be stopped.

Ever.

Especially now. I've made if this far with next to nothing. I hung in there and currently have so much I never had before. There's a family behind me and an amazingly beautiful woman by my side. I've met dear people along the way who gave me the kind of education no school could have. I've partied with and befriended legends that have instilled an insane amount of wisdom in me, both professionally and personally. There's nothing more I could ask for.

This story… my story… it's given me the unique chance to look back at my life, and work through it all in my head. I've wrestled with the demons for decades. Truth be told, my original intention of writing this account was going to be little more than working out my kinks, and then burning it. Just light a fire, man, and watch it all go up in smoke. Some of this shit has been very hard to live with. Even now… even though it's on paper (if you bought a hard copy), these things are still rattling around inside, and I don't think that they're even going to go away. That's okay though… my pain through my experiences is what makes me, me. No one can take those feelings, the tears that they caused, or anything else away from me.

Life's been odd. I spent my early years just not giving a fuck, and the rest of it trying to find out who I am, and why I deserve to be here. For a spell I was concerned with trying to make everyone happy. I thought that maybe I could find my happiness through theirs. That's just not possible. No matter how hard you try, you're never going to be able to make everyone happy, or have everyone like you. People can say whatever they want. You're always gonna be the super villain in someone's story, and there's no controlling that. However, what you have absolute control over is how you choose to

A Comedy of Tragedies

react to these things. Only you can choose to let something or someone make you angry. You can also choose to give that person or situation the finger. I've become a pro at that.

At the end of the day, I know who I am, what I've accomplished, and what I'm capable of. I'm proud of every triumph and failure, and I'm comfortable with every choice that I've ever made.

So what have we learned? Fuck if I know. I just keep on going. I guess the lesson here is—at the end of the day it's possible to take all of the best and worst that life has chosen to throw at you. You can overcome it. In fact, you WILL overcome it.

You see, being happy? That's the easy stuff. Smiling and having a good time can be effortless. It's when you're down in that hole, man. When the walls seem so very high from your point of view on the floor. That's really living. It's the choices you make and the things you do during that ever-so-fragile time that defines both your character and who you will become. Embrace the chaos. Hold the pain when you have to, and release it when you can. There's always gonna be something else. Another road. Another obstacle. Another kick to the gut. If you just keep on punching... even if it feels as if you have nothing left—you will make it through to the other side. I promise you that.

Welcome the idiots in your life who try and inhibit who you are. The ones who tell you that you cannot do anything. That you'll never be anyone. They're just upset that they've forgotten how to dream and will probably be nothing more than they are right now. Let them fuel you. Prove them wrong. It doesn't matter what your race, gender, sexual preference, or political affiliation is. None of that shit matters. We're ALL the same. We're all just people, and the only limits that you have to adhere to in your life, are the ones which you put upon yourself. Keep dreaming. Keep being different. Keep it creepy, funny, disturbing, sexy... whatever your bag is! Open it and flaunt it.

Despite everything, professionally I'm lucky enough to have several projects cooking with some big names in various states of production, so you're NOT done hearing from me. Not by a long-shot. I got a lot more to give, kids, and you haven't seen ANYTHING yet.

This was where I had originally intended to end this book. I've been writing it for four years, and that was a damn good stopping point... but... I had an epiphany recently. It came during the Christmas holiday. Dani and I were laying in bed and about to watch *Absolutely Fabulous* after feeding our hognose snake, Hisstat. Bridget had just left the room after whatever random and thoroughly silly giggle-fest had just occurred.

I turned and looked at Dani. She was lying there smiling. I then noticed I was smiling too. I didn't even realize that I was until that moment.

Apart we have both lived lives that were filled with many challenges, strife, and obstacles, some of which had broken us several times. Yet we always found ways to put the pieces back together. We both talked about these tribulations at length, and wondered how or why we managed to keep going. In this moment though? None of that darkness mattered. We were both content. We were both—not just happy—but truly happy. It took over 50 years, but here we are. This was the reason we kept going. This very second.

It's these small moments that can lead to the biggest realizations and have the most impact. Never give up. Miracles can happen and it doesn't matter how long it takes—it will be worth it. Just hang on.

If this street kid with a GED level education who 99 percent of the populace of this planet said was nothing and never will be anything can end up one day pooping in the personal toilets of his idols and legends (thanks Sid, George, and John), then there's nothing that you cannot accomplish as long as you're willing to put in the work and keep fucking breathing. Do it.

THE END... FOR NOW!

About the Author

Seriously? You just read an entire book about the author and you still want more? Fine.

Steve "Uncle Creepy" Barton is a horror icon. He is king of the horror nerds. He currently lives in New Jersey. He... You know what? Re-read the book. Everything is in there. I swear.

Printed in the USA
CPSIA information can be obtained
at www.ICGtesting.com
CBHW071043211124
17424CB00035B/58/J